The Taste for the Other

The Social and Ethical Thought of C. S. Lewis

GILBERT MEILAENDER

WILLIAM B. EERDMANS PUBLISHING COMPANY
GRAND RAPIDS, MICHIGAN / CAMBRIDGE, U.K.

TO MY PARENTS
*Wisest and best of my
unofficial teachers*

© 1978 Wm. B. Eerdmans Publishing Co.
255 Jefferson Ave. SE
Grand Rapids, Michigan 49503 /
P.O. Box 163, Cambridge CB3 9PU U.K.

This edition published 1998

Library of Congress Cataloging-in-Publication Data

Meilaender, Gilbert, 1946-
The taste for the other.
ISBN 0-8028-4492-8
1. Lewis, Clive Staples, 1898-1963 — Religion and ethics.
I. Title.
PR6023.E926Z795   230'.092'4   78-16506

Acknowledgments

Grateful acknowledgment is given to the following publishers for permission to quote from their publications.

WILLIAM B. EERDMANS PUBLISHING COMPANY

God in the Dock, ed. by Walter Hooper, copyright © 1970 by The Trustees of the Estate of C. S. Lewis.

The Pilgrim's Regress, by C. S. Lewis, copyright © 1933, 1943 by Clive Staples Lewis.

HARCOURT BRACE JOVANOVICH, INC.

The Four Loves, by C. S. Lewis, © 1960 by Helen Joy Lewis.

Letters to Malcolm: Chiefly on Prayer, by C. S. Lewis, © 1963, 1964 by the Estate of C. S. Lewis and/or C. S. Lewis.

MACMILLAN PUBLISHING COMPANY, INC.

The Abolition of Man, by C. S. Lewis, copyright © 1947 by Macmillan Publishing Co., Inc.

The Last Battle, by C. S. Lewis, copyright © 1956 by C. S. Lewis.

The Magician's Nephew, by C. S. Lewis, copyright © 1955 by C. S. Lewis.

Mere Christianity, by C. S. Lewis, copyright © 1943, 1945, 1952 by Macmillan Publishing Co., Inc.

Miracles: A Preliminary Study, by C. S. Lewis, copyright © 1947 by Macmillan Publishing Co., Inc.

Out of the Silent Planet, by C. S. Lewis, Macmillan Publishing Co., Inc.

Perelandra, by C. S. Lewis, copyright © 1944 by Clive Staples Lewis.

Contents

Preface to the Second Edition

As we arrive in 1998 at the centenary of C. S. Lewis' birth, interest in his writings and his life shows little sign of diminishing. In the twenty years since *The Taste for the Other* was first published, many useful studies of Lewis' thought have appeared; yet, relatively few of them seek to provide a coherent, critical account of the theological vision that he develops throughout his work. In that respect, at least, this book may still have a useful contribution to make.

More is known now about Lewis' life than was known twenty years ago, although new puzzles have also arisen. Several biographies have appeared, the most helpful of which is, I believe, that by George Sayer (*Jack: C. S. Lewis and His Times*). The more widely known biography by A. N. Wilson (*C. S. Lewis: A Biography*) tells us more, alas, about its author than its subject. Harder to classify but enjoyable to read is William Griffin's *Clive Staples Lewis: A Dramatic Life*. Walter Hooper's *C. S. Lewis: A Companion and Guide*, published in 1996, is more than just a biography, and it brings to fruition Hooper's decades of labor in Lewisiana. The several versions of "Shadowlands" have made details of Lewis' life and marriage well known to many people, and, while some may quibble about historical accuracy, I myself think the movie version powerfully captures central elements in Lewis' thought about suffering.

With all this added knowledge, however, new puzzles arise. Kathryn Lindskoog has raised important questions about the authenticity of a few of Lewis' posthumously published writings. And it becomes increasingly clear that we may never be confident in our knowledge of some important details of the life, no matter how many C. S. Lewis societies spring up around the globe with people dedicated to ferreting out such detail. And, in the long run, the writings are — to my mind, at least — more important for us than the life.

Much of the best writing about Lewis in the past twenty years has, I think, been on his fiction. Far more has appeared than I can mention here, but surely among the best such works one must note Peter Schakel on Narnia and on *Till We Have Faces*, Paul Ford on Narnia, Lindskoog on *Pilgrim's Regress*, and Chad Walsh on the entire literary legacy of Lewis. Scholars have also treated particular themes in Lewis' philosophical and theological thought, but relatively few have attempted to provide a sense of the whole of his theological vision. Some have, of course, among whom one might mention Richard Purtill's *C. S. Lewis's Case for the Christian Faith* and Lindskoog's *C. S. Lewis: Mere Christian*.

This is a book about Lewis' "social and ethical thought." Only in chapter 5, however, do I discuss some of the standard issues in ethical theory; for the book is not about ethics but about Lewis' understanding of what it would mean fully to realize our nature as human beings. And that understanding is an intensely moral one, deeply Augustinian in its basic contours, in which ethics and theology are closely intertwined. We are made for God. And because God truly loves us, he intends to do whatever can be done to form and shape us into people who genuinely desire to look upon his face, praise his glory, and live in harmony with him. To fall short of that would ultimately mean to fail as human beings, for no true humanity — or, for that matter, humanism — can flourish, or even survive, apart from our relation to God.

That is the goal of life, but there is no jumping ahead to it. The way must be traversed. Just as important in Lewis' vision of life, therefore, is his attention to our pilgrimage toward that end and his constant suggestion that this journey is likely to be a painful one. Bloated with self-concern and self-importance as we are, we may not really want to be with God, in whose presence there are no "private affairs" and who may seem to us to be the Great Interferer in our life and plans. And therefore, the way to self-fulfillment is likely to seem more like a way of self-sacrifice. This constant theme in Lewis' writings becomes especially pronounced in some of his later work, no doubt because of the influence of his marriage late in life and his wife's suffering. Especially in *Till We Have Faces, The Four Loves,* and *A Grief Observed* Lewis develops his sense that "the Divine Nature wounds and perhaps destroys us merely by being what it is"; his sense that "to love at all is to be vulnerable"; his sense that the better and more conscientious a surgeon is, "the more inexorably he will go on cutting."

Lewis firmly believes that God will make us happy — indeed, that we cannot be happy apart from God. But he never says, "Believe in God; he'll make you happy and you'll live the abundant life." His is, in many respects, a much starker and more austere vision of life, and it is precisely this element in his thought, I believe, that continues to draw readers into his work and that makes his vision of the Christian life so compelling. But just when we begin to feel that, however compelling it is, we cannot endure the starkness of the vision any longer, Lewis will remind us again of the goal at which this pilgrimage aims: that, as Screwtape puts it, God is, finally, "a hedonist at heart"; or that, as the children discover in *The Last Battle,* one day the term really will be over and the holidays will begin.

The coherence of these themes throughout Lewis' writings — including his writings on topics that do not, at first sight, appear theological in character — is very striking. Yet, relatively few works have developed the many topics Lewis takes up in relation to what is at the center of his theological vision. That is what I attempt in *The Taste for the Other.* I have made only a few changes for this second edition, correcting here and there a mistake or an infelicitous expression. It was — and is, in some respects — a young man's book. But I think it stands the test of time reasonably well and continues to offer an illuminating way of entry into Lewis' theology. I am pleased that Eerdmans has seen fit to make it available once again at the centenary of Lewis' birth.

Preface to the First Edition

Josef Pieper, explicating St. Thomas, has written that "the world is not to be kept in order through justice alone. There are obligations and debts which of their very nature cannot be adequately fulfilled and discharged." Any reader of this book with some background in contemporary Christian ethics will recognize my indebtedness to my teachers, Paul Ramsey and Gene Outka, under whom this work began as a dissertation. The questions I think it important to address, though certainly not always the answers I find persuasive, are quite obviously the result of their influence. If this is in any measure a good book, that is largely the result of their guidance. In particular I must—a "must" which transcends the requirements of justice alone—thank Paul Ramsey for his unfailing help and encouragement in the years since this manuscript was first drafted. He has, in his help to me, manifested the fidelity about which he has so often written.

I am grateful in addition to others who read and commented on earlier drafts of this manuscript in whole or in part: Horton Davies, Stanley Hauerwas, my colleagues Julian Hartt and David Little, and especially David Smith for his criticisms and encouragement in equal measure. I cannot possibly mention all those from whom I first learned to think about matters theological, but I must say that in ways too subtle to describe this book has been greatly influenced by years of conversation with an occasionally misguided theologian but excellent friend, Ron Thiemann.

When I think of the years spent writing and revising this

book, I do not think primarily of the book or even of academic endeavors. I think of them as years spent with my wife Judy and our children—Peter, Ellen, and most recently, Hannah. Were it not for them I would be far more pedantic than I am, and this would be, I am sure, a far worse book. My wife Judy has never typed a word of this manuscript in any stage of its development. Despite that grave omission I must say of her what Mark Studdock says of Jane in *That Hideous Strength*: that when she first crossed the dry and dusty world which my mind inhabited she was like a spring shower, and that in opening myself to her I was not mistaken.

And finally, the dedication expresses, I hope, my recognition of perhaps the greatest of these "obligations and debts which of their very nature cannot be adequately fulfilled and discharged."

G.M.

Introduction

"For we are discussing no trivial
subject, but how a man should
live."—Plato, *Republic*, 352d

Chad Walsh, whose guess on this matter may at least be said
to be well educated, has stated his belief that between 1943
(the year of the American publication of *The Screwtape
Letters)* and 1963 (the year of Lewis' death) C. S. Lewis

> had an impact on American religious thinking and indeed on
> the American religious imagination which has been rarely, if
> ever, equalled by any other modern writer.[1]

Furthermore, there is no sign that interest in Lewis' writings has diminished since his death.

Nevertheless, in an earlier work than the essay cited
above, Walsh has also written that "for a Christian social
philosophy one turns to Maritain, Niebuhr, Berdyaev,
George MacLeod and many others—not to C. S. Lewis."[2]
The very fact that I have undertaken to discuss in some
detail Lewis' social and ethical thought suggests that I think
Walsh's judgment on this matter mistaken. If he means that
Lewis seldom gives specific answers to concrete political
problems, we may grant the point—although we may also
wonder whether all of those Walsh names offer, for the most
part, anything more than a theological framework within

---

[1]"Impact on America," in *Light on C. S. Lewis*, ed. Jocelyn Gibb (New
York: Harcourt, Brace & World, 1965), p. 106.
[2]*C. S. Lewis: Apostle to the Skeptics* (New York: Macmillan, 1949),
p. 160.

which one may think about politics and society. If, on the other hand, he means to say that Lewis offers no sustained vision of man in society, I suggest that the discussion in the pages that follow may lead to an opposite conclusion. Indeed, I do not think it inaccurate to say that in his own way Lewis treats some questions of central importance for Christian social thought.

In the pages that follow the reader will not find any lengthy biographical data on Lewis. Such material is now readily available elsewhere and, indeed, is rather wearisomely repeated in just about every book written on Lewis. Anyone interested in biography can hardly do better than begin with Lewis' own autobiography of his early years, *Surprised by Joy*. In addition, several recent works provide at least some of the story of Lewis' life in a trustworthy manner.[3] Instead, I have tried to get at the heart of Lewis' vision of human community and his understanding of morality.

What is the heart of this vision? Any full answer must, of course, await the discussion that follows, and even that discussion ought do no more than send one back to Lewis' own writings. Walter Hooper, Lewis' biographer and the editor of several posthumous collections of Lewis' essays, has written that the central premise of Lewis' theological works is that all men are immortal.[4] Somewhat more precise, I suggest, is this premise: All human beings are made for life in community with God (and, thereby, with one another). Thus, in writing of our first parents who fell into sin, Lewis says: "They wanted, as we say, to 'call their souls their own'. But that means to live a lie, for our souls are not, in fact, our own."[5] I will call this Lewis' "reality

---

[3]Roger Lancelyn Green and Walter Hooper have written what, though rather perfunctory, comes close to being an authorized biography: *C. S. Lewis: A Biography* (New York: Harcourt, Brace, Jovanovich, 1974). For a stunningly beautiful pictorial biography with accompanying commentary (often in Lewis' own words) see Douglas Gilbert and Clyde S. Kilby, *C. S. Lewis: Images of His World* (Grand Rapids: Eerdmans, 1973).

[4]In the "Preface" to Lewis' *Christian Reflections*, ed. Walter Hooper (Grand Rapids: Eerdmans, 1967), p. vii.

[5]*The Problem of Pain* (New York: Macmillan, 1962), p. 80. Hereafter this volume will be referred to with the abbreviation *PP*.

principle," suggesting thereby his belief that fellowship with God is the destination for which the human being is actually created and that to fall short of this destiny is to fall short of full humanity. At the same time, however, Lewis is keenly aware that within the limits of our history we never reach that destination. We are not yet home, and, hence, the image of the Christian as pilgrim will be important in the following pages. The vision of community pictures for Lewis the end toward which the creation moves, and the whole Christian story outlines the course of that movement.

I hope it will be evident that I have tried to treat Lewis as a serious thinker and theologian. That he is often considered a "popular" author and that he aims at a wider readership than do most professional theologians is certainly true. But it may be mere prejudice to hold against an author the fact that he is widely read, and I am hopeful that my discussion of Lewis will provide some reason to think that insofar as he is being widely read by non-theologians, his readers are getting a fairly heavy dose (in alluring literary form) of relatively serious theological reflection.

It is true, though, that anyone attempting to write systematically about Lewis' thought faces the great difficulty of coping with the many genres in which Lewis expresses his ideas. He writes theological treatises, short essays on a variety of topics, science fiction and fantasy, children's stories, myth, and literary criticism. And, beyond that, one would be hard pressed to specify the genre of a work like *The Screwtape Letters*. This fact has seduced many into commenting on Lewis' works in piecemeal fashion. While such an approach has some benefits, it fails to do justice to the coherence of Lewis' vision, a coherence which pervades his very diverse writings. Furthermore, although the scope of his work presents a special difficulty, it is equally true that it accounts for much of the richness of his thought.

Lewis once wrote in reference to a critic: "My chief criticism of the Professor's article is that, wishing to criticize my philosophy (if I may give it so big a name) he almost ignores the books in which I have attempted to set it out and concentrates on my romances."[6] I have tried, conceptually at least, to avoid this danger and have concentrated on Lewis' "standard" theology. In the order of exposition, however, I have made use of one of Lewis' many genres—the children's story—by beginning each chapter with some material from the Chronicles of Narnia which relates to themes under discussion in that chapter. I have also felt free to draw on other writings, especially his fiction, to elucidate themes being discussed. This does not, I think, do any injustice to Lewis. He himself distinguished between the author as author and the author as man.[7] He felt that, in his own experience at least, the material for a story simply "bubbles up" in the mind of the author (as *The Lion, the Witch and the Wardrobe* began for him with an image of "a faun carrying an umbrella"). However, it is the author as man who has to supply the form for the story, and in so doing he may, according to Lewis, consider whether his "message" is likely to be "wholesome." Whether or not this is a good theory about literature I leave to others to discuss. However, it does seem true to Lewis' own fiction, which is often didactic as well as imaginative. In drawing on his fiction, therefore, we can be faithful to Lewis' own intentions.

Michael Oakeshott has written that

> philosophy in general knows two styles, the contemplative and the didactic, although there are many writers to whom neither belongs to the complete exclusion of the other. Those who practice the first let us into the secret workings of their minds and are less careful to send us away with a precisely formulated doctrine. Philosophy for them is a conversation, and, whether or not they write it as a dialogue, their style reflects their conception. . . . [Those who practice the second provide] only a residue, a distillate that is offered to the reader. The defect of such a style is that the reader must either accept or reject; if it inspires to fresh thought, it does so only by opposition.[8]

[6]"A Reply to Professor Haldane," *Of Other Worlds: Essays and Stories* (London: Geoffrey Bles, 1966), p. 75.

[7]"Sometimes Fairy Stories May Say Best What's to be Said," *Of Other Worlds*, pp. 35f.

[8]Introduction to Hobbes' *Leviathan* (Oxford: Blackwell, 1955), p. xviii.

My impression is that most people would probably consider Lewis' theological works to belong to the didactic rather than the contemplative style. Yet, in the course of studying his thought I have come to believe that this is far from true. If his fiction can be didactic as well as imaginative, his "standard" theology does far more than argue for certain propositions believed to be true. He is serious of course; for he has read his Plato well and knows that discussion of how a man ought to live is no trivial subject. And, indeed, he strives to present his theology consistently. But it is, he thinks, a consistent picture of an untidy world. The world as Lewis experiences it resists complete systematization— which is what we should expect from one who knows himself to be a pilgrim. Not all questions can be answered this side of "the land of the Trinity."

Very often Lewis does manage to take us inside his thinking as he reflects theologically about a world in which many different things interest him and arouse his questioning intellect. This, indeed, is much of the key to reading Lewis: recognizing the degree to which he is focussing on things *outside* himself and trying to make sense of them *for* himself. Lewis compares the conversation of Adam and Satan in Milton's *Paradise Lost*:

> Adam talks about God, the Forbidden Tree, sleep, the difference between beast and man, his plans for the morrow, the stars and the angels. He discusses dreams and clouds, the sun, the moon, and the planets, the winds and the birds. He relates his own creation and celebrates the beauty and majesty of Eve.[9]

Satan, on the other hand, no matter what he begins talking about, must quickly return to himself, his position, his "injured merit."

> Adam, though locally confined to a small park on a small planet, has interests that embrace 'all the choir of heaven and all the furniture of earth'. Satan has been in the Heaven of Heavens and in the abyss of Hell, and surveyed all that lies between them, and in that whole immensity has found only one thing that interests Satan. . . . Satan's monomaniac con-

[9]*A Preface to Paradise Lost* (London: Oxford, 1961), pp. 101f.

cern with himself and his supposed rights and wrongs is a necessity of the Satanic predicament. . . . He has wished to 'be himself', and to be in himself and for himself, and his wish has been granted.[10]

In that last sentence the "reality principle" reasserts itself. Satan has purchased a tidy view of life at the cost of the world. His being is constricted. Lewis, on the contrary, seems to believe that the theologian must give himself, as it were, to the amazing multiplicity of experience and wrestle with the data of a pilgrim existence. Though he never says so, this is nothing more than to understand the task of theological reflection in terms of what is probably his most often cited biblical passage: "he who loses his life will save it." Thus, it is not just Lewis the mythmaker but also Lewis the theologian who puts into Orual's mouth the words near the close of *Till We Have Faces*:

> I ended my first book with the words *no answer*. I know now, Lord, why you utter no answer. You are yourself the answer. Before your face questions die away. What other answer would suffice? Only words, words; to be led out to battle against other words.[11]

Yet, of course, Lewis does provide many of those "words," and we will make it our business to investigate them. He does not attempt to make his vision of human nature and community a strikingly original one, and there is, of course, no guarantee that originality would be a mark of truth. But in reading Lewis we do meet one whose thought is deeply grounded in much that has lasted in Western Christendom. Augustinian themes, in particular, abound. In explicating his social and ethical thought, therefore, we have some claim to be explicating a view which has been influential and which represents at least one of the major strands in Christian thought. No one ought to write on Lewis and seek more originality than that, since no other approach would be faithful to the Lewis who wrote:

No man who bothers about originality will ever be original:

[10]*Ibid.*, p. 102.
[11]Eerdmans, 1966, p. 308.

whereas if you simply try to tell the truth (without caring twopence how often it has been told before) you will, nine times out of ten, become original without ever having noticed.[12]

---

[12]*Mere Christianity* (New York: Macmillan, 1960), p. 174. Hereafter this volume will be referred to with the abbreviation *MC*.

CHAPTER I

THE SWEET POISON
OF THE FALSE INFINITE

What do we see if we look rightly at our world? We see,
C. S. Lewis thinks, an "astonishing cataract of bears, babies,
and bananas: this immoderate deluge of atoms, orchids,
oranges, cancers, canaries, fleas, gases, tornadoes and
toads."[1] What sort of attitude is appropriate for a human
being confronting this "astonishing cataract" and "immoderate deluge" of things? We are, Lewis writes in the same
context, to offer nature "neither worship nor contempt."
This is a theme to which Lewis often returns. To be fully
human involves a certain stance toward the things of creation: delighting in things without seeking security in
them.

The Chronicles of Narnia provide more than enough
examples of a wrong attitude toward things—of, that is,
inordinate love. In *The Lion, the Witch and the Wardrobe*
Edmund's inordinate love for Turkish Delight is the cause
of great sorrow and, finally, of Aslan's death. When Edmund
finds that he (like Lucy) has gotten into Narnia through the
magic wardrobe, it is not long before he encounters the
White Witch (posing as Queen of Narnia). He is, at first,
fearful and apprehensive in her presence. But all that is
soon forgotten when she asks him what he would like most
to eat and then grants his request by magically providing a
box containing several pounds of Turkish Delight. While
Edmund eats, she plies him with questions about how he
had gotten in and about his brothers and sisters.

[1]*Miracles: A Preliminary Study* (New York: Macmillan, 1947), p. 67.

8

> At first Edmund tried to remember that it is rude to speak with one's mouth full, but soon he forgot about this and thought only of trying to shovel down as much Turkish Delight as he could, and the more he ate the more he wanted to eat, and he never asked himself why the Queen should be so inquisitive.[2]

The key is given us right there: "the more he ate the more he wanted to eat." At that moment Edmund wants nothing more than he wants Turkish Delight; and his inordinate love makes a god of Turkish Delight, a god that leads him on and controls him.

The Queen promises Edmund more Turkish Delight if, on any other occasion when he should get into Narnia, he will bring his brother and sisters to her. (She knows the ancient prophecy that Narnia will be freed from her spell when two Sons of Adam and two Daughters of Eve sit on the four thrones of Cair Paravel, and she wants to avoid that at all costs.) When the four children do get back into Narnia through the magic wardrobe, Edmund tries to do what she had asked. He goes with the others to the home of Mr. and Mrs. Beaver. There the children are served a delicious meal: fresh fish, potatoes and butter, a jug of creamy milk, and freshly baked marmalade rolls. But of Edmund we are told:

> He had eaten his share of the dinner, but he hadn't really enjoyed it because he was thinking all the time about Turkish Delight—and there's nothing that spoils the taste of good ordinary food half so much as the memory of bad magic food. (p. 71)

Edmund has made for himself a god, and it will finally destroy all true pleasures. Not only that; it makes him a traitor. He sneaks off in an attempt to betray his brother and sisters—simply to gain more Turkish Delight.

Thus, what began in a seemingly unimportant craving for Turkish Delight ends in disaster. First, other ordinary pleasures are destroyed for Edmund. Then he becomes willing for the sake of his idol to betray those who trust him. And finally, when the Witch points out that according to the

---

[2]*The Lion, the Witch and the Wardrobe* (New York: Macmillan, 1950), pp. 28f.

"Deep Magic from the Dawn of Time" traitors belong by right to her, Aslan offers himself as a sacrifice in place of Edmund. That is where his inordinate love finally leads: to the Stone Table, where Aslan is tortured and killed.

This is probably the most important example of inordinate love in the Chronicles of Narnia, but there are others worth mentioning. Digory's Uncle Andrew is a fine example of greed. When as a result of his own magic and treachery he ends up in Narnia with Digory, Polly, and Jadis, he quickly shows his true colors. They are present at Narnia's creation. Jadis had brought into Narnia the lamppost which she had uprooted in London. Now she throws it at Aslan. It falls to the ground and immediately begins growing into a new lamppost; evidently this is what happens in a "young" world. Suddenly Uncle Andrew realized the truth about this world.

> I have discovered a world where everything is bursting with life and growth. Columbus, now, they talk about Columbus. But what was America to this? The commercial possibilities of this country are unbounded. Bring a few bits of scrap iron here, bury 'em, and up they come as brand new railway engines, battleships, anything you please. They'll cost nothing, and I can sell 'em at full prices in England. I shall be a millionaire.[3]

Uncle Andrew reminds us of Devine in *Out of the Silent Planet*, who thinks only of bringing back to earth the gold of Malacandra so that he can have "ocean-going yachts, the most expensive women and a big place on the Riviera."[4] The Oyarsa correctly analyzes him: he is only a "talking animal" in whom nothing but greed is left (p. 139). Devine misses the beauty and majesty of Malacandra; Uncle Andrew is completely unable to appreciate the awesome spectacle of the creation of Narnia. A wrong attitude toward things has killed in them the capacity for pleasure.

The seductive lure of things is an ever present danger in Narnia. One of the episodes in *The Voyage of the "Dawn Treader"* finds Caspian and the children in a narrow bay of water. There they discover a pool of water which turns

[3]*The Magician's Nephew* (New York: Macmillan, 1955), pp. 98f.
[4]*Out of the Silent Planet* (New York: Macmillan, 1965), p. 30.

anything immersed in it into solid gold. Instantly, an idol begins to take possession of them.

> "The king who owned this island," said Caspian slowly, and his face flushed as he spoke, "would soon be the richest of all kings of the world. I claim this land for ever as a Narnian possession. It shall be called Goldwater Island. And I bind all you to secrecy. No one must know of this. Not even Drinian— on pain of death, do you hear?"
> "Who are you talking to?" said Edmund. "I'm no subject of yours. If anything it's the other way round. I am one of the four ancient sovereigns of Narnia and you are under allegiance to the High King my brother."
> "So it has come to that, King Edmund, has it?" said Caspian, laying his hand on his sword-hilt.[5]

Only the appearance of Aslan in the distance breaks the hold of their inordinate love and prevents the quarrel from becoming a fight. They suddenly realize what they had been about to do.

> "Sire," said Reepicheep, "this is a place with a curse on it. Let us get back on board at once. And if I might have the honour of naming this island, I should call it Deathwater." (p. 106)

And that, indeed, is what—save for the appearance of Aslan—it would have been. The seductive lure of things, "the sweet poison of the false infinite," might have meant death for all of them.[6]

Yet, having said all this, we can never forget that Narnia is a land of many delights. Feasting and revelry are common. If self-denial must be practiced, it is only when the cause of Aslan is at stake. Things must be renounced in order to guard oneself against unfaithfulness to The Lion. But such renunciation is never an end in itself, and when in the final chapter of *The Last Battle* the children enter Aslan's world, they find beauties and delights beyond imagination or description. All that must wait, however. In Nar-

---

[5]*The Voyage of the "Dawn Treader"* (New York: Macmillan, 1952), p. 105.

[6]The phrase from which this chapter takes its title is found in the second book of Lewis' space trilogy, *Perelandra: A Novel* (New York: Macmillan, 1965), p. 81.

nia there is both enjoyment *and* renunciation. These must
stand together if either is to remain healthy. As Aslan's
creatures, Narnians are meant to enjoy created things. As
those who are always tempted to put second things first,
they are ever in danger of succumbing to the sweet poison
of the false infinite.

PLEASURES ON MALACANDRA AND PERELANDRA

Lewis weaves many themes into his space trilogy, but because it is not directly related to the main plot we might
overlook the treatment of pleasures in *Out of the Silent
Planet* and *Perelandra*. Yet, almost everything which Lewis
has to say about the proper attitude toward things is encap-
sulated in these two books. They provide, therefore, a good
starting point for discussion.

In *Out of the Silent Planet* Ransom, after escaping from
Weston and Devine, encounters and comes to know one of
the *hrossa* named Hyoi. He stays with Hyoi and lives for a
time in a community of *hrossa*. Ransom spends much time
pumping Hyoi for information about Malacandra and its
inhabitants. He begins a conversation one day by asking
Hyoi whether the *seroni, hrossa,* and *pfifltriggi* ever make
war upon one another (pp. 72ff.). "What for?" asks Hyoi.
Ransom suggests that certain needs might lead to this—a
need for food, for example. He wonders whether it might
not be possible for several species of Malacandrians to fight
over food supplies.

> "If the other *hnau* wanted food, why should we not give it
> to them? We often do."
> "But how if we had not enough for ourselves?"
> "But Maleldil will not stop the plants growing." (p. 72)

Hyoi has, it seems, a sense of possessions but no sense of
possessiveness with respect to what is his. He does not
think of possessions as something which one necessarily
keeps for oneself.

Ransom presses on. He is bothered by the problem of
scarce resources. However, Hyoi and his world are untrou-

bled by this, for Malacandra is a world so radically different from ours that the problem does not arise. In picturing such a world Lewis is expanding our vision and helping us see things about our own world which we might otherwise miss.

Ransom tries to make Hyoi see how a food shortage could arise. Suppose, he suggests, the *hrossa* were to have more children than they do at present. What would Maleldil do then? It would not suffice then just to keep the plants growing; for population would outstrip food production. Hyoi's response is simple: "But why should we have more young?" (p. 72). Ransom is puzzled and has difficulty making his point clear. Don't the *hrossa* find pleasure in the begetting of young? Hyoi responds that they surely do; they call it love. Ransom then points out that (in his world) when a *hman* experiences a pleasure he wants it again. "He might want the pleasure more often than the number of young that could be fed" (p. 72).

Now it is Hyoi's turn to be puzzled. "You mean," he said slowly, "that he might do it not only in one or two years of his life but again?" (p. 72). Finally Ransom understands that for Hyoi the notion of love involves far more than the pleasure of begetting. When a *hross* is young he looks for a mate, courts her, begets young by her, rears the young, and finally boils the memories of all this down inside himself, and shapes them into poems and wisdom. "A pleasure is full grown only when it is remembered" (p. 73). That is Hyoi's view. There is one process in which the specific pleasure of begetting occupies a part, but the process reaches its culmination only when the experience is remembered and memorialized in a great ballad. To continue grasping at one stage of the process would destroy the greater pleasure still to come; for the poem is the end of the pleasure.[7]

[7]Compare the words of the hermit to John in *The Pilgrim's Regress: An Allegorical Apology for Christianity, Reason and Romanticism* (Grand Rapids: Eerdmans, 1958), p. 162: "First comes delight: then pain: then fruit. And then there is joy of the fruit, but that is different again from the first delight. And mortal lovers must not try to remain at the first step. . . . Manna kept, is worms."

In response Ransom takes up Hyoi's reference to poetry. Are there not moments when a line in a poem is so splendid that one longs to hear it over again—to repeat the pleasure?

> Hyoi's reply unfortunately turned on one of those points in their language which Ransom had not mastered. There were two verbs which both, as far as he could see, meant to *long* or *yearn*; but the *hrossa* drew a sharp distinction, even an opposition, between them. Hyoi seemed to him merely to be saying that every one would long for it (*wondelone*) but no one in his senses could long for it (*hluntheline*). (p. 73)

We meet here Lewis' concept of *Sehnsucht*—longing for joy.[8] The experience of *Sehnsucht* is, Lewis says, one of intense longing; yet this want is itself felt as a delight. "The hunger is better than any other fullness; this poverty better than all other wealth."[9] The experience of almost any thing can arouse this "inconsolable longing."[10] It seems always to be a longing for something not given in experience; it comes as a by-product of focussing attention and desire on something else. Hence, Lewis can say: "All joy reminds. It is never a possession" (*SJ*, p. 66). Few writers can evoke the experience better than Lewis, and it is worth quoting at length a passage in which he does so.

> Are not all lifelong friendships born at the moment when at last you meet another human being who has some inkling (but faint and uncertain even in the best) of that something which you were born desiring, and which, beneath the flux of other desires and in all the momentary silences between the louder passions, night and day, year by year, from childhood to old age, you are looking for, watching for, listening for? You have never *had* it. All the things that have ever deeply possessed your soul have been but hints of it—tantalising glimpses, promises never quite fulfilled, echoes that died away just as they caught your ear. But if it should really become manifest—if there ever came an echo that did not die away but swelled into the sound itself—you would know it. Beyond all

---

[8]For a book-length treatment of *Sehnsucht*, see Corbin Carnell, *Bright Shadow of Reality: C. S. Lewis and the Feeling Intellect* (Grand Rapids: Eerdmans, 1974).

[9]Preface to *The Pilgrim's Regress*, p. 7.

[10]*Surprised by Joy: The Shape of My Early Life* (New York: Harcourt, Brace & World, 1956), p. 165. Hereafter this volume will be referred to with the abbreviation *SJ*.

possibility of doubt you would say "Here at last is the thing I was made for." We cannot tell each other about it. It is the secret signature of each soul, the incommunicable and unappeasable want, the thing we desired before we met our wives or made our friends or chose our work, and which we shall desire on our deathbeds, when the mind no longer knows wife or friend or work. While we are, this is. If we lose this, we lose all. (*PP*, pp. 146–47)

The key to understanding the concept—a key which Lewis himself was a long time finding—is that it is a longing for something never directly given in experience. This is, in effect, Lewis' description of the restless heart which Augustine said can rest only in God. To try to satisfy this longing with any object given in experience will be futile and will inevitably spoil the genuine pleasure which the object might have given. This is what Hyoi intends to say about the splendid line in a poem. It might indeed create a longing in him, but he would not mistake that simply for a longing to hear the poem again (hence, the two different words in the Malacandrian language). Instead, he would recognize that in this splendid line a shaft of Maleldil's glory had gotten through and awakened in him sweet desire for Maleldil himself—a desire which no repetition of the poem could possibly satisfy. To go back in the poem would kill the beauty of the line.

Ransom puzzles over this conversation, amazed that he should have chanced upon "a species naturally continent, naturally monogamous" (p. 74). He finds in the *hrossa* a species whose instincts differ greatly from the human beings he knows—whose instincts, in fact, correspond to the unattained ideals of humanity. This is for him a source of bewilderment. "At last it dawned upon him that it was not they, but his own species, that were the puzzle" (p. 74). Lewis wants the same light to shine on each reader; he wants a different attitude toward pleasures and the things of creation to develop.

In *Perelandra* we find more detailed treatment of a similar theme. This time Ransom is taken to a newly created world of almost indescribable beauty. He finds himself in "a part of the wood where great globes of yellow fruit hung from the trees" (p. 42). He intends to take just a small "experimental sip" of the juice from the fruit, since it might not be healthful for a human being. But at the first sip he forgets such caution.

> It was like the discovery of a totally new *genus* of pleasures, something unheard of among men, out of all reckoning, beyond all covenant. For one draught of this on earth wars would be fought and nations betrayed. It could not be classified. He could never tell us, when he came back to the world of men, whether it was sharp or sweet, savoury or voluptuous, creamy or piercing. "Not like that" was all he could say to such inquiries. (p. 42)

Having drained one gourd, Ransom is about to pick another when he suddenly realizes that he is no longer hungry or thirsty. Yet, although he is drawn by the desire to repeat this intense pleasure, it seems better for him not to eat another at this time.

Shortly thereafter he has a similar experience when he finds a group of "bubble trees." These trees draw up water from the ocean, enrich it in some way, and produce spheres which swell until they burst and emit a delicious fragrance. Before Ransom has discovered the nature of these trees, he puts out his hand to touch one. Instantly (since he has popped it) he gets what seems like a shower with a delicious scent. Now, having discovered the secret of the trees, Ransom thinks of new possibilities. He could plunge through the trees, breaking many of the spheres at once, and enjoy the experience "multiplied tenfold" (p. 48). But, as in the case of the fruit, something restrains him.

> He had always disliked the people who encored a favourite air in the opera—"That just spoils it" had been his comment. But this now appeared to him as a principle of far wider application and deeper moment. This itch to have things over again, as if life were a film that could be unrolled twice or even made to work backwards . . . was it possibly the root of all evil? No: of course the love of money was called that. But money itself— perhaps one valued it chiefly as a defence against chance, a security for being able to have things over again, a means of arresting the unrolling of the film. (p. 48)

Ransom has another similar experience when he finds some bushes which bear oval green berries. These are good to eat, though they do not give "the orgiastic and almost alarming pleasure of the gourds, but rather the specific pleasure of plain food" (p. 49). As he eats, Ransom finds that a few of the berries have a bright red center and are especially tasty. He is tempted to look only for those with the red center but is again strongly restrained from doing so.

> "Now on earth," thought Ransom, "they'd soon discover how to breed these redhearts, and they'd cost a great deal more than the others." Money, in fact, would provide the means of saying *encore* in a voice that could not be disobeyed. (p. 50)

Later when Ransom meets the Lady, the conversation turns to the topic of food. The Lady has no concept of an event which would not be pleasing or welcome. She thinks of events as waves which Maleldil rolls toward her (p. 68). Ransom, somewhat to his own shame, helps her to a new understanding. She comes to realize that when she goes into the forest to pick fruit, she normally has only one particular fruit in mind.

> Then, it may be, one finds a different fruit and not the fruit one thought of. One joy was expected and another was given. But this I had never noticed before—that the very moment of the finding there is in the mind a kind of thrusting back, or setting aside. The picture of the fruit you have *not* found is still, for a moment, before you. And if you wished—if it were possible to wish—you could keep it there. You could send your soul after the good you had expected instead of turning it to the good you had got. You could refuse the real good; you could make the real fruit taste insipid by thinking of the other. (p. 69)

The Lady learns, in other words, to conceive of a heart which does not simply receive the offered good but clings instead to its original desire. She learns that events are not simply waves Maleldil sends toward her; rather, she herself plunges into the wave.

What Lewis provides in *Perelandra* and *Out of the Silent Planet* is his picture of the appropriate attitude toward created things. What we are to remember—and what is so easy to forget—is that they are *created*; they are gifts of the

Creator meant to be received. This is the key to understanding the picture Lewis paints. The proper posture for the creature is one of receptivity. In *Perelandra* we see several ways in which this posture could be corrupted or destroyed. First it is always possible to seek ways to assure ourselves of repeating the pleasure. This is what makes money so suspect in Lewis' eyes—it is a means by which we assure ourselves that we can have the pleasure whenever we want it. It provides a measure of independence. One no longer has to throw oneself into the wave. Second, even when one pleasure is given, it is (as the Lady discovered) possible to turn from what is given to something which is (thought to be) preferred. And this, in turn, is what makes a life oriented toward the future suspect for Lewis—to commit too much of one's hopes and happiness to the future will make impossible the posture of receptivity appropriate to a creature.

In either case—whether we try to secure means for repeating the pleasure at will or turn from what is given to something else which is desired—Lewis thinks that we will eventually lose the capacity for delighting in what is received. For to treat a created thing as something more than that is to destroy its true character. To seek in any created thing a complete fulfillment of the longing which moves us is to make of it an object of infinite desire and, because it is only a created thing, a false infinite. It may still be sweet, at least for a time, because it is intended by its Giver to be a source of delight. But in the end it will be poison for the person who gives his heart only to it. Hence the constant temptation: the lure of the sweet poison of the false infinite.

This theme comes out most clearly in *Perelandra* in the symbolism of the Fixed Land. Perelandra is largely a world of floating islands, but it also has a Fixed Land. The Lady (and the King) are permitted to go onto the Fixed Land but not to dwell there or sleep there (p. 74). When Ransom learns this, he points out how different things are in his world. There, the very thought of a world like Perelandra would make people unhappy and afraid (p. 75). Indeed, the Fixed Land provides the UnMan with material for tempting the Lady. She misses the King, and the UnMan calls her attention to the fact that when people live on a fixed land they cannot be so suddenly separated (p. 104). They can control their own destinies to some extent; they are not constantly thrown into the wave. The command to live on the floating islands makes no sense, he says. "It stands between you and all settled life, all command of your days" (p. 117). However, in the end, when Ransom has triumphed over the UnMan, the Lady comes to see the meaning of the command.

> The reason for not yet living on the Fixed Land is now so plain. How could I wish to live there except because it was Fixed? And why should I desire the Fixed except to make sure—to be able on one day to command where I should be the next and what should happen to me? It was to reject the wave—to draw my hands out of Maleldil's, to say to Him, 'Not thus, but thus'—to put in our own power what times should roll toward us . . . as if you gathered fruits together to-day for tomorrow's eating instead of taking what came. That would have been cold love and feeble trust. And out of it how could we ever have climbed back into love and trust again? (p. 208)

Receptivity to what is given in the present: that is the proper posture for a creature. In Gunnar Urang's words, the image of the Fixed Land operates "in an almost Spenserian manner, to suggest the contrast between living by faith and seeking a rigid kind of security."[11]

This sort of trust involves a willingness to receive what is given (even if it was not originally desired) as well as a willingness to let it go again without grasping after repetition of the pleasure. Always, one must throw oneself into the wave. We can, in passing, note how this attitude contrasts with that exhibited by Weston in *Out of the Silent Planet*. What better description of his behavior in that story could we give than to say that it is an attempt to avoid having to live out of trust? We see him oriented entirely toward the future, willing to offer up human sacrifice on the altar of human survival. That dream embodies the sweet

[11]*Shadows of Heaven: Religion and Fantasy in the Writing of C. S. Lewis, Charles Williams, and J. R. R. Tolkien* (Philadelphia: Pilgrim Press, 1971), p. 17.

poison of the false infinite, and stands in opposition to the posture of receptivity which ought to characterize a creature.

THE DIALECTIC OF ENJOYMENT AND RENUNCIATION

In the space trilogy Lewis offers an imaginative vision of the proper posture for unfallen creatures. However, we live neither on Malacandra nor Perelandra. The picture will have to be complicated if it is to be adequate to our experience. Lewis achieves this in the whole body of his writing by placing us, as it were, in a still larger story: the Christian story of creation, fall, incarnation, redemption, and *eschaton*. Within the context of this story we see that a proper attitude toward things involves more than receptivity. Creatures like us must, Lewis thinks, take up a kind of double attitude toward things—a dialectical movement between enjoyment and renunciation.[12] The dialectic is nicely captured in a couplet by William Dunbar of which Lewis was fond.

> Man, please thy Maker, and be merry,
> And give not for this world a cherry.[13]

This double movement is grounded, in the first place, in creation itself. The things of our world are genuine sources of delight, but they are still *created* things. They call us out of ourselves, but they cannot satisfy the heart which seeks in them a full answer to its longing. All pleasures, Lewis says, are "shafts of the glory as it strikes our sensibility."[14]

---

[12]This is clearly related to Charles Williams' treatment of the Way of Affirmation of Images and the Way of Rejection of Images summarized in his phrase, "This also is Thou; neither is this Thou." For an excellent discussion of Williams' theology (focussing on the Way of Affirmation) see Mary McDermott Shideler, *The Theology of Romantic Love: A Study in the Writings of Charles Williams* (Grand Rapids: Eerdmans, 1966).

[13]Quoted by Lewis in *The Four Loves* (New York: Harcourt Brace Jovanovich, 1960), p. 127. Hereafter this volume will be referred to with the abbreviation *FL*.

[14]*Letters to Malcolm: Chiefly on Prayer* (New York: Harcourt, Brace & World, 1964), p. 89.

But no thing is the glory itself. Rather, the glory of the One
shines through the multiplicity of created things. Hence,
from one point of view we reverence the thing as the gift of
the Creator. We receive it with joy and delight in it. Yet,
from another perspective the thing itself is of little consequence, for our life is directed toward God and not only
toward the pleasures of his creation.[15]

Lewis thinks he can discern meaning in the pattern of
creation.

> The settled happiness and security which we all desire, God
> withholds from us by the very nature of the world: but joy,
> pleasure, and merriment He has scattered broadcast. We are
> never safe, but we have plenty of fun, and some ecstasy. It is
> not hard to see why. The security we crave would teach us to
> rest our hearts in this world and oppose an obstacle to our
> return to God: a few moments of happy love, a landscape, a
> symphony, a merry meeting with our friends, a bathe, or a
> football match, have no such tendency. Our Father refreshes
> us on the journey with some pleasant inns, but will not encour-
> age us to mistake them for home. (*PP*, p. 115)

This is the message Lewis claims to find in the works of
William Morris, an author who was a lifelong favorite of his:
a vision of "the ravishing sweetness and the heartbreaking
melancholy of our experience" and a sense of how the one
passes over into the other. In presenting this, says Lewis,
Morris presented "the *datum* which all our adventures,
worldly and otherworldly alike, must take into account."[16]
That datum is the character of the creation. In it we are
struck by shafts of the Creator's glory which call us out of
ourselves; yet, in the things of creation we never fully find
the glory itself. The glory is not *in* the things; it comes
through them.[17] Thus, the nature of the creation itself requires us to say that both an affirmation and a negation of
things—both enjoyment and renunciation—are part and

[15]*God in the Dock: Essays on Theology and Ethics*, ed. Walter Hooper
(Grand Rapids: Eerdmans, 1970), p. 148.

[16]"William Morris," *Selected Literary Essays*, ed. Walter Hooper
(Cambridge, 1969), p. 231.

[17]"The Weight of Glory," *The Weight of Glory and Other Addresses*
(Grand Rapids: Eerdmans, 1965), p. 4. Hereafter this volume will be
referred to with the abbreviation WG.

parcel of a right attitude toward created things. This is what
the Lady learned from Ransom; that a receptive enjoyment
of Maleldil's gift involved renunciation of the fruit she had
originally intended to eat.

To fasten on only one half—either half—of the dialectic
involves not only a wrong attitude but a misunderstanding
of created things. Lewis thinks that this is a very common
mistake. He calls it "the Fool's Way" and "the Way of the
Disillusioned 'Sensible Man'" (MC, pp. 105f.). The fool
knows only the path of enjoyment of things. Consequently,
when he finds that a certain thing fails to satisfy his longing,
he assumes that he must simply have gotten the wrong
object and ought to try another. Because his vision is con-
fined to created things, he is unable to find the point of view
from which these things are of little moment; for

> only Supernaturalists really see Nature. You must go a little
> away from her, and then turn round, and look back. Then at last
> the true landscape will become visible. . . . To treat her as God,
> or as Everything, is to lose the whole pith and pleasure of her.
> Come out, look back, and then you will see . . . this astonishing
> cataract of bears, babies, and bananas: this immoderate deluge
> of atoms, orchids, oranges, cancers, canaries, fleas, gases, tor-
> nadoes and toads. . . . She is herself. Offer her neither worship
> nor contempt.[18]

The Disillusioned Sensible Man is far less optimistic about
the enjoyment of things. The Sensible Man knows that our
longings can never be satisfied, so he trains himself not to
ask too much of things and to suppress his seemingly infinite longings. Indeed, this is the counsel John receives from
Mr. Sensible in The Pilgrim's Regress. Mr. Sensible, who
holds that contentment is the best riches, tells John that the

> great art of life is to moderate our passions. Objects of affection
> are like other belongings. We must love them enough to enrich
> our lives while we have them—not enough to impoverish our
> lives when they are gone. (p. 83)

[18]Miracles, p. 67. Cf. what Lewis says about medieval poets in The
Discarded Image (Cambridge, 1967), pp. 38–39: "They believed from the
outset that Nature was not everything. She was created. . . . It is precisely
this limitation and subordination of Nature which sets her free for her
triumphant poetical career. By surrendering the dull claim to be everything, she becomes somebody."

Lewis believes that this is, on the whole, a better way than that of the Fool. Nevertheless, it is just as true to say that the Sensible Man does not see created things aright. He finds in them too little; he misses the shaft of glory as it strikes his sensibility or, at any rate, he will not permit it to call him out of himself. To answer the call might occasion disappointment and sorrow, and rather than risk that he prefers always to qualify his enjoyment of things.

Neither of these ways will do. One must, Lewis thinks, enter into the movement of the dialectic and practice both enjoyment and renunciation. Neither simply qualifies the other, but instead, life is seen as a constant movement back and forth between the poles of the dialectic. The things of creation are intended to arouse delight without fully satisfying desire. Turning from them can be justified only as part of a total movement intended to honor, esteem, and affirm them for what they are: shafts of the Creator's glory. By the same token, they must not be mistaken for the glory itself; for then too they are not honored as *created* things.

There is an *almost* Franciscan character to Lewis' attitude toward things. G. K. Chesterton, in his masterful little biography of St. Francis, tries to explain how it is that St. Francis could praise the sun and hide in a dark cave, how he could rejoice in the gaiety of the fire and roll in the snow. We can understand it, Chesterton suggests, only if we see that he is drawn by the deepest and most personal of passions: love.

> The clue to the asceticism and all the rest can be found in the stories of lovers when they seemed to be rather like lunatics. Tell it as the tale of one of the Troubadours, and the wild things he would do for his lady, and the whole of the modern puzzle disappears. . . . The reader cannot even begin to see the sense of a story that may well seem to him a very wild one, until he understands that to this great mystic his religion was not a thing like a theory but a thing like a love-affair.[19]

Something similar can be said of Lewis' attitude toward created things. Drawn by longing for One never fully given in our experience, we are caught up in the dialectic of

---

[19]G. K. Chesterton, *St. Francis of Assisi* (Image Books, 1957), pp. 15f.

enjoyment and renunciation. Lewis offers this not so much as a theory but as a description of how we respond to a vision of things as created.

However, there is more to the Christian story than this. We are to speak not simply of creatures but of fallen creatures. People as we know them are not like the inhabitants of Malacandra or Perelandra whom Ransom befriended. To say that men are fallen is, for Lewis, to say that they have learned to live without

> directing their lives to their Creator and taking all their delights as uncovenanted mercies, as 'accidents' (in the logical sense) which arose in the course of a life directed not to those delights but to the adoration of God. (*PP*, p. 80)

In this way a right attitude toward created things is corrupted, and we fall out of the posture of receptivity. Furthermore, we inevitably kill many genuine pleasures. The thrill of delight which comes as an "uncovenanted mercy" when we eat a particular food cannot be recaptured if we make it the object of our search. For we have turned then from enjoyment of the thing itself to a quest for *self*-gratification. Lewis believes this to be characteristic of fallen creatures. What once was innocently received becomes an object which is desired only because of the pleasure it can give the self.

It is important to repeat here what we have already said above: Lewis does not think this a reason for making renunciation of things the only principle of life. Even in a fallen world renunciation remains only part of a dialectical movement. Simply to turn from things is just as dangerous as seeking from them nothing but self-gratification. Either is a misuse of the thing. In fact, principled renunciation may be more dangerous than principled enjoyment; for the thing itself is a channel through which the glory strikes us. Enjoyment of the thing may call us out of ourselves. Thus,

> to love and admire anything outside yourself is to take one step away from utter spiritual ruin; though we shall not be well so long as we love and admire anything more than we love and admire God. (*MC*, p. 98)

In his autobiography *Surprised by Joy,* Lewis describes his ideal day (which consists largely of the pleasures of good reading, eating, walking, and conversation). He comments that it is a life almost entirely selfish but not self-centered: "for in such a life my mind would be directed towards a thousand things, not one of which is myself" (*SJ,* p. 143). Lewis is by no means recommending the selfish way, but he does think that for such a person there is, at least, the possibility that the lure of things may call him out of himself and begin the process of recovering a posture of receptivity.

On several occasions Lewis has Screwtape take note of this fact in his advice to Wormwood. Screwtape warns that though pleasures are a fine source of temptation, they contain certain dangers. "Never forget that when we are dealing with any pleasure in its healthy and normal and satisfying form, we are, in a sense, on the Enemy's ground."[20] Indeed, the Enemy encourages liking for things. Wormwood's task is to see that his patient will reject his spontaneous likings for the likings of some fashionable group. In that way he can concentrate the attention of his patient not on the thing but on himself and the way in which he can use the thing (as opposed simply to enjoying it). Hence, Screwtape suggests as a general rule that Wormwood try to uproot every strong personal taste of his patient, even tastes which seem trivial.

Lewis commonly—and perhaps rarely for an intellectual —makes a similar point with reference to culture. The Christian, he thinks, will take it a little less seriously than many others, for he knows how easily a supposed cultural interest can become a sophisticated form of concern for self and how easily this can undermine genuine delight in things. Lewis writes about how warmed his heart would be if, after a certain kind of sherry party with a great deal of talk about culture, he were to see a boy on a bus reading a science fiction book and obviously delighting in it.

[20]*The Screwtape Letters, with Screwtape Proposes a Toast* (New York: Macmillan, 1961), p. 41. Hereafter this volume will be referred to with the abbreviation *SL.*

I should have hopes of that boy. Those who have greatly cared
for any book whatever may possibly come to care, some day,
for good books. The organs of appreciation exist in them. They
are not impotent. And even if this particular boy is never going
to like anything severer than science fiction, even so
> The child whose love is here, at least doth reap
> One precious gain, that he forgets himself.[21]

This has been a long but necessary digression. If fallen
creatures cannot adopt the posture of receptivity, if they
inevitably use things for self-gratification instead of simply
delighting in these things, if therefore renunciation takes
on increased importance; it remains true that renunciation
is not rejection of the thing. Yet, of course, it is just as
important to remind ourselves that Lewis is a man who
could write: "Self-renunciation is thought to be, and indeed
is, very near the core of Christian ethics."[22] We have already
seen that a kind of negation of things is built into the notion
of creation itself. But this element of the dialectical movement becomes more pronounced and takes on a more ascetic character when we add the element of fallenness to the
Christian story.

For a fallen creature—that is, one who wants to grasp
and retain, to store up rather than receive, to turn from what
is given to what is desired—for such a creature the movement of negation will often be felt as self-negation. The
moment of renunciation will be experienced as self-
renunciation. It will involve a kind of killing of the self; for
a fallen creature does not truly desire to enter into a dialectical movement premised on trust in the Giver. Lewis
writes:

> Even in Paradise I have supposed a minimal self-adherence to
> be overcome, though the overcoming, and the yielding, would
> there be rapturous. But to surrender a self-will inflamed and
> swollen with years of usurpation is a kind of death. (PP, p. 91)

The natural self-centered life in us is ready "to fight tooth
and nail" to avoid being put to death (MC, p. 139). This

[21]"Lilies That Fester," The World's Last Night and Other Essays (New
York: Harcourt Brace Jovanovich, 1960), p. 39.
[22]God in the Dock, p. 193.

explains why Lewis is so fond of the paradox that he who loses his life will save it. And this is only a variation of a theme we will meet later; namely, that in a fallen world self-giving love becomes self-sacrificing. To turn from the image in the thing to the glory itself, from created thing to Creator, is to find one's life and the end for which one was created. But for a fallen creature to do this will seem like a death of the self. It cannot be experienced simply as a turning from one good to a higher good but instead must often be experienced as a negation not only of the thing but of the self. Thus, for a fallen creature the dialectical movement becomes more severe.

We are turned quite naturally, then, to a discussion of the legitimacy of self-love. Lewis points out that the self can be considered in two ways. It is, on the one hand, God's creation. From this perspective the self provides an occasion for love and delight, for pity and healing (where these are needed). On the other hand, the self is also that ego— one self among others—which continually makes claims to be preferred. Such a claim, Lewis says, is not simply to be hated. It is to be killed.

> The Christian must wage endless war against the clamour of the *ego* as *ego*: but he loves and approves selves as such, though not their sins. The very self-love which he has to reject is to him a specimen of how he ought to feel to all selves; and he may hope that when he has truly learned (which will hardly be in this life) to love his neighbour as himself, he may then be able to love himself as his neighbour: that is, with charity instead of partiality.[23]

Characteristically, Lewis adds a few sentences later that "it is better to love the self than to love nothing," since the latter is for him a description of hell.

There is in *That Hideous Strength* an interesting example of what seems to be legitimate self-love (or, perhaps better, legitimate delight in oneself). Jane has met the Director and is now returning home. Within the one Jane various "Janes" are present; various feelings and emotions

[23]*Ibid.*, p. 194.

bombard her.[24] Above all, she finds herself in a state of joy—an almost ecstatic state. Whatever she thinks of reminds her of the Director and, through him, leads to joy. She delights in the sunlight streaming through the windows of the train, in the rabbits and cows, in the speech of the old man who shares her compartment. She considers what she will do when she gets home and can think of nothing which does not delight her—she may listen to Bach, or read Shakespeare's sonnets, or have buttered toast and tea. She rejoices in all this.

> She rejoiced also in the consciousness of her own beauty. . . . In such a mood it was only natural, after the old countryman had got out at Cure Hardy, to stand up and look at herself in the mirror which confronted her on the wall of the compartment. Certainly she was looking well: she was looking unusually well. And, once more, there was little vanity in this. For beauty was made for others. (p. 152)

Recognizing her beauty as not her own, Jane is permitted to delight in it. It is hers, but she is conscious of having received it; hence, she has no sense of possessiveness with respect to it. She enjoys it as everything is enjoyed when rightly received. This sort of delight in the self is not incompatible with a self-giving love. Indeed, it results from the fact that Jane has given herself to the Director—through him her beauty leads to joy.

Therefore, the dialectic which applies to created things applies also to the self. Since the beloved may be the self, it is not safe to think of love only as a steady wish for the good of the loved one. That alone might not call for a movement out of the self. It is safe to characterize love as commitment to the well-being of the loved one only when we also characterize it in terms of self-giving. Neither half of the dialectic can stand alone. Just as no principled rejection of the created thing is permitted—since that would destroy the dialectic—so also, it is an abuse of the dialectic to reject *in*

---

[24]*That Hideous Strength: A Modern Fairy-Tale for Grown-Ups* (New York: Macmillan, 1965), pp. 150ff. Hereafter this volume will be referred to with the abbreviation *THS*.

principle any desire for one's fulfillment or happiness. The notion that it is wrong ever to desire our own good is, in Lewis' view, an accretion which has crept into Christian thinking from Kant and the Stoics (*WG,* p. 1). Nevertheless, it is accurate to think of self-giving as fundamental to the dialectic, since self-fulfillment is, in Lewis' view, possible only as the by-product of a self-giving love.

When all this has been said, it remains true according to Lewis that we cannot for more than a passing moment attain a state of wholly legitimate self-esteem in this present life. The Fall continues to be part of the story by which we must understand ourselves. The self must be honored as God's creature, yet put to death. That is simply the dialectical movement of enjoyment and renunciation applied to the self, and in this application the dialectic acquires a decidedly ascetic tone. The pole of renunciation, when lived out in a fallen world, will often be experienced as self-renunciation. One can believe that the journey leads toward self-fulfillment, but one cannot experience it to be that.

If the addition of fallenness to the story adds a severe, somewhat ascetic note, the opposite can be said for the climax of the story: incarnation, redemption, and *eschaton.* There is, of course, "in our present pilgrim condition plenty of room (more room than most of us like) for abstinence and renunciation."[25] But it is clear that the story speaks of the end as something quite different from release from the body and the things the body knows through the senses. Renunciation is for the sake of these things, so we can learn to approach them once again from the posture of receptivity. With his natural talent for metaphor, Lewis puts it this way:

> These small and perishable bodies we now have were given to us as ponies are given to schoolboys. We must learn to manage: not that we may some day be free of horses altogether but that some day we may ride bare-back, confident and rejoicing, those greater mounts, those winged, shining and world-shaking horses which perhaps even now expect us with impatience, pawing and snorting in the King's stables. Not that the gallop would be of any value unless it were a gallop with

[25]*Miracles,* p. 169.

the King; but how else—since He has retained His own charger—should we accompany him?[26]

Incarnation is the sign that things and bodies—the creation—remain objects of delight even in a fallen world. It is the promise that abstinence and renunciation are not the final word. We cannot, Lewis admits, adequately picture what a redeemed creation will be like, but he believes it is far better to affirm the very human images of the Bible than to lapse into any negative spirituality. He points out, for example, that life in the new creation will no longer be sexual. For us this seems to mean that it will amount to something like a fast. But our outlook, he suggests, is like that of a small boy

> who on being told that the sexual act was the highest bodily pleasure, should immediately ask whether you ate chocolates at the same time. On receiving the answer "No," he might regard absence of chocolates as the chief characteristic of sexuality. In vain would you tell him that the reason why lovers in their carnal raptures don't bother about chocolates is that they have something better to think of. The boy knows chocolate: he does not know the positive thing that excludes it. We are in the same position.[27]

What the end of the story brings is not release from things but instead new and unimaginable splendors.

Lewis follows the same pattern in everything he says about created things. At any point in life a thing may have to be renounced because it threatens to become an idol. In heaven one will find that what he abandoned (even if he plucked out his right eye) "was precisely nothing."[28] Thus, when the end of all worlds, including Narnia, comes in *The Last Battle,* the children find that England (along with many other lands) is within Aslan's country. Mr. Tumnus the Faun tells them: "You are now looking at the England within England, the real England just as this is the real Narnia. And in that inner England no good thing is de-

[26]*Ibid.*
[27]*Ibid.*, p. 165.
[28]*The Great Divorce: A Dream* (New York: Macmillan, 1946), p. 6. Hereafter this volume will be referred to with the abbreviation *GD*.

stroyed."[29] But this is a "retrospective vision" which we ought not try to anticipate (*GD*, p. 7). The story must be lived, and for now the end of the story can serve only to offer hope and encouragement to the weary traveler. The journey itself, however, is one in which we are never free of "our present pilgrim condition."

LIVING THE DIALECTIC

The person who wants the Christian story to shape the contours of his life will want to enter into this dialectical movement between enjoyment and renunciation. Lewis is more willing to discuss the dialectic than to offer practical suggestions for the living of it. But any reader of his works will recognize certain themes which fit well into this pattern. There is, in the first place, his constant concern that we remember the necessity of both affirming and negating created things. Neither side of the movement can be turned into a principle. Ordinarily it is the side of self-denial or renunciation which is formalized and turned into a policy. (One who follows the way of enjoyment is perhaps less likely to be consciously formulating a policy.)

In any case, no principle can be derived from the dialectic. Enjoyment and renunciation are both required. "One of the marks of a certain type of bad man is that he cannot give up a thing himself without wanting everyone else to give it up" (*MC*, p. 62). Hence, the particular way in which one enters into the dialectic involves personal decision. In this Lewis seems to agree with Charles Williams' understanding of the manner in which the Way of Affirmation and the Way of Negation co-inhere. Mary McDermott Shideler might almost be speaking of Lewis when she summarizes Williams' view.

> The choice between the Ways, the manner of choosing, and the kind of balance to be maintained between them, is an intensely personal business that cannot be regulated by another person, or possibly even by oneself. It does not matter very

[29]*The Last Battle* (New York: Macmillan, 1956), p. 172.

much, so long as they are held together. But it is not altogether easy to unite them. The perversions of both Ways are more comfortably sustained than the tension. . . .[30]

What is especially clear in Lewis is that both movements of the dialectic should ordinarily be lived by everyone. He does not think that one movement should be lived by one group of Christians while others content themselves with the remaining attitude toward things. Nevertheless, even here he adheres to the belief that no general statement of principle is possible. He accepts the fact that some Christians will want a life characterized primarily by renunciation, especially in a society intensely concerned with the acquisition of luxuries.

Lewis speaks of "the blessedly two-edged character" of Christianity.[31] The Christian God is the God of nature who sends rain into the furrows, who causes the wild deer to bring forth their young. He is the God of wheat and wine and oil.[32] Yet, writes Lewis, he is not a nature-god. Indeed, the central image in the Christian faith is that of a man slowly dying by torture. It is a religion of martyrdom and fasts, and the Christian lives both sides of that faith—or tries to. True Christian asceticism never involves a rejection of the created thing. One must say: "Marriage is good, though not for me; wine is good, though I must not drink it; feasts are good, though today we fast."[33] What is sought is an attitude which leaves a person free both to enjoy his breakfast *and* to mortify his inordinate appetites.[34] In other words, entry into the movement between enjoyment and renunciation is seen by Lewis as the closest we can come to capturing in our lives the posture of receptivity which ought to characterize creatures. Renunciation is necessary lest we immerse ourselves only in the thing, trying to grasp and retain it. Enjoyment is necessary lest renunciation become a principled rejection of the creation itself. Both

[30]Shideler, p. 27.
[31]*God in the Dock*, p. 147.
[32]*Miracles*, pp. 119, 168.
[33]*God in the Dock*, p. 149.
[34]*Ibid.*

movements are required for anyone who tries to approach things in the light of the Christian story. The point is well made by Charles Williams when he notes that—at least in its dogma—the church always checked asceticism by requiring that even the rejected thing had to be declared good.

> Rejection was to be rejection but not denial, as reception was to be reception, but not subservience. Both methods, the Affirmative Way and the Negative Way, were to co-exist; one might almost say, to co-inhere, since each was to be the key of the other. . . .[35]

Enjoyment and renunciation will be asked of all—but in different ways, in different measures, and at different times. Thus, the first thing to be said is this: that the manner in which one lives the dialectic can never be prescribed or universalized. Lewis also believes that a right attitude toward things will be difficult to maintain for anyone who lives too much in the future, who rests too much of the heart's longing in what is not yet given. A proper appreciation of created things is characterized by a willingness to receive and delight in what is given. In *Letters to Malcolm*, Lewis speaks of the need to cultivate in ourselves "a preliminary act of submission" toward whatever is given in the present moment (p. 26). And in words which echo Ransom's reflections on Perelandra, he writes:

> It seems to me that we often, almost sulkily, reject the good that God offers us because, at that moment, we expected some other good. . . . God shows us a new facet of the glory, and we refuse to look at it because we're still looking for the old one. . . .
> It would be rash to say that there is any prayer which God *never* grants. But the strongest candidate is the prayer we might express in the single word *encore*.[36]

The dialectic is lived for the sake of a receptive enjoyment of the good things of creation. To be preoccupied with what is not yet given—and may never be given—is to turn from

---

[35]Charles Williams, *The Descent of the Dove: A Short History of the Holy Spirit in the Church* (Grand Rapids: Eerdmans, 1939), p. 57.
[36]*Letters to Malcolm*, pp. 26f.

the actual things which here and now offer delight and call us out of ourselves.

Lewis consistently recommends that luxuries be sacrificed, but he is a stout defender of what he calls "middle things." He finds in the writings of Addison, for example, this "tranquil ground of quiet sentiments and pleasing melancholies and gentle humor."[37] Addison does not, he writes, stir one's depths as Johnson does.

> And yet, if I were to live in a man's house for a whole twelve-month, I think I should be more curious about the quality of his small beer than about that of his wine; more curious about his bread and butter and beef than about either.[38]

Addison stands on this "common ground of daily life" and deals with "middle things." Middle things are created things, never the Creator. But they are to be honored for what they are, and one cannot read Lewis without sensing that an esteem for the commonplace things of life was an essential part of living the dialectic.

At the same time we can point to another element in Lewis' own life which illustrates the pole of renunciation. When in *Perelandra* Ransom is preparing to be sent off in the coffin-like box, he discusses matters with his confidant (a fictional Lewis) and asks him to look after various matters.

> I got to know a lot more about Ransom than I had known before, and from the number of odd people whom he recommended to my care, 'If ever I happened to be able to do anything,' I came to realise the extent and intimacy of his charities. (p. 28)

This is quite in keeping with what Lewis believed to be an appropriate way of entering into the dialectic. In the direct manner which characterizes his approach in the radio broadcasts he says that "if our charities do not at all pinch or hamper us, I should say they are too small" (*MC*, p. 67). The great obstacle to charity lies not simply in a desire for luxury but in fear of insecurity. That fear is symbolized by

---

[37]"Addison," *Selected Literary Essays*, p. 168.
[38]*Ibid.*, p. 167.

Lewis in the image of the Fixed Land. And it was a fear well known to Lewis. He writes that his father

> represented adult life as one of incessant drudgery under the continual threat of financial ruin. In this he did not mean to deceive us. Such was his temperament that when he exclaimed, as he frequently did, "There'll soon be nothing for it but the workhouse," he momentarily believed, or at least felt, what he said. (*SJ*, p. 23)

Lewis had the same fear throughout his adult life—a legacy from his father which he was unable to shake off. Yet, despite this, it is known that his private charities were immense. (A good example of the way in which he provided help can be seen from reading his *Letters to an American Lady*.)[39] One will not keep fear of insecurity from becoming a possessive demon by making oneself ever more secure. The hold of the god must be broken by flying in the very face of the drive for security. That is what Lewis believed and practiced.

Entry into the dialectical movement between enjoyment and renunciation, a life directed largely to the present, an appreciation of the commonplace, a relatively severe practice of charity—Lewis sees all these as ways by which a right attitude toward created things can be cultivated. It is no easy task to learn to delight in things without seeking security in them; yet, this is part of what it means to be human. Here, though, a persistent theological issue as-

---

[39]Ed. Clyde S. Kilby (Grand Rapids: Eerdmans, 1967). Cf. also the comment by Lewis' brother, W. H. Lewis, in "Memoir of C. S. Lewis" which serves as a preface to *Letters of C. S. Lewis* (New York: Harcourt, Brace & World, 1966). His brother comments (pp. 20f.): "It was with the publication of *The Screwtape Letters*, in the autumn of 1942, that Jack first achieved wide public success of the kind that brings money rolling in. He was not used to this—his early penury had not trained him for relative affluence—and he celebrated by a lavish and improvident scattering of cheques to various societies and individual lame dogs. Before the situation got completely out of hand, his solicitor intervened: a charitable trust was set up into which two-thirds of his royalties was thereafter paid automatically, and from which payments both large and numerous were made for all manner of charitable purposes. The financial side of his charity was by no means limited to this particular arrangement, and the total of his benefactions will never be known. . . ."

serts itself. What is the motive for trying to cultivate this attitude? Is this part of a concerted quest for holiness?

In one sense it surely is, but Lewis does not think we can describe it simply in those terms. The Christian is engaged in an attempt not to be holy but to be Christ-like. Lewis can summarize the whole of Christianity as "putting on Christ" (*MC*, p. 152). What Christ asks is that the Christian give himself up entirely to be re-made. Lewis conceives of this process as a perfecting which takes place over time—a process which is never completed in this life. It goes on until a life of sanctity makes possible a real union of will between creature and Creator.[40] However, at the same time that he stresses the attempt to put on Christ, Lewis can say that it is God who is doing everything in the Christian (*MC*, p. 150).

> It is like a small child going to its father and saying, "Daddy, give me sixpence to buy you a birthday present." Of course, the father does, and he is pleased with the child's present. It is all very nice and proper, but only an idiot would think that the father is sixpence to the good on the transaction. (*MC*, pp. 110f.)

Lewis is aware that the cultivation of a right attitude toward things could become another form of the self's quest for its own good at the expense of others. But here the paradox reasserts itself. Saving one's life requires losing it. To regain the posture of receptivity would be to achieve self-fulfillment. But fulfillment of the self cannot be the end aimed at; one must lose one's life. "Christ will indeed give you a real personality; but you must not go to Him for the sake of that" (*MC*, p. 175).

It is at this point—and only at this point—that faith (in the sense of trust) becomes central for Lewis. It is not central in his understanding of Christianity. Much nearer to the heart for him is the goal of fellowship with God and all creatures, a fellowship which is the culmination of a long process of sanctification. Faith as trust enters in at one point—though a vital one. Lewis believes that anyone who

---

[40]*Letters to Malcolm*, p. 69. Note, though, that this union of wills is said here to be reached "under grace."

seriously attempts to "put on Christ" will sooner or later have to face failure. At some point he will realize that he has failed to regain the posture proper to a creature and that, even if he could, he would be doing nothing more than giving back to God what God had given (*MC*, p. 112). And at that point, when he is in danger of despairing, the Christian comes to say to God in faith, "You must do this, I can't" (*MC*, p. 113). He leaves it to God and recognizes even—though Lewis sees dangers in the formulation—that Christ not only offers something for nothing but offers everything for nothing (*MC*, p. 114). The formulation is dangerous only if it is removed from the existential context in which it first sprang up: the context of one who is at the point of despair because of his own failure. It is interesting to notice the way in which Lewis begins the chapter of *Mere Christianity* which discusses faith as trust. He writes:

> I want to start by saying something that I would like everyone to notice carefully. It is this. If this chapter means nothing to you, if it seems to be trying to answer a question you never asked, drop it at once. Do not bother about it at all. There are certain things in Christianity that can be understood from the outside, before you have become a Christian. But there are a great many things that cannot be understood until after you have gone a certain distance along the Christian road. These things are purely practical. . . . They are directions for dealing with particular cross-roads and obstacles on the journey and they do not make sense until a man has reached those places. (p. 112)

Faith as trust is not for Lewis the foundation stone on which to build an exposition of Christian theology. Hence, the Christian life is not conceived largely as a turn from consciousness of sin to the proclamation of grace. Instead, it is conceived as a journey, a process of sanctification. The Christian is one who has found in Christ what he yearned for: the way to community with the Father. And he is one who has now entered upon an imitation of Christ. From start to finish his journey is the work of grace, but it remains true that grace is conceived not as the announcement of a right relationship with God but as the means by which one may travel the path which leads to such a relationship.

Faith as trust can be fruitfully discussed only with one who is already seriously attempting the *imitatio Christi*. It is a practical consideration designed, not to lay the foundation for all theological construction, but to deal with a certain kind of problem which will inevitably confront anyone making this journey.

We will approach this issue again, though from a slightly different angle, in Chapter Three. It should be obvious, however, that we here touch upon an aspect of Lewis' theology which might properly be termed "Anglo-Catholic." It is the vision of God, not justification by grace through faith, which is the cornerstone of his theological system. Protestants might well ask whether Lewis has not seen what they have sometimes missed: that what is central for the task of preaching to troubled consciences may not be central for theological endeavor as a whole. One must do justice both to the vision of God which Lewis' reality principle articulates and to the pilgrim condition in which we presently find ourselves. Lewis tries to do this by conceiving of the pilgrim's journey as a process of sanctification.

This need not mean that the Christian is engaged in a quest for holiness. That danger hovers rather near to Lewis' way of organizing theology (just as the danger of ignoring the call to holiness may threaten a theology which makes faith as trust central). The theologian is himself a pilgrim, whose experience is unfinished. For precisely that reason, one's theological system must necessarily remain unfinished, a witness to that vision toward which it points but which it cannot capture. Whatever organizing principle the theologian chooses will bring with it certain risks and dangers as well as certain strengths. Lewis makes his choice and pays the concomitant price: the lack, at times, of a clear affirmation of grace and the faith which grace elicits.

What should be clear is that in this discussion the centrality of the story has reasserted itself. The story of creation, fall, incarnation, redemption, and *eschaton* shapes the contours of the entire Christian life. The Christian understands his life by locating it within that story, and it is no accident that in his first attempt to recount his conversion

Lewis reached back to the pattern of Bunyan in order to write *The Pilgrim's Regress*. The key to the story, for Lewis, is its central element: incarnation. Hence, to enter the story and understand one's life by it is not to seek holiness but to follow Christ—to respond to the lure of his call. That is the motive which guides Lewis' search for a right attitude toward the things of creation.

Everything we have said thus far about living the dialectic has been concerned with the way in which individuals do this in their personal lives. There can be little doubt that this is Lewis' central concern—a concern reinforced by his belief that there are no ways to make a principle of the dialectic. Yet, it is also true that individuals live in societies, and in societies scarcity of resources exists, and money serves as a medium of exchange (a means of satisfying the itch to have things over again). Lewis recognizes this but does not think it reason for opposing civil society. Civilization is commanded, yet dangerous.[41] And money, while it may be suspect in certain ways, does serve to facilitate civilization. Emil Brunner has clearly and simply expressed the rather ambivalent view which Lewis holds.

> Money is the abstract form of material goods. This abstraction, like all abstraction, includes both great potentialities and great dangers.... Where money has become the main material good, quantity tends to prevail over quality. The desire for wealth becomes infinite. I cannot imagine an infinite number of concrete material goods, but I can easily add an indefinite number of ciphers to any given figure. That is why money becomes a great danger to social life. In itself it is a most valuable invention, freeing the exchange of goods from chance and other limitations and giving economic life a new mobility.[42]

Lewis points out that British society of his day is based in important ways on investment and the lending of money at

[41]"Williams and the Arthuriad," *Arthurian Torso: Containing the Posthumous Fragment of 'The Picture of Arthur' by Charles Williams and a Commentary on the Arthurian Poems of Charles Williams by C. S. Lewis* (London: Oxford, 1948), p. 134. Lewis here is commenting on Williams' poetry, but this much of the comment seems at least to reflect his personal view as well.

[42]Emil Brunner, *Christianity and Civilisation, Second Part: Specific Problems* (London: Nisbet & Co., 1949), pp. 87f.

interest—a practice which was, he says, condemned in ancient Greece, Israel of Old Testament times, and medieval Christendom (*MC*, p. 66). He recognizes that there may be important differences between usury as practiced then and modern practices, and he makes no attempt to decide the issue himself. But he does make clear his own deep ambivalence about a society based on money as a medium of exchange, and in the light of Ransom's reflections on Perelandra this is not hard to understand. If money really does provide a way to grasp inordinately after things (and, thus, a way to deny one's creaturely role), it is a kind of institutionalized evil.

We can see here the importance which Lewis gives to the fact that we are embodied creatures in a world of things. For example, Emil Brunner, after the passage cited above, goes on to suggest that "within the Christian faith motive is more important than structure."[43] Thus, for Brunner an economic system built on money as a medium of exchange is not inherently suspect. It is, simply, subject to misuse by sinful people. Lewis' suspicions seem to cut deeper. He is inclined to believe that certain forms of work, which can be done only for the sake of money, are alienating in themselves. He is less willing to separate structure and motive than Brunner might seem to be. For Lewis, the way we structure the things of our world may often impinge on our attitudes and motives. Delight in work may become impossible in an economy in which money (or, a still greater abstraction, credit) has become the main material good.

Lewis offers no alternative program for society, for he doubts whether radical change would be, on the whole, beneficial. He believes that life within society is commanded, and, hence, he rules out a kind of Christian sectarianism. Nevertheless, his entire work constitutes a sustained vision of other possibilities for human existence. The closest he comes to specifying what a "Christian civilization" would be like comes in one passage in *Mere Christianity* (p. 66). It would, he says, please no one entirely. Its economic life would strike us as rather socialistic, its family

[43]*Ibid.*, p. 93.

life and code of manners as quite old-fashioned and even aristocratic. Everyone would like some parts of the picture and dislike others, and for precisely that reason Lewis doubts whether it can be achieved. It has been suggested that the community at St. Anne's in *That Hideous Strength* offers a few hints about Lewis' economic views.[44] We are told that Denniston has become a Distributivist (*THS*, p. 19). This may be a reference to "Distributism," an economic program advocated by G. K. Chesterton (whom Lewis had certainly read). If so, we can get a slightly clearer view of what an ideal economic life would be. It would not involve (as the *Mere Christianity* passage might suggest) socialism in the sense of government ownership of the means of production. Instead, it would involve the widest possible distribution of private property. Every man would own his small shop, small farm, small factory, and so forth. It is difficult to tell whether this truly represents Lewis' economic position when he wrote *That Hideous Strength*, but the hypothesis has inherent plausibility. Yet, as Jared Lobdell notes, such a position amounts to a call for an industrial counter-revolution.[45] Lewis may have desired such an ideal, but he was far from issuing this call (partly because he did not believe it his vocation to do so).

What we find then in Lewis is genuine reservation about the economic organization of modern Western societies combined with an equally genuine belief that no feasible alternative system has presented itself. There can be little doubt about Lewis' basic hostility to industrialized society in which planned obsolescence is an economic necessity. In his inaugural lecture at Cambridge he maintained that the greatest division in Western history is "that which divides the present from, say, the age of Jane Austen and Scott."[46] And his trump card in defense of this case is the birth of machines. As a result we have come to speak of

[44]In what follows I draw upon Jared C. Lobdell, "C. S. Lewis, Distributist: His Economics as Seen in *That Hideous Strength*," *Orcrist*, 6 (1971–72), pp. 20f. For an excellent recent discussion of Chesterton's socio-economic views, see Margaret Canovan, *G. K. Chesterton: Radical Populist* (New York: Harcourt Brace Jovanovich, 1977).

[45]*Ibid.*, p. 21.

[46]" 'De Descriptione Temporum'," *Selected Literary Essays*, p. 7.

'stagnation' where we once spoke of 'permanence,' and that
purely linguistic observation is not unrelated in Lewis'
mind to economic matters. In advertising, 'latest' means
'best,' though there is no reason why this should necessarily
be the case.[47] The reason, or so Lewis thinks, lies in the
power the machine has exercised over thought and imagination; for old machines are forever being replaced by new
and better ones.

What is to be said about living in such a society? In
commenting on Charles Williams' Arthurian poems Lewis
points to a need for a continuous redemption of society. In
one of the poems coinage comes to Logres, and the question
arises whether this is good or bad. On the one hand, coinage
facilitates exchange; on the other, it can become a way of
seeking autonomy and independence. It can encourage

> a deadly oblivion of the fact that we all live in and on each
> other, a deadly illusion that the laws of the city permit inde-
> pendence. . . . The city, by reason of its legitimate complexity,
> does really need instruments such as coinage which them-
> selves need to be continually redeemed if they are not to
> become deadly. Civilization is commanded, yet civilization
> can safely be practised only by those to whom it is promised
> that 'if they drink any deadly thing it shall not hurt them.'[48]

We should not forget, however, that this passage is a commentary on Williams' poem. Lewis was less sanguine about
the possibilities of the city. In her address memorializing
Lewis, Helen Gardner notes that, despite the fact that much
of his work concerned the debt of English literature to the
literature of the Renaissance, no vision of "cities, large and
small, with splendid public monuments" ever played a
large role in his imagination. For Lewis, she suggests, "the
simple loyalties of the *comitatus* were never replaced . . .
by the more complex loyalties of the 'city'."[49]

Her observation rings true. Lewis tends to turn to solutions for the individual or small group of like-minded persons rather than for society as a whole. His reservations

[47]*Ibid.*, p. 10.
[48]*Arthurian Torso*, p. 134.
[49]Helen Gardner, "Clive Staples Lewis, 1898–1963," *The Proceedings
of the British Academy*, Vol. 51 (London: Oxford, 1965), p. 420.

about offering larger answers grow out of his beliefs that
such larger answers are not likely to be very ready at hand
just now and that, even if they were, it is not his vocation to
offer them. Christians ought, Lewis thinks, to seek work of a
particular kind—work which would be worth doing even if
no one paid for it, work which would have to be done even
by a family or small group living in primitive isolation and
concerned only with meeting basic human needs. Work,
that is, in which a person can take genuine delight in what
he is doing *at present.* As examples Lewis points to jobs
such as agricultural worker, policeman, doctor, teacher, artist, and priest. This is to be contrasted with work "whose
sole purpose is the earning of money; work which need not
be, ought not to be, or would not be, done by anyone in the
world unless it were paid."[50] Lewis' favorite example of this
sort of work is advertising—which, on his view, is dedicated
largely to creating superfluous desires. Lewis notes that the
professional prostitute is "an extreme example of an activity
which has no possible end in view except money."[51] This is
significant, since it is for Lewis axiomatic that inordinate
love and a refusal to adopt the posture appropriate to a
creature will finally kill all genuine pleasures. Creaturely
rebellion can be institutionalized, and the end will be a
destruction of true humanity.

Enough has been said to clarify Lewis' reservations
about modern society as well as his unwillingness or inability to provide solutions to large-scale problems of social
organization. We need to be clear, though, about what he
objects to. He is not against division of labor and specializa-
tion. Indeed that is to be applauded, since it brings home to
men their need for one another. His targets seem to be (1)
money and an economy dependent on buying and selling;
(2) luxuries and the desire for luxury; and (3) large factories
(he seems happy only with small manufactures where the
etymology of the word—from the Latin *manus,* for
"hand"—has not been forgotten).[52] His target in general

---

[50]"Good Work and Good Works," *The World's Last Night* . . . , p. 72.
[51]*Ibid.*
[52]Lobdell, p. 20.

seems to be anything which stimulates or reinforces greedy accumulation or the power to repeat pleasures at will. The institutionalizing of such motives has, he thinks, forced large numbers of people into work which no one can delight in and which can be done for no motive other than the earning of money. This is a condition for which he—unlike some other social critics—blames no one in particular. "It has stolen upon us, unforeseen and unintended."[53]

What is important, he believes, is not to assign blame but to learn to live within such a society. Here again he returns to personal entry into the dialectic. To seek really good work—work which offers possibility for delight—may require "considerable mortification of our avarice."[54] The reward for doing so could be genuine enjoyment of what we do; a real appreciation of created things. The penalty for refusing the renunciation (if it is required of us) could be work in the world of "business," of buying and selling— work done only for the sake of some future benefit. To learn to live means to learn to enter into the dialectic and live *it*. There is no other way Lewis knows by which we can break the hold of "the sweet poison of the false infinite." But break it we must if we are to be fully human. Human beings have been created in a world of things; created to delight in things but never to seek security in them. That vision is captured by Lewis in imaginative worlds, and that task is defined by him in terms of the Christian story.

[53]"Good Work and Good Works," *The World's Last Night* . . . , p. 72.
[54]*Ibid.*, p. 78.

CHAPTER II

THE REVELRY
OF INSATIABLE LOVE

Part of the magic of C. S. Lewis' Chronicles of Narnia is the
picture of community which they imprint on the imagination. Narnia is a land where rule is respected and hierarchy
accepted with delight. The Talking Animals of Narnia know
that, though it is a country for animals, a man is supposed to
be king in Narnia.[1] And the king, in turn, stands under the
Lion Aslan. It is a land of courtesy and courage (best
exemplified by Reepicheep, the valiant mouse). Obedience
to proper authority is a delight. In *Prince Caspian*
Trumpkin the Dwarf doubts that the blowing of the magic
horn will bring help; nevertheless, he is willing to under-
take a perilous journey to meet those who are to come and
help if Caspian his king so commands. He has, he says,
given his counsel; now he will take orders from the king.[2]
The fruits of such attitudes are obvious. Except when evil
enters from without, peace and harmony prevail within
Narnia despite the tremendous diversity to be found there.
In Narnia one meets talking horses, talking badgers, talking
mice, marsh-wiggles, centaurs, giants, dwarfs, fauns,
dryads—yet, under the rule of Aslan there is harmony and
true community.

The secret of community lies in the relation of each
inhabitant of Narnia to Aslan. All beauties of Narnia are his
creation and images of his splendor; all relationships must
be based on one's relation to him. Apart from him no

[1]*Prince Caspian* (New York: Macmillan, 1951), p. 57.
[2]*Ibid.*, p. 80.

genuine self-fulfillment is possible. A repeated theme of
The Horse and His Boy is that each learns only his own
story—that is, the story of how he has been called by Aslan
and what is required of him.[3] Loyalty to Aslan is asked of
each, and that common bond is the source of Narnia's unity.

All this describes Narnia as it was meant to be and as it is
when undisturbed by evil. However, almost from the moment of its creation evil had entered Narnia in the person of
Jadis, who had been Queen of Charn (in another world) and
who became the White Witch of Narnia. If we understand
evil as Jadis represents it, we also understand how such evil
could threaten the community of Narnia. In Charn, Jadis
and her sister had fought over the throne. When the battle
went against Jadis and it seemed that she must surrender,
she had preferred the destruction of Charn to loss of the
throne. Using her magical powers, she had uttered the
"Deplorable Word" which snatched victory from her sister
by destroying the object for which they were contending:
Charn.[4] Jadis is the personification of a pride which would
rather reign in hell than serve in heaven. And the lesson is
clear: Pride leaves no city, no possibility of community.

The entry of such pride brings division into Narnia.
When right rule and hierarchy are no longer respected by
all, the inhabitants of Narnia are divided into two communi-
ties between which there can be no ultimate harmony.
Shift, the wicked Ape, tries to claim that there is no real
distinction between Tash (the idol of the Calormenes) and
Aslan. Tash, he says, is simply another name for Aslan.[5]
However, as Shift himself learns, the conflict between
loyalties is real and decisive. In the great scene of es-
chatological judgment at the conclusion of *The Last Battle* a
division is made between those who look on Aslan with love
and those who do not. More accurately, the creatures of
Narnia themselves make the division. As they come streaming up to the door of the stable at which Aslan stands, all
must look on his face. Some look and find with delight the

[3]New York: Macmillan, 1954. Cf. pp. 139, 171, 176.
[4]*The Magician's Nephew*, p. 53.
[5]*The Last Battle*, p. 31.

face for which they have always been searching. Others look and see only a source of fear and terror. They veer off to the left into the nothingness created by Aslan's shadow, and, significantly, they cease at that moment to be Talking Beasts. In turning from Aslan they turn from their true selves; for loyalty to self in opposition to Aslan has turned out to be a *self*-destructive loyalty.[6]

What the Chronicles of Narnia provide, then, is a vision of a genuine community, of its perversion by evil, and of the war between good and evil until the end of Narnia's history. In itself Narnia is a land of feasting, singing, revelry; of courtesy and courage; of obedience and gratitude; of diversity and harmony. And undergirding all that is good in Narnia is the tie of loyalty to Aslan. Love for Aslan is the secret of Narnia's festive spirit. Here obedience is not servitude, and every duty is a delight. This is "the revelry of insatiable love."[7]

The entry of pride into Narnia brings great sorrow, but it cannot finally conquer love. The triumph is Aslan's in the moving scene of death and resurrection in *The Lion, the Witch and the Wardrobe*. Yet, a share in the battle belongs to every loyal Narnian. They can participate in this struggle with joy, not because they are assured of victory (there is no hint of that in Narnia), but because joy lies in being on the side of The Lion. That kind of joy is exemplified by Roonwit the Centaur who, when dying, sends a message to Tirian, last of the kings of Narnia, telling him "to remember that all worlds draw to an end and that noble death is a treasure which no one is too poor to buy."[8]

[6]*Ibid.*, pp. 145f.
[7]Lewis uses the phrase in a very different context. In *The Discarded Image* he describes the way a person who accepted the Medieval Model of the universe would feel when looking at the darkness of the night sky. "You would feel like one looking *in*. The Earth is 'outside the city wall'. When the sun is up he dazzles us and we cannot see inside. Darkness, our own darkness, draws the veil and we catch a glimpse of the high pomps within; the vast, lighted concavity filled with music and life. And, looking in, we do not see, like Meredith's Lucifer, 'the army of unalterable law', but rather the revelry of insatiable love. We are watching the activity of creatures whose experience we can only lamely compare to that of one in the act of drinking, his thirst delighted, yet not quenched" (p. 119).
[8]*The Last Battle*, p. 86.

What can such a vision of community offer? On one
occasion Lewis, after giving a talk on children's literature to
a conference of librarians, responded to such a question.
One questioner pointed out that it had become the trend to
offer children more practical books, such as a book on how
to build a boat. And

> he wondered what practical use fantasy, such as Dr. Lewis
> advocated, would have for the child. Dr. Lewis agreed that
> practical things were first class, but that although fantasy might
> not help a boy to build a boat, it would help him immensely
> should he ever find himself on a sinking ship.[9]

Indeed, what Lewis provides is not so much an argument as
the embodiment of an ideal. This can do for others what it
did for Puddleglum, the dour Marsh-wiggle in one of
Lewis' stories. The Witch tries to enchant him, Eustace, and
Jill by making them believe that they had only dreamed of a
land of Narnia and that Aslan was simply a big cat created
by their imaginations. In that moment of danger the vision
sustains Puddleglum. Stamping out the fire from which the
enchanting fumes were coming, he declares that he prefers
Aslan's world even if it should not be real. For, he says, it is
at least a better world than any the Witch can provide.[10]
This alone does not guarantee the truth of the vision; however, it demonstrates how the vision may serve to shape
character and action as well as expose the dangers of other
visions of community.

THAT MYSTICAL DEATH WHICH IS
THE SECRET OF LIFE
Images of Community

In the Chronicles of Narnia Lewis created a whole
world in which he could incarnate his vision of community.

[9]From the proceedings of the 1952 Bournemouth Conference of the
London Library Association. Quoted in John Warwick Montgomery, "The
Chronicles of Narnia and the Adolescent Reader," *Myth, Allegory and
Gospel: An Interpretation of J. R. R. Tolkien, C. S. Lewis, G. K. Chesterton,
Charles Williams*, ed. J. W. Montgomery (Minneapolis: Bethany Fellow-
ship, 1974), p. 115.
[10]*The Silver Chair* (New York: Macmillan, 1953), pp. 148ff.

He could not do that in writings of a very different character. Nevertheless, throughout his work the social vision
which is incarnate in Narnia is suggested by various images. These images are intended to suggest the difference
between two opposite solutions to the problem of isolation
and the selfishness which divides individuals from one
another. To search for community in the face of recalcitrant
claims of human selves one must turn either to love, a
relation between persons, or to the abolition of persons (of
"mine" and "thine") in the collective.[11] In order to picture
his vision of a community bound by love, Lewis uses images of players in a band, of organs in a body, of the city, and
of the dance.[12] For the moment we will confine ourselves to
images of the dance and the body in order to see why he
uses them and to note one way in which they stand in
tension.

Lewis is willing to apply, with caution, his image of the
dance to the divine life itself. He writes in *Mere Christianity:*

> In Christianity God is not a static thing—not even a person—
> but a dynamic, pulsating activity, a life, almost a kind of drama.
> Almost, if you will not think me irreverent, a kind of dance.
> The union between the Father and Son is such a live concrete
> thing that this union itself is a Person. ... What grows out of
> the joint life of the Father and Son is a real Person, is in fact the
> Third of the three Persons who are God. (p. 136)

And immediately Lewis applies the image to mankind.

> The whole dance, or drama, or pattern of this three-Personal
> life is to be played out in each one of us: or (putting it the other

---

[11]"A Reply to Professor Haldane," *Of Other Worlds*, p. 83.
[12]For the images of the band and the body, see *MC*, p. 128. Lewis
nowhere develops the image of players in a band as he does that of organs
in the body. The image of the city is central in *THS*, which will be
discussed later in several places. Despite its importance for that book, I
believe Mariann Russell is correct in saying that Lewis' characteristic
image is that of the dance, whereas the city is the chief image of Charles
Williams (*The Idea of the City of God* [Columbia University: Unpublished
Ph.D. Dissertation, 1965], p. 166). The obvious Augustinian roots of
Lewis' social vision should not lead us to concentrate on the image of the
city and forget that of the dance; for it adds certain features which are very
characteristic of Lewis' vision.

way round) each one of us has got to enter that pattern, take his place in that dance. (*MC*, p. 137)

The image of the dance makes Lewis' vision of community seem infectiously festive, and he, of course, intends that it should. But in his hands the image has other effects as well. In the eternal dance of love between Father and Son in the Trinitarian life of God, the Father delights in the Son and the Son looks up to the Father (*MC*, p. 135). In a dance, as Lewis conceives it, considerations of equality do not arise. Some dancers must bow to their partners; some must lead and others follow. What is especially interesting about the image, however, is that those who lead now may have to follow as the dance moves on. In *Miracles* Lewis discusses whether the redemption of man means that man has a central position in the universe. His answer is that, although this is reasonable from man's point of view, from another perspective one might look upon the redemption of man as only a preliminary to the rebirth of the whole creation. Lewis does not think we have to choose, and in making the point he turns to the image of the dance.

> What is subservient from one point of view is the main purpose from another. No thing or event is first or highest in a sense which forbids it to be also last and lowest. The partner who bows to Man in one movement of the dance receives Man's reverences in another. To be high or central means to abdicate continually; to be low means to be raised. ... (p. 129)

Continual abdication: that is "the mystical death which is the secret of life."[13] Similarly, in the vision of the Great Dance with which *Perelandra* closes one of the voices says: "Thus each is equally at the centre and none are there by being equals, but some by giving place and some by receiving it" (p. 217). The dance as an image of community pictures a festive union of individuals in which considerations of equality do not arise. To participate in the dance is to abdicate continually and continually to be raised.

Lewis also uses the image of the dance to picture a union of individuals in which freedom and order are har-

[13]*Miracles*, p. 135.

moniously combined. We must, he writes, "suppose the life
of the blessed to be an end in itself, indeed The End: to be
utterly spontaneous; to be the complete reconciliation of
boundless freedom with order. . . ."[14] Hence, the freedom
and spontaneity of the dance do not stand in tension with
the order and precision it requires. The image combines
these; for each participant enters into the festive spirit of
the dance only when he freely submits to its rules. Milton
also pictured life as an intricate dance, and Lewis says this
of the central paradox of Milton's vision:

> Discipline, while the world is yet unfallen, exists for the sake
> of what seems its very opposite—for freedom, almost for ex-
> travagance. : . . The heavenly frolic arises from an orchestra
> which is in tune; the rules of courtesy make perfect ease and
> freedom possible between those who obey them. Without sin,
> the universe is a Solemn Game: and there is no good game
> without rules.[15]

It is important that we not miss the words "without sin."
Lewis does not for a moment think that freedom and discipline can be harmoniously combined in our present life.
Nor does he think considerations of equality are unimportant for us. (We will investigate later what he has to say
about these matters.) But he does insist that we not forget
the image; for it points to the final reality. If we forget the
image we may come to believe that equality rather than the
continual abdication of the dance is desirable as an end
in itself, or we may come to think of rules of morality as an
end. Lewis wants none of this, and he uses the image of the
dance to picture a community which questions the lesser
unions for which we must often settle. He writes in *Letters
to Malcolm,*

> I know that my tendency to use images like play and dance for
> the highest things is a stumbling-block to you. . . .
> I do *not* think that the life of Heaven bears any analogy to
> play or dance in respect of frivolity. I do think that while we
> are in this 'valley of tears' . . . certain qualities that must belong
> to the celestial condition have no chance to get through, can

[14]*Letters to Malcolm,* p. 92.
[15]*A Preface to Paradise Lost,* p. 81.

project no image of themselves, except in activities which, for us here and now, are frivolous. (p. 92)

Another image which he uses extensively is the body or organism. For Lewis the search for true community is at the same time a search for true personality. Individuals need to be united yet remain themselves; what one seeks is "extreme differentiation of persons in harmonious union" (WG, p. 34). The principle of such union is love, exemplified first in the divine life where distinction exists "so that the union of reciprocal loves may transcend mere arithmetical unity or self identity" (PP, p. 151). Lewis finds similar implications in the concept of creation. To say that God creates is to say that everything is no longer God. The fact of creation means that in place of mere sameness there must now be a union of love.

To image such diversity within unity Lewis often turns to the organism. He sometimes thinks in specifically Christian terms of being taken up into the divine life itself: the mystical body (MC, p. 125). The person who shares in it becomes just that—a person. He is no longer an individual in isolation, but neither has he been absorbed into a collective. However, Lewis does not use the image only in theological contexts. In his essay "Membership," he points out that one can lose one's individuality and depart from isolation in two ways: when a convict has a number but not really a name and when a man in his home loses his name and becomes "Father" (WG, p. 35). He emphasizes that in an organic unity one becomes a member not of a class but of a body. The members of a class are interchangeable; not so the organs of a body. They are "things essentially different from, and complementary to, one another: things differing not only in structure and function but also in dignity" (WG, p. 33). The image, again, is hierarchical.

We should note a certain tension between the concepts of hierarchy in the images of the dance and the body. The image of the dance seemed to picture a union which was hierarchical in the sense that equality never pertained among the participants. Some would always lead and others follow; some give reverence and others receive it. In the next movement of the dance positions might be reversed. The hierarchies were never fixed. The image of the body, on the other hand, seems to point in the direction of more stable hierarchies, and we will see later that Lewis believes this to be true of certain relationships.

Understanding the meaning of community seems to have been an almost lifelong concern of Lewis. In 1926 he published "Dymer," a narrative poem. When it was issued in a new edition in 1950, Lewis wrote a preface in which he commented on the strength of anti-totalitarian feeling in the poem and the fact that he had been by temperament "an extreme anarchist."[16] Yet, he came to believe that it was as dangerous to isolate the self as to absorb it into a whole, for he later said, "There are no private affairs" (GD, p. 35).

Primarily, the images of the dance and the body function as a critique of false notions of community. Lewis writes in Mere Christianity that it is important to have a right picture of community so that one can be protected against two opposite and equally destructive errors: individualism, which fails to see that men are related to one another; and totalitarianism, which seeks to suppress differences throughout the whole of life (p. 145).

Some sense of how the vision can function is captured fictionally in Out of the Silent Planet. Weston's dedication to the continuation of human life (the species) makes him quite willing to sacrifice particular persons (i.e., Ransom) for the sake of the survival of the species. And it is significant that when Ransom has to translate Weston's philosophy into the language of the unfallen Malacandrians, it is impossible for him to make Weston's program sound anything other than terribly evil. The image of the Malacandrian community casts a clarifying light on programs and ideals which are potentially dangerous and destructive.

When we realize how deeply embedded these images are in Lewis' work we can begin to appreciate what Austin Farrer said not of Lewis' fiction but of one of his most

---

[16]Preface to *Narrative Poems*, ed. Walter Hooper (London: Geoffrey Bles, 1969), pp. 3, 6.

obviously apologetic works. "We think we are listening to
an argument, in fact we are presented with a vision; and it is
the vision which carries conviction."[17] It would be going
much too far to say that Lewis is not interested in the
argument; nevertheless, it is true that his social thought is
first of all a vision intended to appeal to the imagination just
as much as to the intellect. He believed that "what we learn
from experience depends on the kind of philosophy we
bring to experience."[18] Much of his writing can be understood as an attempt to provide compelling Christian images
which might shape and mold men's thinking about the kind
of life they live and the kind they ought to live. He maintained that literature functioned not to make people morally
better but to broaden their minds and open them to new
possibilities. In *Out of the Silent Planet* Ransom says,
"what we need for the moment is not so much a body of
belief as a body of people familiarized with certain ideas"
(p. 154). The whole human race is like a local pocket of evil
in the universe, and it needs visions of other and better
possibilities for community than those which naturally
occur to it (*PP*, p. 64). Lewis attempts to provide such a
vision: to paint a picture of community, of harmony between God and his creatures.

The Love Which Creates Community

Love is the guiding principle of true community and the
central mode of relationship among persons. However,
Lewis speaks of love in many different ways, and it is
important that we achieve an understanding of his meaning
behind this term.

Love brings men together in community because it
overcomes the problems of selfishness and self-
centeredness. Screwtape tells Wormwood that the
philosophy of hell rests upon the simple axiom that one self
is not another, and hence one self's good is not another's.
No shared good is possible and, therefore, competition

[17]Austin Farrer, "The Christian Apologist," *Light on C. S. Lewis*, ed.
Jocelyn Gibb (New York: Harcourt, Brace & World, 1965), p. 37.
[18]*Miracles*, p. 7.

rather than community is the end of human existence. But, writes Screwtape,

> the Enemy's philosophy is nothing more nor less than one continual attempt to evade this very obvious truth. He aims at a contradiction. Things are to be many, yet somehow also one. The good of one self is to be the good of another. This impossibility he calls *Love*. . . . Thus He is not content, even Himself, to be a sheer arithmetical unity; He claims to be three as well as one, in order that this nonsense about Love may find a foothold in His own nature. At the other end of the scale, He introduces into matter that obscene invention the organism, in which the parts are perverted from their natural destiny of competition and made to cooperate. (*SL*, pp. 81f.)

Lewis bases his understanding of love both upon specifically theological data (the trinitarian nature of God) and upon the image of the organism. Later we will see that in explaining the nature of love Lewis also appeals to the command to love the neighbor as we love ourselves and to the example of the incarnate God in whom we are to see "the Divine life operating under human conditions."[19]

The distinction between *eros*, which desires to possess the beloved and longs for union, and *agape*, which seeks to give and to spend oneself in service of the beloved, is now a commonplace.[20] In *The Four Loves* Lewis makes a similar distinction between what he calls "need-love" and "gift-love." Need-love is what sends a frightened child back to his mother's arms. Gift-love moves a man to work for the future of his family even if he will not himself be alive to share that future. And Lewis is quite clear that God's love is gift-love.

[19]*FL*, p. 17. For an example of Lewis' use of the great commandment, see *MC*, p. 100.

[20]See especially Anders Nygren, *Agape and Eros*, trans. Philip S. Watson (New York: Harper & Row, 1969). In *The Discarded Image*, his prolegomena to medieval studies, Lewis uses the distinction. He writes that both Christian theology and the medieval model "can speak about the 'love of God'. But in the one this means the thirsty and aspiring love of creatures for Him; in the other, His provident and descending love for them. The antithesis should not, however, be regarded as a contradiction. A real universe could accommodate the 'love of God' in both senses" (pp. 113–14). Lewis makes a similar contrast in his essay, "Edmund Spenser, 1552-99," in *Studies in Medieval and Renaissance Literature* (Cambridge, 1966), p. 144.

> Divine love is Gift-love. The Father gives all He is and has to
> the Son. The Son gives Himself back to the Father, and gives
> Himself to the world, and for the world to the Father, and thus
> gives the world (in Himself) back to the Father too. (*FL*, p. 11)

Indeed, Lewis can often sound as unremitting as Nygren in
maintaining that nothing could be less like God than need-
love.

Nevertheless, Lewis believes that need-love is a legitimate part of the love of human beings for God and for one
another.[21] He points first to the simple fact that we would
do violence to most languages if we refused to call need-
love 'love'.[22] He then goes on to suggest that we do *in
reality* need one another, and therefore ought not write off
all need-love as mere selfishness. Indeed, if it is the case
that we do need one another, failure to demonstrate need-
love might well be "the mark of the cold egoist." Lewis
appeals to the example of mother and child. "A tyrannous
and gluttonous demand for affection can be a horrible thing.
But in ordinary life no one calls a child selfish because it
turns for comfort to its mother; nor an adult who turns to his
fellow 'for company'." Lewis' third reason for thinking
need-love legitimate is that our spiritual health requires it.
Not only do men need one another; they need God as well.
And this love must almost always be largely a need-love. In
relation to God "our whole being by its very nature is one
vast need."

This view of love is grounded, quite simply, in Lewis'
beliefs about the nature of reality. That is, a truly human
existence is not lived in isolation. Men are made for community, for fellowship with God and with other men. They
have that need because divine love (which in itself is entirely gift-love) has so created them. To deny the legitimacy

[21]His discussion can be found on pp. 11–14 of *FL*. The citations in
this paragraph are taken from that discussion.

[22]This is not for Lewis just a point about the way we talk. He thinks the
evidence from language important because there is in language "a good
deal of stored insight and experience" (*FL*, p. 12). Contrast this with Nygren's belief that the "power of language over thought" has served to
confuse the originally sharp distinction between *eros* and *agape*. This is, in
Nygren's view, a "spell" cast upon us, which spell must be broken (p. 32).

of this component of human love would, for Lewis, amount
almost to a denial of our creaturely status. If we are made for
a fellowship with God and others which at present is not
fully realized, we cannot help but desire it. With self-
fulfillment understood in that sense Lewis will not quarrel.
He does, however, retain a certain ambiguity even here.
Although it is legitimate for a person to long for union with
God, Lewis is hesitant to affirm this too strongly—lest one
make a principle out of this at the expense of self-giving.
Thus, he speaks of the legitimacy of such desire but immediately adds:

> Such is my opinion; and it may be erroneous. Perhaps this
> secret desire also is part of the Old Man and must be crucified
> before the end. . . . The thing you long for summons you away
> from the self. Even the desire for the thing lives only if you
> abandon it. (*PP*, p. 149)

Thus the self needs God, but love concerns itself with God,
not with the self.

The contrast between *eros* and *agape* is not entirely
suitable as a "translation" of Lewis' contrast between
need-love and gift-love. For he is not making a simple
contrast between human love and divine love. To say that
God's love is gift-love is not necessarily to say that all
gift-love is God's love, and Lewis does not want to claim
that it is. There is a gift-love which is just as natural to
human beings as need-love. Hence, it is natural to expect of
a father that he work and save for the future of his family.
Both need-love and gift-love are natural components of
human love. Neither is simply disguised selfishness though
each can degenerate into that. If there is a natural gift-love
built into our natures, we can begin to play some verbal
tricks. Do we need to express a gift-love? Lewis does not
seem to object to such a formulation, but he eschews such
expressions, preferring to accept the clarification his distinction provides without denying the possible verbal ambiguities. Need-love grows out of lack, out of desire to be
filled. Gift-love grows out of abundance, out of desire to
reach out. Once we make that distinction it is perhaps
possible to say that a creature who must give in order to be

the sort of creature he is meant to be needs to give. Theologically viewed, this means that *agape* is not alien to our human nature; that when Christ came in gift-love, he came to his own.

What is *not* natural to human beings is participation in the love of the divine life itself. Human need-love and human gift-love both need to be transformed by divine love if they are to achieve their own fruition. Need-love is natural, but it is not natural for men to feel nothing but a "glad acceptance" of their bottomless need for God (*FL*, p. 179). Nor does our need-love readily accept a love of charity from others which is not based on our own merits (*FL*, p. 182). It is only when need-love is taken up into the life of God that a man "is not sorry at all for the innocent Need that is inherent in his creaturely condition" (*FL*, p. 181).

Lewis' anthropological assumption here is obvious: Not only are human beings made for fellowship with God and their fellows, they are also alienated from that fellowship and in rebellion against it. Need-love calls out for community but cannot provide it because of the sin that dwells within. Men rebel against their own needs. We are, of course, familiar with something like this in our everyday experience. When a young child—so tired that he can hardly stop crying—fights the idea of a nap and does everything possible to keep from falling asleep, we recognize that he is fighting what he needs most. And when we see a person who obviously desires to enter a circle of companions hang back because he is too embarrassed or proud to join them, we see him as a person who cannot accept the need that is inherent in his nature. Human need-love by itself is not enough to create community.

Similarly, the gift-love that is natural to man must also be transformed by divine love, for divine love is not the same as the gift-love which has been built into our natures. The gift-love natural to man is deficient in two ways. First, our gift-loves, even at their best, are biased in favor of the gifts which we ourselves can bestow. "But Divine Gift-love—Love Himself working in a man—is wholly disinterested and desires what is simply best for the beloved" (*FL,* p. 177). Second, "only the lovable can be naturally loved" (*FL,* p. 183). The gift-love natural to man is directed to objects that are intrinsically lovable: the deserving, or those whose very helplessness itself is of an appealing kind. It is important to remember that Lewis in no way condemns such natural gift-love. It is not wrong; it is incomplete. And true community requires that it be completed by divine love which enables one to love even what is not naturally lovable.

Thus far we have said that love binds persons together in community, that this love (in human beings) is legitimately composed of both need-love and gift-love, and that human love is insufficient apart from participation in the divine life of love. Throughout Lewis' social vision there is a reality principle: Persons truly stand in need of one another; they need to give to one another; and they need to be joined with God in harmonious union. Human life is dependent life because it is created life. The naturally human loves will find their fulfillment only when transformed by God's love, which is pure gift-love.[23] But how do we characterize divine gift-love?

When we begin to ask what Lewis means by divine gift-love we encounter a dizzying variety of formulations. We can begin by noting the positive character of love over against the negative unselfishness which Screwtape and his cohorts seek to foster. They want, Screwtape writes, to "teach a man to surrender benefits not that others may be happy in having them but that he may be unselfish in forgoing them" (*SL,* p. 121). Deftly, Lewis shows how a

[23]One must be careful in pressing talk even of divine love as pure gift-love. Lewis is willing to recognize a sense in which it may be said that God needs man. God's original act of creation is one of pure giving; however, in that very act of giving he binds himself to man so that he forever desires fellowship with him. But Lewis insists on the primacy of the divine gift. "Before and behind all the relations of God to man, as we now learn them from Christianity, yawns the abyss of a Divine act of pure giving—the election of man, from nonentity, to be the beloved of God, and therefore (in some sense) the needed and desired of God, who but for that act needs and desires nothing, since He eternally has, and is, all goodness. And that act is for our sakes" (*PP,* p. 51).

commitment to unselfishness can lead to the "Generous
Conflict Illusion." Something trivial, such as having tea in
the garden, is proposed. A member of the group consents to
this while making clear that he would rather not but is
prepared to be unselfish. At once the other members of the
group, also eager to be unselfish, withdraw their proposal.
The first insists on doing what the others want. They insist
on doing what he wants, and an argument quickly ensues.
This, Lewis means to say, is not the positive affection of
Christian love. This is good to remember when we find
Lewis saying that love is a matter of the will rather than the
feelings and that one does not have to be fond of those
whom he loves (*MC*, p. 90). That is Lewis' way of saying
that it is possible to have Christian love for a person without
feeling affection, friendship, or erotic love for him. He does
not mean, however, that love involves nothing more than
refraining from injuring the neighbor.

It is in trying to characterize this positive, active love
that difficulties begin. Speaking of the love that exists
within God from all eternity Lewis refers to "the concrete
reciprocities of love," thinking evidently of a mutual fellowship in love (*PP*, p. 29). In another context he writes that
"love is not affectionate feeling, but a steady wish for the
loved person's ultimate good as far as it can be obtained."[24]
This steady wish for the other's good is something different from kindness. For kindness is "the desire to see others
than the self happy; not happy in this way or in that, but just
happy" (*PP*, p. 40). But love, on this definition, is different.
It wills the *good* of the neighbor and is therefore willing to
cause suffering and unhappiness if they are necessary to
bring about the neighbor's good. God's love for men never
wearies and as a consequence "is quite relentless in its
determination that we shall be cured of . . . sins, at whatever
cost to us, at whatever cost to Him" (*MC*, p. 103). Love, on
this definition, can punish and even kill an enemy, but it
cannot wish the enemy were evil. It must hope that in this
world or another he may be cured. It must, in that sense,
seek his good (*MC*, pp. 92f.). Lewis has still other formula-

[24]*God in the Dock*, p. 49.

tions which sound like definitions of love. In self-giving, he writes, we touch a rhythm of all creation (*PP*, p. 152). Vicariousness (what Charles Williams called 'Exchange') is a law of the natural universe.[25] In this life—an important qualification—love involves sacrifice (*PP*, p. 102).

What are we to make of these varying formulations? Why should wishing the neighbor's good always involve sacrifice? How can a love which concerns itself solely with the neighbor's good concern itself with the reciprocities of mutual love?[26] Does self-giving mean the same thing as wishing the good of the neighbor? How can self-giving permit itself to cause pain and suffering to another?

Our problem will be eased somewhat by an (admittedly) intuitive grasp of what is central to Lewis' thought. If we remember that we are investigating Lewis' social vision —his picture of community—and that he often reverts to images such as the dance and the organism to characterize that vision, we will begin unraveling the knot with the concept of vicariousness. All life is interdependent. As Lewis writes in explicating Williams' concept of Exchange, "The courtesy of the Emperor has absolutely decreed that no man can paddle his own canoe and every man can paddle his fellow's. . . ."[27] In all created life, no being can exist on its own resources. Each profits by the work of

[25]*Ibid.*, p. 85.

[26]These are closely related to questions Paul Ramsey has put to Reinhold Niebuhr's ethics. In *Nine Modern Moralists* (Englewood Cliffs, N.J.: Prentice-Hall, 1962) Ramsey has written: "Love is mainly intent on the good of another. It is not intent on the *overt* sacrifice or the suffering this entails, any more than it intends the mutuality that sometimes (perhaps often) follows" (p. 136). And again: "Love is simply love, the genuine article; and it intends the good of the beloved one and not the response of mutuality; it intends the good of the other and not its own actual self-sacrifice or suffering. It is the *neighbor*, and not mutuality or heedlessness or sacrifice or suffering, who stands ever before the eyes of love" (p. 146). In general, we may say that the problem of reconciling Lewis' descriptions of love bears some similarity to that of reconciling Niebuhr's harmony of mutual love with his self-sacrificial love. Light cast on the one case may help to illumine the other. In Lewis' thought, however, there is another problem. One of his formulations sounds like Ramsey's "intending the good of the neighbor." However, that description may stand in some tension with another formulation: love as self-giving.

[27]*Arthurian Torso*, p. 123.

another. This interdependence is, in the first place, a fact about the divine life. In the mystery of that life none of the persons lives independently; yet, distinction remains. Within the life of God something analogous to society exists (*PP*, p. 29).

If we begin with this concept, we can see that vicariousness is not so much a definition of love as of community. We have simply come to see in another way that a genuine community unites individuals who, though separate and different, really do need one another. And from this point of view we can perhaps say that love is something different from mutual reciprocity. Lewis does speak of "the concrete reciprocities of love" in the life of God, but that seems to indicate only that in a genuine community reciprocity will result. It does not yet define the love which makes such community possible. The mutuality of intimate fellowship is the fruition of love, even its desired outcome.[28] But the concrete reciprocities of love are part of the picture of a community which practices vicariousness, not the definition of love itself.

If we seek a definition of love we must ask what makes a vicarious community possible. For that is what Lewis means by love: a relation among persons which— overcoming the recalcitrant claims of self—can generate and maintain a community of vicariousness and reciprocity. The question to ask therefore is, what is needed to create and maintain such a community? To find that will be to find what Lewis means by love. We will read him most consistently if we turn to "self-giving" as his basic understanding of love.

> For in self-giving, if anywhere, we touch a rhythm not only of all creation but of all being. For the Eternal Word also gives Himself in sacrifice; and that not only on Calvary. . . . From before the foundation of the world He surrenders begotten Deity back to begetting Deity in obedience. . . . From the

---

[28]Lewis might to some extent agree with Dorothy Sayers' discussion in *The Mind of the Maker* (London: Methuen & Co., 1941). She discusses the love of a creator for his work and says that what the creator desires is "the complete independence of the creature combined with its willing co-operation in his purpose" (p. 111).

highest to the lowest, self exists to be abdicated and, by that abdication, becomes the more truly self, to be thereupon yet the more abdicated, and so forever. ... What is outside the system of self-giving is not earth, nor nature, nor 'ordinary life,' but simply and solely Hell. (*PP*, p. 152)

Throughout his writings Lewis scatters references to the truth that "he who loses his life will save it." This is for him neither a prudential maxim nor a higher law. It is merely the truth of the universe on which all community must finally be based.[29] Without such a willingness to give of self, the vicariousness needed for community could not arise. The family would be a very different institution if the mother were not willing (even eager) to give of her strength and substance that the child, both before and after birth, might live vicariously from her. But at the same time, if there never comes a day when the child wants to give as well as receive, the relationship between mother and child can never reach its fruition in a mutual giving and receiving. Love, therefore, is "that mystical death which is the secret of life." Life requires that the self be not grasped but given up. Through self-giving we find our true selves; for it makes community possible, and we cannot be ourselves until we have left isolation and entered into fellowship.

We have yet to ask how love as self-giving will cohere with the remaining two descriptions of love cited at the beginning of this discussion: love as self-sacrifice and love as wishing the neighbor's good. Love as self-sacrifice is the incarnation of love as self-giving. Lewis grounds the need for self-sacrifice in an imitation of Christ but even more so in anthropological assumptions. Self-giving becomes self-sacrifice when incarnate in the human flesh because that flesh cannot, with a whole heart, will to surrender the self.

[29]Cf., for example, *MC*, p. 175 and *PP*, p. 149. Lewis' point is similar to that made by Reinhold Niebuhr in relating sacrificial love and mutual love. "Sacrificial love thus represents a tangent towards 'eternity' in the field of historical ethics. It is nevertheless the support of all historical ethics; for the self cannot achieve relations of mutual and reciprocal affection with others if its actions are dominated by the fear that they may not be reciprocated. Mutuality is not a possible achievement if it is made the intention and goal of any action." *The Nature and Destiny of Man: Vol. II* (New York: Scribner's, 1964), p. 69.

To surrender the self would be "to tread Adam's dance backward"; it would mean not seeking to grasp life as one's own but, instead, being willing to entrust one's life to the Creator in obedience (*PP*, p. 100). And such a willingness is no longer natural for those who are fallen. Hence, love must be sacrificial because it is seeking to be active in sinful people in a sinful world.

Sacrifice will also characterize the love of the incarnate God. Lewis points to the sacrifice of Christ—but more as an exemplification than a basis for the concept of sacrificial love (*PP*, p. 102). Christ's sacrifice is repeated among his followers in varying degrees. Sacrifice, as it is supremely realized in Jesus' death, is not asked of all. There are, after all, "some old people whose state of grace we can hardly doubt who seem to have got through their seventy years with surprising ease" (*PP*, p. 104). Nevertheless, it remains true that

> as suicide is the typical expression of the stoic spirit, and battle of the warrior spirit, martyrdom always remains the supreme enacting and perfection of Christianity. (*PP*, p. 102)

If love as self-sacrifice can in this way be brought into harmony with the concept of self-giving, it is not clear that the same can be done for the one remaining formulation: love as a steady wish for the loved person's ultimate good. Lewis usually introduces this formulation when he is pointing out that loving the neighbor is not the same as feeling fond of him.[30] But we must also note what he proceeds to do with the formulation. Though we love the neighbor, we may have to punish him or even kill him (*MC*, pp. 91f.). One loves the neighbor who is unlovable—but with an interesting twist. To love such a neighbor means to labor to make him lovable (*PP*, p. 48).

The difficulties become most acute when, in *The Problem of Pain*, Lewis discusses God's love for men. God knows the end for which he has created us and knows that we will not ultimately be happy if we remain alienated from that end: fellowship with him and with other human be-

---

[30]As in *MC*, pp. 90ff. and *God in the Dock*, p. 49.

ings. Hence, he seeks our good by doing whatever may be necessary to bring us to that end. He may even cause us great pain in order to achieve this. But he does more than take us as his beloved; he actively seeks to perfect us (*PP*, pp. 46, 48). The resultant sufferings should not be described as necessary evils which love permits. Rather, divine love itself inflicts these pains in order to do us good— to bring us to the end for which we were created.

What has happened? How does one bring this notion of love into coherent relation with a love that is pure self-giving? It is not easy to see how this can be managed if Screwtape speaks the truth (as he often does) about "the Enemy" when he says: "He cannot ravish. He can only woo" (*SL*, p. 38). In moving from love as self-giving to love as wishing the good of the neighbor the focus shifts. In love as self-giving the neighbor is present, since such love is always the bond of a relation among persons. Nevertheless, the point of a self-giving love is that claims of self are never permitted to stand in the way of community. One continually abdicates those claims and thereby makes community with the other person possible.

In the other formulation the focus is on the neighbor's good and what one does to help him achieve that good. It becomes a characterization, not of what must move a man if the claims of self are to be overcome within him, but of what must be done to and for the neighbor. This description of love can permit a great deal of suffering to be inflicted on the neighbor in the name of love since it is inflicted for the neighbor's good. The contrast between Lewis' two formulations is close to the contrast between Jesus' parable of the Prodigal Son and Anders Nygren's different version of that parable. Nygren tells

of a father whose son had wasted his substance with riotous living in a far country and then returned to his father destitute but with good intentions; but the father, who knew from experience what such good intentions are usually worth, met his son's entreaties with the stern reply, "My house is closed to you until by your own honest work you have earned a place for yourself and so made amends for the wrong you have done"; and the son went out into the world and turned over a new leaf, and when he afterwards returned to his father he thanked him for the unyielding severity that had led to his recovery. . . .[31]

Perhaps this is what the son needed. Perhaps such action by the father would be for his ultimate good. But—and this is Nygren's point—this is not the same as a self-giving love.

Lewis' two characterizations of love stand in tension with one another. On the one hand we have an agent who fosters the neighbor's good by punishing or even killing him. And we are forced to ask whether that sort of love can be the same as the love which seeks only to give of itself in order that community may be established and maintained. In short, Lewis is in the same position in which Reinhold Niebuhr found himself. If he wants to say both that love is self-giving and that it is sometimes permissible to punish or kill the neighbor, he may have to call the latter something other than love. He may have to say, as Niebuhr did, that

> it is not even right to insist that every action of the Christian must conform to *agape,* rather than to the norms of relative justice and mutual love by which life is maintained and conflicting interests are arbitrated in history.[32]

It may be that in the case of *human* love Lewis could do this within his system. He does not think that love is or need be the sole principle by which human action is guided. To consider the neighbor-in-community one will have to consider the neighbor's freedom; for the ideal community is never a coerced union. To consider the neighbor-in-community one will have to take account of considerations of justice, what makes the neighbor *this* person rather than another. In a fallen world one will have to consider punitive justice, how to preserve the neighbor for and towards life-in-community. And one will have to consider earthly forms of love which, though related to *agape,* differ from it. In every case, of course, one would have the problem of relating such considerations to a love which is pure self-giving. But that is only to say that Lewis would face a problem which haunts anyone who thinks about

---

[31]Nygren, pp. 83f.
[32]Niebuhr, p. 88.

Christian love. And we will see in a later chapter that—at least in the case of the earthly loves—he considers this problem carefully. Furthermore, though it is not developed in his thought, he does have a notion of the state where punitive justice reigns as a kind of second-best community—necessary to preserve life but not desirable as an end in itself.

Even if this can be done, it will be harder to admit other principles in the case of *divine* love. The greatest difficulty lies in reconciling punitive justice with a love which is pure self-giving. How can a God who seeks only to give himself to his creatures in order to awaken community with them mete out punishment? And how can such punitive justice ever create the sort of community which Lewis holds up as an ideal? Ought not a loving God simply practice the principle of vicariousness and seek as best he can to love community into existence?

On the other hand, a God who tries simply to love community into existence seems to be issuing man a blank check to exploit his love endlessly.[33] Lewis might point to the cross as evidence of submission to just such exploitation. But it is one thing for God to permit himself to be exploited in that way. It is another for him to permit some persons to be exploited by others because his self-giving love cannot do otherwise. At that point some other principle seems needed.

Yet, simply to make of punitive justice another principle alongside love within God would seem to destroy the unity of the God who *is* love. Still worse, hell (in the reality of which Lewis believes) would mean that the dualism within the being of God is never overcome. At one point Lewis equates two ways of talking about punishments sent by God; the force of our discussion has been to ask whether the two pictures should really be equated. He writes:

> I have begun with the conception of Hell as a positive retributive punishment inflicted by God because that is the

[33]Cf. the discussion in Gene Outka, *Agape: An Ethical Analysis* (New Haven: Yale, 1972), pp. 21ff.

form in which the doctrine is most repellent, and I wished to tackle the strongest objection. But, of course, though Our Lord often speaks of Hell as a sentence inflicted by a tribunal, He also says elsewhere that the judgement consists in the very fact that men prefer darkness to light, and that not He, but His "word," judges men. We are therefore at liberty—since the two conceptions, in the long run, mean the same thing—to think of this bad man's perdition not as a sentence imposed on him but as the mere fact of being what he is. The characteristic of lost souls is "their rejection of everything that is not simply themselves." (*PP*, pp. 122–23)

The two conceptions may, in the long run, mean the same thing for the state of the man who ends in perdition, but it is not clear that they mean the same thing about what sort of being God is.

Quite often at other places in his writings Lewis thinks of punishment (and, ultimately, hell) in the second of these ways: not as the work of love but as the natural result of turning from the One who is love. When Narnia is coming to an end in *The Last Battle*, the dwarfs—who are always only "for the dwarfs"—find themselves in the stable along with the children and King Tirian. For the children the stable door has proved to be the entrance to Aslan's world. But the dwarfs think they are in a stable. The children plead with Aslan to do something for the dwarfs and he responds: "I will show you both what I can, and what I cannot, do." With that a glorious feast appears before the dwarfs. But they think they are eating hay and turnips. They have chosen cunning instead of belief, and there is nothing more Aslan can do for them (pp. 137ff.). Similarly, one of the central statements in *The Great Divorce* is: "There are only two kinds of people in the end: those who say to God, 'Thy will be done,' and those to whom God says, in the end, 'Thy will be done' " (p. 72).

In places such as these Lewis tends to think of the punitive element simply as the inevitable result of turning against God. It is just as true, however, to note that he is not consistent about this. In *Letters to Malcolm* he seems to repudiate such a position.

You suggest that what is traditionally regarded as our experience of God's anger would be more helpfully regarded as what inevitably happens to us if we behave inappropriately towards a reality of immense power. As you say, "The live wire doesn't feel angry with us, but if we blunder against it we get a shock."

My dear Malcolm, what do you suppose you have gained by substituting the image of a live wire for that of angered majesty? You have shut us all up in despair; for the angry can forgive, and electricity can't. (p. 96)

All this suggests that Lewis has not, cannot, or does not wish to reconcile his varying formulations. And that, of course, may be a wise decision. We will need to wait until the next chapter to suggest fully why, for Lewis, no complete reconciliation may be possible.

What we have, at any rate, are two descriptions of love which continue to stand in some tension with one another. On the one hand, Lewis speaks of love as self-giving. The emphasis here is on love as the means by which claims of self are overcome and community made possible. This formulation, while it perhaps can allow infliction of pain on other grounds, can hardly permit such activity to be drawn into the characterization of love itself. On the other hand, Lewis speaks of love as a steady and active wish for the other's good. Since the other's good may require infliction of harm, this description of love can include within love's scope many acts that the first cannot. Neither formulation is without problems. The first more narrowly restricts what love will do. Having done that, however, we seem to need to supplement self-giving love with other principles—most especially, punitive justice. The second broadens the notion of love and draws considerations such as infliction of punishment into it. But when we do that, our characterization of love seems less than satisfactory. The difficulties become most obvious when we speak of God's love. If his love is pure self-giving, we will either have to supplement his love with a principle of punitive justice (and endanger thereby his unity as One who is love) or we will have to find some other way to talk about punitive justice. If, on the other hand, his love can and does inflict suffering, we will

have solved these problems—but possibly at the cost of a
clear affirmation of his love.

It may be wrong to ask which of these two concepts of
love lies closer to the heart of Lewis' position. If we are
speaking—as we have been in this chapter—of Lewis' vision of the ideal community for which the human heart
longs, then it seems correct to focus on love as self-giving.
For only it can make such community possible. If on the
other hand we think—as we did in the first chapter and will
again—of the Christian as pilgrim toward that community,
we may have to come to terms with a love that needs to
punish. The simple truth is that we find both views in
Lewis, and we find them even within a single work (e.g.,
The Problem of Pain). The human heart, Lewis thinks,
longs for a God who can never be fully experienced in
human history. Earthly life, however, is understood in
terms of a story of pilgrimage toward that God—who must
often be believed to be other than he seems.

Hierarchy in Community

In the previous discussion of the images of community it
was noted that Lewis' social vision was non-egalitarian.
Nowhere does he develop this case in a sustained manner,
but it is not hard to glean from his writings at least some of
the reasons which lie behind this aspect of his vision.
There is, first, simple delight in diversity. Equality for
Lewis is always "flat equality"; true community is full,
varied, and rich. The fullness of diversity we will know
only in heaven, which will, Lewis is certain, display far
more variety than hell.[34] Screwtape informs Wormwood that
"the Enemy" prefers the parochial to the congregational
principle of organization. It is a unity of place rather than of
likings. As such it unites people of widely different classes
and tastes (*SL*, p. 73). Thus, Lewis' first reason for advocating a non-egalitarian social vision is simply that he believes
it far more attractive than a world in which equality is the
rule. Delight is the key. "It delights me that there should be

[34]*Letters to Malcolm*, p. 10.

moments in the services of my own Church when the priest stands and I kneel" (*WG*, p. 38).

Equality, for Lewis, is possible only in a collective. An essential concern of his is the search for ways to overcome individual isolation without destroying personality. And the collective is for him always a term which denotes a false solution to this problem. It overcomes isolation at the cost of personality. All are submerged because all are alike. The members of a collective become interchangeable. Equality implies interchangeability, and that in turn means the destruction of individual personality (*WG*, p. 34).

In "De Descriptione Temporum," his famed inaugural address at Cambridge, Lewis advances the thesis that the most significant division in western history is "that which divides the present from, say, the age of Jane Austen and Scott."[35] We noted this in a different context in the previous chapter and saw that the trump card Lewis offers in defense of his thesis is the observation that it was this period that saw the birth of machines. And, we may now note, the machine age has made full use of the concept of interchangeable parts (not to mention interchangeable workers on the assembly line). Arguments for equality were, of course, known long before the age of the machine. Nevertheless, Lewis thinks they may take on a kind of obvious character for one whose every image is molded by the dominance of the machine. It is not surprising, therefore, to find him turning to natural rather than artificial images for community. The household, he notes, may be made up of the grandfather, parents, grown-up son, child, dog, and cat; and all are true members precisely because they are not interchangeable (*WG*, p. 34). In that kind of organic union personality is preserved.

On at least one occasion Lewis hints at another reason for his opposition to equality within true community. "Equality," he writes, "is a quantitative term and therefore love often knows nothing of it" (*WG*, p. 38). What Lewis means, I think, is this: Within a relationship of love there is

[35]In *Selected Literary Essays*, p. 7.

neither need nor desire to assert one's equality. The defiant
claim "I'm as good as you" is out of place in such a relationship; for love seeks not to measure claim against claim but
to give and, then, give again. If such love is the guiding
principle of community, claims to equality must in principle be excluded. How, after all, shall we abdicate continually if we are concerned to give just the right amount—and
no more?

Finally, Lewis is fond of noting that certain pleasures,
which he thinks essential to any genuine fellowship, are
impossible without inequality. These are the specific pleasures of the inferior: delight in being praised; modesty;
gratitude; obedience; admiration; and humility.[36] We do
not, he thinks, want a world in which these are lacking.

> A world in which I was *really* (and not merely by a useful legal
> fiction) 'as good as everyone else,' in which I never looked up
> to anyone wiser or cleverer or braver or more learned than I,
> would be insufferable. The very fans of the cinema stars and
> the famous footballers know better than to desire that.[37]

Lewis believes, in fact, that the pleasures of admiration are
among our most important pleasures both in number and
intensity. Without them we would be impoverished. The
"I'm as good as you are" attitude is, of course, common; but
that is because we are sinful and naturally prone to seek
fulfillment in ourselves rather than in fellowship with
others. At one time, Lewis notes, people had a name for
such an attitude—they called it envy and considered it a
vice (*SL*, p. 163). Such a state of mind is dangerous; for,
excluding humility, gratitude, and admiration, it will turn
one away from almost any road leading to community (*SL*,
p. 170).

Still, we may ask, cannot a case be made for equality
even when all this has been said? Even if we grant that
individuals differ greatly in talents, abilities, beauties, and
so forth, cannot we say that every person possesses within
himself an irreducible dignity equal to that of his fellows?
Lewis sounds, at least, as if he were dubious.

[36]Cf., for example, *WG*, p. 9; *Miracles*, p. 122; *God in the Dock*, p. 85.
[37]*Miracles*, p. 122.

The infinite value of each human soul is not a Christian doctrine. God did not die for man because of some value He perceived in him. The value of each human soul considered simply in itself, out of relation to God, is zero. . . . He loves us not because we were lovable, but because He is Love. It may be that He loves all equally—He certainly loved all to the death—and I am not certain what the expression means. If there is equality it is in His love, not in us. (WG, p. 38)

This is related to remarks often made by Lewis on the theme of originality. To begin with a concept of the value of the individual human being leads to a search for ways whereby each individual may express what is valuable in his being. Lewis turns to the New Testament and finds a different approach. As Christ is the image of God, so the Christian is the image of Christ. As Christ submits to God, so the wife submits to her husband. As Paul imitates Christ, so the new believer is exhorted to imitate Paul. The whole art of life becomes one of imitation.[38] The goal is not expression of one's individual value:

> Our whole destiny seems to lie in the opposite direction, in being as little as possible ourselves, in acquiring a fragrance that is not our own but borrowed, in becoming clean mirrors filled with the image of a face that is not ours.[39]

Personality is found when we submit to the function for which we were created.[40]

We can illuminate Lewis' thought if we use a distinction made by Charles Williams between hierarchies of merit and hierarchies of function.[41] Although Lewis does not use this terminology, it fits nicely with what he says. Hierarchies of merit (based on talents, abilities, beauties, etc.) are genuine hierarchies but are constantly changing. He who is master of one skill may be pupil in another (as is easily recognized by many an academician in those moments when his car

[38]"Christianity and Literature," *Christian Reflections*, pp. 4ff.
[39]*Ibid.*, p. 7.
[40]Cf. Charles Williams, *The Descent of the Dove: A Short History of the Holy Spirit in the Church* (Grand Rapids: Eerdmans, 1939). Williams quotes Dante to the effect that "the essence is created for the sake of the function and not the function for the essence" (p. 132).
[41]Charles Williams, "A Dialogue on Hierarchy," *The Image of the City* . . . , pp. 127f.

breaks down). Thus, in hierarchies of merit the ranked degrees are being continually reordered. "Equality is the name we give to the whole sum of such changes."[42] Hierarchies of function, on the other hand, are fixed. They do *not* depend on merit and there is always, Lewis thinks, something opaque and mysterious about them.

Lewis finds both kinds of hierarchies within the spheres of creation and redemption. The delightful variety of talents and abilities gives rise to numerous hierarchies of merit for those with a willingness to see them. And only for those who do see them will the immense pleasures of admiration be possible. Lewis also seems to find fixed hierarchies within nature. There is a natural authority of learned over simple, man over beast, parent over child, and husband over wife (*WG,* p. 37). Within the realm of redemption there are also countless hierarchies—or, perhaps better, the sphere of redemption (the mystical body) is itself a hierarchically ordered community. There is, first of all, the authority of the Head of the body over its members. The hierarchies of husband/wife and parent/child are taken up within this body. Priest stands over laity. "There is, in forms too subtle for official embodiment, a continual interchange of complementary ministrations" (*WG,* p. 36).

The sources of Lewis' hierarchical vision are many. The New Testament concept of the Church as the Body of Christ is obviously influential, and the mysteries of the trinitarian relationship within the Godhead are never far from his thinking. Then too, Lewis was well versed in the classics, and he was surely influenced to some extent by Aristotle. More important, though, must have been the "medieval model" which Lewis made it his business to study and expound. In *A Preface to Paradise Lost* he discusses the concept of hierarchy which Milton shared with many others.

> According to this conception degrees of value are objectively present in the universe. Everything except God has some natural superior; everything except unformed matter has some

---

[42]*Ibid.,* p. 127. The parallel to Lewis' concept of continual abdication within the dance is clear.

natural inferior. The goodness, happiness, and dignity of every being consists in obeying its natural superior and ruling its natural inferiors. When it fails in either part of this twofold task we have disease or monstrosity in the scheme of things. (pp. 73f.)[43]

Lewis did not want to take over the medieval model in its full-blown complexity, nor did he think it took the effects of sin seriously enough. But he did believe firmly that a vision of community based on equality could neither command assent nor elicit delight.

In *Out of the Silent Planet* Lewis deliberately creates a world in which community without equality can be seen. On Malacandra the three rational species of *hnau* (*sorns, hrossa,* and *pfifltriggi*) live together in peace. All recognize that the *sorns* are unsurpassed in scientific knowledge, the *hrossa* in poetry, and the *pfifltriggi* in craftsmanship. Ransom, having come from a planet in which sin has disturbed such relationships, is amazed. He inquires about political relationships, trying to determine which of the three species rules the others, only to be told that Oyarsa rules. All the inhabitants of Malacandra accept the rule of Oyarsa and therefore are free to live in harmony with one another. Ransom is amazed at what he has learned about the political structure (or lack thereof) on Malacandra, but the *sorns* find Ransom's account of the evils on earth equally incredible. They are not, however, without an explanation.

"They cannot help it," said the old *sorn.* "There must be rule, yet how can creatures rule themselves? Beasts must be ruled by *hnau* and *hnau* by *eldila* and *eldila* by Maleldil. These creatures have no *eldila.* They are like one trying to lift himself by his own hair—or one trying to see over a whole country when he is on a level with it—like a female trying to beget young on herself." (p. 102)

Thus, Lewis finds in another world something of what the medievals had seen in our own.

Up to this point our concern has been simply to understand Lewis' beliefs about hierarchy and equality. It is,

[43]Cf. also *The Discarded Image*, pp. 12f., and *The Allegory of Love: A Study in Medieval Tradition* (London: Oxford, 1958), pp. 347f.

however, important to consider as well some of the unre-
solved difficulties in his view. I used the distinction between hierarchies of merit and hierarchies of function in
explicating his position, but it will also illuminate some of
the ambiguities. Hierarchies of merit involve inequalities
in merit but, as we noted, also a kind of equality. This is
because none of these hierarchies is stable throughout the
whole of life. The person who merits headship in one context does not in another. Hence, though it is always true
(since persons are not interchangeable parts) that some lead
and others follow by virtue of the special characteristics
they possess, it is not likely to be true that in all contexts the
same person always merits headship. Roles of super- and
subordination constantly shift, introducing an equality different from the "flat equality" which considers individuals
as interchangeable parts.

In hierarchies of function headship is not exercised by
virtue of any special merit. This sort of headship does not
belong by right to a person but to an office. And there is
always something a little opaque and mysterious about *why*
these hierarchies should exist. No reason can be given to
explain them fully, precisely because such reasons tend to
focus on certain characteristics by which a person merits
headship. Yet, exactly that sort of reason is ruled out here;
for to appeal to it would be to transform hierarchies of
function into hierarchies of merit. When he argues against
priestesses in the church, Lewis quite explicitly recognizes
this. He is willing, even eager, to affirm that women are as
capable as men of the piety, zeal, and learning which the
pastoral office requires.[44] He nevertheless believes that the
roles of man and woman in the church are to symbolize the
relation between Christ and church. And he grants that
there will always be something opaque, even irrational
about this.[45] For no reason can be given in support of the
man's headship if by reason we mean some distinguishing
feature by which men merit the office.

[44]*God in the Dock*, p. 235.
[45]*Ibid.*, p. 238.

Hence, just as hierarchies of merit left room for a kind of equality (i.e., the whole set of exchanges), so too may hierarchies of function indirectly suggest a basic level of equal human worth. The very fact that hierarchies of function such as that of husband over wife or parent over child cannot be justified by pointing to superior worth or merit indicates that such considerations are not involved here. However, Lewis does not—or not always—seem clearly to recognize this. Thus, he can write that the members of an organic union (as opposed to items in a class) are "things differing not only in structure and function but also in dignity" (*WG*, p. 33). What the reader of such a line cannot tell is whether superior dignity does or does not imply superior worth—or exactly what the difference between the two might be. In his arguments Lewis tends indiscriminately to mix examples from hierarchies of merit (which do involve a kind of superior merit) and hierarchies of function (which do not). Yet, even if neither is compatible with "flat equality," the two need to be carefully distinguished. The image of the dance is not the same as the image of the body. Lewis is quite correct to say that either sort of hierarchy is incompatible with the kind of equality which characterizes units of a class. But need hierarchy of either sort conflict with the belief that, at some fundamental level, individuals ought to be valued equally?

Having pressed the argument to this point, we can now note that any advocate of equality might—without asserting a doctrine of inherent worth of human personality—ask whether Lewis does not confuse valuing individuals equally with treating them identically.[46] The argument could take several forms. The motive for valuing persons equally might be grounded in the action of God, which could be seen as the prototype for such equal valuing. After all, valuing individuals equally need not depend on *discovering* in them equal worth or merit. Worth can be *ascribed* or *bestowed*, not simply discovered.[47] In fact, Lewis hints

[46]Cf. Outka, pp. 19f.
[47]*Ibid.*, pp. 154ff.

as much in the passage cited above in which he rejects any
notion of inherent worth.[48] For there he suggests that God
loves all equally—or, at any rate, to the death. Thus, he
comes close to distinguishing between (1) a doctrine of the
infinite, inherent worth of human personality, and (2) infinitely valuing the person, no matter what his inherent
worth.[49] Lewis' reluctance to talk about equality or, even,
about valuing individuals equally stems from his contention that love knows nothing of comparison or of quantitative terms. Thus, there is nothing in his position which
prohibits *infinitely* valuing each human being. Valuing
them *equally* is suspect because it introduces comparison
where it is out of place. And, in this connection, infinitely
valuing the individual should probably be understood (in
imitation, no doubt, of God's action) as bestowal of value
rather than discovery of inherent worth.

There is another way in which one might argue (against
Lewis) that valuing individuals equally need not imply
identical treatment. The argument this time would turn on
the fact that each person, simply as a human being, may
possess certain generic characteristics which entitle him to
a minimal respect equal to that given any other person.[50]
This, though obviously similar, is different from a simple
claim of inherent worth of human personality. To say that
basic respect is due every individual would be to say that
persons, since they share these fundamental generic
characteristics, ought to be valued equally. A ground-floor
level would be established, below which our regard for any
human being ought never fall. But this need not mean that
all discriminations among persons are forbidden. Presumably there is some point at which equally valuing individuals
implies treating them similarly, but it need not involve
identical treatment. Having regard for the humanity of each
person can still leave us free to deal with persons in ways

48See p. 73 above.
49Cf. Paul Ramsey, *Basic Christian Ethics* (New York: Scribner's,
1950), pp. 59, 94.
50Outka (pp. 263–65) isolates three such generic characteristics: (1) the
God-relation; (2) welfare (including basic psycho-physical needs); and (3)
freedom.

appropriate to their particular personalities and their relations to us.[51] Hence, to value individuals equally is not the same as to treat them identically.

If we consider Lewis' views in light of this second form of the objection, we may be led to distinguish more carefully among the arguments he gives in support of his hierarchical vision. At the outset of our discussion we listed four: (1) sheer delight in diversity over against "flat equality"; (2) the belief that equality concerns interchangeable units rather than persons; (3) the statement that love knows nothing of quantitative assessments; and (4) the belief that our most important pleasures require hierarchy. Certainly the first and last of these need only rule out treating persons identically. They require nothing more than hierarchies of merit which give free play to the variety in life. However, Lewis' second and third arguments cut more deeply. He is, these arguments suggest, opposed not simply to identical treatment but to equal valuation of persons—for to introduce considerations of equality here is to fall short of the level of personality and to introduce comparison where it is out of place. Here again, however, there seems to be nothing in Lewis' position which would prohibit us from infinitely—as opposed to equally—valuing any human being in all his concrete particularity.

Thus, Lewis' position is not without safeguards for the treatment of persons. He firmly believes that every person is made to share in the enjoyment of God. If for Lewis it is inadequate to think in terms of valuing one person equally with another, it is just as mistaken to forget the God-relatedness of every human being. "There are no *ordinary* people. ... Next to the Blessed Sacrament itself, your

[51] It is an important question, which we cannot discuss here, whether even minimal respect can so easily make room for further attention to the particularities of individual personalities and special moral relations. This can probably be done if the minimal respect is interpreted as certain negative duties—interpreted, that is, simply as an injunction never to do certain things to any human being. If, on the other hand, we are in any positive way to give attention equally to every person's psycho-physical needs alone, there may be neither time nor resources for proceeding further and taking account of all the differences which make up someone's personal history.

neighbour is the holiest object presented to your senses"
(*WG*, p. 15). In this sense, all are created to share the same
end. But—and this is the core of Lewis' social vision—to
have a share in the life of God is to share in *infinite* goodness; it is to enter a relationship in which no one need fear
that he will get an inadequate measure of the goodness
shared.

We can also note, in anticipation of a later chapter, one of
the normative moral beliefs which Lewis holds. He believes that certain fundamental duties central to any seriously held morality are owed to persons simply by virtue of
their humanity. But to concentrate on these duties is to
view persons simply as human existents rather than as particular personalities with differentiated individual his-
tories. It is, in other words, to fall short of the ideal of true
community. We badly misunderstand Lewis, therefore, if
we think that his criticisms of equality arise out of any
aristocratic bias. (The picture he paints in *That Hideous
Strength* of the community at St. Anne's, if nothing else,
ought to divest us of that notion.) His criticisms stem,
rather, from his ideal of a community in which persons
could truly be themselves and yet be joined in a union of
love.

If genuine community is the place where personality is
found, we cannot (Lewis would say) be content in our social
vision to focus on those characteristics which fail to distinguish persons from one another. Behind this lies a view of
the self which Lewis nowhere develops in detail. On one
occasion he wrote:

> A man I know dreamed that he was at Falstaff's funeral; and as
> the mourners were saying that they had lost only the mortal
> husk of Sir John and that the real man awaited them in a better
> world, my friend awoke crying out, "But we've lost his *fat-
> ness!*" I am not sure about the theology of this, but I approve
> the sentiment. Where personality is in question I will not give
> up a wrinkle or a stammer. I am offended when a man whom I
> heartily love or hate starts wearing a new kind of hat.[52]

[52]"Open Letter to Dr. Tillyard," *Essays and Studies by Members of the
English Association,* Vol. XXI, collected by Herbert Read (Oxford: Clarendon, 1936), pp. 156f.

Commitment to persons means commitment to them in their particularity.[53] That is central to Lewis' thought. His strictures against equality are not intended to deny that in certain important ways men—simply because they are men—are to be treated equally. He hopes, rather, to make clear that fellowship with another person involves all there is of the person, not simply or even primarily his generic characteristics; for fellowship is built on a love which does not concern itself with quantitative assessments.

Despite all the strictures, something akin to equality remains in Lewis' social vision. The glory of the One for whom individuals are created shines in and through each participant in the great dance. One of the scenes in *The Great Divorce* involves a meeting between the ghost of an artist and a Solid Person who had also been a painter and had known the ghost in their earthly lives. The ghost is eager to paint the beauties of heaven but is told that he must first learn to appreciate them. Perhaps then a time will come when he can paint, for he will see some things better than anyone else and will of course desire to let all the others see the glory as he sees it. But, contrary to his desires, he will not be known as a distinguished artist. In heaven all are famous. "The Glory flows into everyone, and back from everyone: like light and mirrors. But the light's the thing" (pp. 82–83). It is the divine beauty and glory that is shared by all. In that sense all are equal, but considerations of equality never arise. They are unimportant, since the divine glory is not diminished when it is shared.

> Each of the redeemed shall forever know and praise some one aspect of the divine beauty better than any other creature can. Why else were individuals created, but that God, loving all infinitely, should love each differently? ... If all experienced God in the same way and returned Him an identical worship, the song of the church triumphant would have no symphony, it would be like an orchestra in which all the instruments played the same note. ... Heaven is a city, and a Body, because the

[53]Cf. Ramsey, *Basic Christian Ethics*, p. 94: "Response to the general worth of human personality always hesitates a little in confronting the neighbor. Hereby the full particularity of neighborly love finding the neighbor out would be lost."

blessed remain eternally different. . . . For doubtless the continually successful, yet never completed, attempt by each soul to communicate its vision to all others . . . is also among the ends for which the individual was created. (*PP*, p. 150)[54]

The above discussion is subject to an important qualification, and we would not have reflected Lewis' position accurately if we were to stop at this point. Good ethics is not necessarily good politics—or so Lewis' view would imply. For, despite the arguments he marshals in favor of the vision, Lewis does not think we should attempt to realize it in all realms of life. We must, therefore, examine how he qualifies his ideal of a community in which inequalities are celebrated. In his volume on English literature in the 16th century Lewis writes of Hooker: "Equality is not a conception that has any charms for Hooker. The charm of inequality is, indeed, the mainspring of erotic love."[55] The view attributed here to Hooker is shared by Lewis; yet he goes on to say this of Hooker:

Sometimes a suspicion crosses our mind that the doctrine of the Fall does not loom quite large enough in his universe. . . . He writes of Man, if fallen, yet now redeemed and already partially glorified.[56]

Lewis attempts to take the Fall into sin and its effects

[54]It is interesting to note that in a similar passage in his later work, *The Four Loves*, Lewis refers to the soul as feminine rather than neuter. He writes of heaven, "where the very multitude of the blessed (which no man can number) increases the fruition which each has of God. For every soul, seeing Him in her own way, doubtless communicates that unique vision to all the rest" (pp. 92–93). This reflects a theme we will take up in a later chapter: Lewis' belief that in relation to God all persons are feminine and God masculine. It also makes clear his belief that the creature/Creator distinction has inextricably written 'hierarchy' into the nature of the universe.

[55]*English Literature in the Sixteenth Century, Excluding Drama.* The Oxford History of English Literature, Vol. III (Oxford: Clarendon, 1954), p. 460. The passage from Hooker's *Ecclesiastical Polity* to which Lewis refers seems to be this: "Woman therefore was even in her first estate framed by nature not only after in time but inferior in excellency also unto man, howbeit in so due and sweet proportion as being presented before our eyes, might be sooner perceived than defined. And even herein doth lie the reason why that kind of love which is the perfectest ground of wedlock [i.e., erotic love] is seldom able to yield any reason of itself" (V, LXXIII, 2).

[56]*Ibid.*, p. 461.

upon human nature seriously. He proclaims himself a believer in political equality, not as an ideal but as a necessary medicine for a humanity sick with sin. The "real reason for democracy" is that mankind is "so fallen that no man can be trusted with unchecked power over his fellows."[57] This, as Lewis is quick to note, casts equality in a rather different light: not something good in itself but something in the same class as medicine or clothes. We need medicine when we are ill and clothes because we are no longer innocent. The point is that, in our present condition, we really do need equality. Lewis states explicitly that we should not even try to reinstitute the hierarchical ideal. That is not his aim (WG, p. 37).

Why then retain the ideal? Because there is "no spiritual substance in flat equality." Only the hierarchical vision can keep alive in us the desire for true community. It can help us realize that we are settling for something which, though necessary, is second-best. And without that realization, without the desire for something better, we have lost an essential ingredient in our humanity.

> The man who cannot conceive a joyful and loyal obedience on the one hand, nor an unembarrassed and noble acceptance of that obedience on the other, the man who has never even wanted to kneel or to bow, is a prosaic barbarian.

If we fail to keep alive that desire for a better, richer, and more satisfying community in which personality is found, we may become "men to whom pebbles laid in a row are more beautiful than an arch."

Furthermore, if we forget that the necessary medicine is only that, we may turn it into an ideal and seek to extend it beyond the political realm into all areas of life. That would, Lewis thinks, be the destruction of personal and spiritual life—a destruction which our natures would not long tolerate. To over-extend the concept of equality would be to invite another romantic attack upon equality even within the political sphere. It is important, therefore, to remember

---

[57]"Equality," *The Spectator,* 171 (August 27, 1943), p. 192. The unidentified citations in the next few paragraphs are from this short essay.

the naked body beneath the clothes. "Let us," Lewis says, "*wear* equality; but let us undress every night."

The Place of Animals

The place of animals in the community at St. Anne's might be considered a rather unimportant topic, but not for Lewis. His vision of ideal community includes animals, though he is careful to make clear that he has nothing but speculations to offer on the topic. At St. Anne's there is a tame jackdaw, there are trained mice whom Jane is permitted to see, and there is Mr. Bultitude the Bear—all incorporated into the còmpany. At the sound of Ransom's silver whistle the mice scurry across the carpet and clean up the crumbs on the floor. "There," he said, "a very simple adjustment. Humans want crumbs removed; mice are anxious to remove them. It ought never to have been a cause of war" (p. 149). And when, at the end of *That Hideous Strength*, Venus descends on St. Anne's, the animals too find their mates.

> "This," said MacPhee with great emphasis, "is becoming indecent."
> "On the contrary," said Ransom, "decent, in the old sense, *decens*, fitting, is just what it is. Venus herself is over St. Anne's." (p. 376)

Behind all this Lewis is making a serious point which he puts in Ransom's mouth in the conversation with MacPhee. Human beings are *embodied* creatures and, as such, are part of the animal creation. They are more than animals but not less and, hence, are not to be isolated from the animal creation. Ransom says,

> "Perelandra is all about us and man is no longer isolated. We are now as we ought to be—between the angels who are our elder brothers and the beasts who are our jesters, servants and playfellows." (p. 378)

It is this concern that humanity not be isolated from the animal creation which leads to the importance of animals in Lewis' social vision. Man stands in ambiguous relation to the animal creation: he is part of it yet transcends it. Man is priest of the animals. Some of Lewis' thoughts on these matters were first developed in *The Problem of Pain* when he dealt with the (to him, almost insoluble) difficulty of pain in the animal creation. There he speculates about a possible redemption of the animals. We must, he says, consider the beasts not in isolation but in relation to man and through man to God. The "natural" animal is one who has been tamed by man; for God intended man to have dominion over the beasts (*PP*, p. 138). This passage brought a protest from Evelyn Underhill, who wrote Lewis that the belief that the natural animal was the tame animal was "an intolerable doctrine."

> Is the cow which we have turned into a milk machine or the hen we have turned into an egg machine really nearer the mind of God than its wild ancestors? . . . You surely *can't* mean that, or think that the robin red breast in a cage doesn't put heaven in a rage but is regarded as an excellent arrangement.[58]

It would seem clear that this was not Lewis' intent. What he seeks is a way of expressing the relation between man and beast which will retain the wildness while nevertheless expressing the obedience of the animal to man, the priest of creation. We get a picture of this in his poem, "Eden's Courtesy."

> Such natural love twixt beast and man we find
> That children all desire an animal book,
> And all brutes, not perverted from their kind,
> Woo us with whinny, tongue, tail, song, or look;
>   So much of Eden's courtesy yet remains.

[58]Quoted in Green and Hooper, *C. S. Lewis: A Biography*, pp. 188f. Norman Pittenger, in his famous article criticizing Lewis ("Apologist Versus Apologist," *The Christian Century*, 75 [1958], pp. 1104-7) wrote of "the callous attitude toward the animal creation . . . which outraged Evelyn Underhill." In his response to Pittenger ("Rejoinder to Dr. Pittenger," *The Christian Century*, 75 [1958], pp. 1359-61) Lewis wrote: "Where he really hurt me was in the charge of callousness to animals. Surprised me too; for the very same passage is blamed by others for extreme sentimentality. It is hard to please all. But if the Patagonians think me a dwarf and the Pygmies a giant, perhaps my stature is in fact fairly unremarkable." There seems to me little doubt that this is one of several places in which Pittenger's critique rather badly misses the point of Lewis' thinking.

> But when a creature's dread, or mine, has built
> A wall between, I think I feel the pains
> That Adam earned and do confess my guilt.
>   For till I tame sly fox and timorous hare
> And lording lion in my self, no peace
> Can be without; but after, I shall dare
> Uncage the shadowy zoo and war will cease;
>   Because the brutes within, I do not doubt,
> Are archetypal of the brutes without.[59]

What Lewis wants is not so much a way to domesticate animals as a way to bring the animal creation into proper relation with human beings. He wants to say that man, though himself an animal, nonetheless rules (and rightly so) the beasts.

> Even now we meet rare individuals who have a mysterious power of taming beasts. This power the Paradisal man enjoyed in eminence. The old picture of the brutes sporting before Adam and fawning upon him may not be wholly symbolical. . . . For man was made to be the priest and even, in one sense, the Christ, of the animals—the mediator through whom they apprehend so much of the Divine splendour as their irrational nature allows. (*PP*, p. 66)

In the science fiction trilogy there are two examples of such a "paradisal" relation between man and beast. There is in *Perelandra* a scene where the beasts run to the Lady (an unfallen Eve) and frolic in her presence.

> It was not really like a woman making much of a horse, nor yet a child playing with a puppy. There was in her face an authority, in her caresses a condescension, which by taking seriously the inferiority of her adorers made them somehow less inferior—raised them from the status of pets to that of slaves. (p. 65)

And there is the case of Mr. Bultitude in the presence of Ransom.

> He felt, in his own fashion, the supremacy of the Director. Meetings with him were to the bear what mystical experiences are to men, for the Director had brought back with him from Venus some shadow of man's lost prerogative to ennoble

[59]In *Poems*, ed. Walter Hooper (London: Geoffrey Bles, 1964), p. 98.

> beasts. In his presence Mr. Bultitude trembled on the very
> borders of personality. . . . (THS, p. 307)

The animals too wait for liberation from a creation in bond-
age. The final answer to Evelyn Underhill's objection was
actually contained in *The Problem of Pain* where Lewis
speculated (in a passage that amazingly foreshadows his
later creation of Aslan, the great lion of Narnia) about what
the lion would be like in the new creation.

> If there is a rudimentary Leonine self, to that also God can give
> a 'body' as it pleases Him—a body no longer living by the
> destruction of the lamb, yet richly Leonine in the sense that it
> also expresses whatever energy and splendour and exulting
> power dwelled within the visible lion on the earth. . . . I think
> the lion, when he has ceased to be dangerous, will still be
> awful: indeed, that we shall then first see that of which the
> present fangs and claws are a clumsy and satanically perverted
> imitation. There will still be something like the shaking of a
> golden mane: and often the good Duke will say, 'Let him roar
> again.' (PP, pp. 142–43)

FOREVER CONJOINED BUT NOT RECONCILED

Images of Hell

"The characteristic of lost souls is 'their rejection of
everything that is not simply themselves' " (PP, p. 123).
Lewis' vision of ideal community is heightened and
clarified by what he has to say about the polar opposite of
such community—which is, ultimately, hell. Human beings
are made for fellowship with God and one another, and only
in that fellowship can personality attain its fruition. Hell is,
therefore, a retreat into the self, a denial of community.
Lewis can speak of "the ruthless, sleepless, unsmiling
concentration upon self which is the mark of Hell" (SL,
p. ix).

This is a theme Lewis shares with Charles Williams. In
Williams' novel *Descent into Hell* the retreat into the self
takes place in the life of Wentworth, a military historian. He
is engaged in an intellectual controversy with Aston Moffatt, another military historian. Their debate, of interest

only to specialists, is a complicated one turning on details about some skirmishes in the Wars of the Roses.

> Aston Moffatt, who was by now almost seventy, derived a great deal of intellectual joy from expounding his point of view. He was a pure scholar, a holy and beautiful soul who would have sacrificed reputation, income, and life, if necessary, for the discovery of one fact about the horse-boys of Edward Plantagenet. He had determined his nature. Wentworth was younger and at a more critical point, at that moment when a man's real concern begins to separate itself from his pretended, and almost to become independent of himself. He raged secretly as he wrote his letters and drew up his evidence; he identified scholarship with himself, and asserted himself under the disguise of a defence of scholarship. He refused to admit that the exact detail of Edward's march was not, in fact, worth to him the cost of a single cigar. . . .
> He was sitting now in his study, his large body leaning forward over the table, and his hands had paused in measuring the plan that lay in front of him. He was finding the answer to Aston Moffatt's last published letter difficult, yet he was determined that Moffatt could not be right. He was beginning to twist the intention of the sentences in his authorities, preferring strange meanings and awkward constructions, adjusting evidence, manipulating words. In defence of his conclusion he was willing to cheat in the evidence—a habit more usual to religious writers than to historical.[60]

Wentworth's descent continues. He awakens one morning to find in the paper an announcement that Aston Moffatt has been knighted.

> There was presented to him at once and clearly an opportunity for joy—casual, accidental joy, but joy. If he could not manage joy, at least he might have managed the intention of joy, or (if that also were too much) an effort towards the intention of joy. . . . With a perfectly clear, if instantaneous, knowledge of what he did, he rejected joy instead. He instantaneously preferred anger, and at once it came; he invoked envy and it obliged him. (p. 80)

Wentworth will not love reality, nor will he care for the neighbor who is given. He cannot get outside himself. He

---

[60]Grand Rapids: Eerdmans, 1949, pp. 38f. Related to this passage is Williams' belief that "Hell is always inaccurate" (*The Image of the City . . .* , p. 30).

ends by preferring a succubus conjured up by his imagination to the flesh and blood of a real woman; he ends, that is, completely isolated within himself. This is the picture Lewis describes in straight prose when he imagines what a thorough egoist would be like.

> The taste for the *other*, that is, the very capacity for enjoying good, is quenched in him except in so far as his body still draws him into some rudimentary contact with an outer world. Death removes this last contact. He has his wish—to live wholly in the self and to make the best of what he finds there. And what he finds there is Hell. (*PP*, p. 123)

Lewis has images beyond that of a retreat into the self. Those who do this may still find themselves in contact with one another. Some form of association will then arise even if no true community is possible. Such a "society" is imaged in *The Screwtape Letters*. There we have an association of those who, in Screwtape's words, are "forever conjoined but not reconciled" (*SL*, p. 171). Lewis' picture of hell is that of a heavily bureaucratized state in which "everyone is perpetually concerned about his own dignity and advancement" (*SL*, p. ix). Envy is the ruling passion, and it soon becomes clear that this association is held together only by fear. At one point Screwtape suffers a momentary lapse and writes that the Enemy really does love the human vermin. This is, of course, a direct denial of the philosophy of hell, which holds that selves are by their very nature in competition. Wormwood evidently questions Screwtape about this lapse and receives a reply.

> I hope, my dear boy, you have not shown my letters to anyone. Not that it matters, of course. Anyone would see that the appearance of heresy into which I have fallen is purely accidental. By the way, I hope you understood, too, that some apparently uncomplimentary references to Slubgob were purely jocular. I really have the highest respect for him. And, of course, some things I said about not shielding you from the authorities were not seriously meant. You can trust me to look after your interests. But do keep everything under lock and key. (*SL*, pp. 85f.)

Later we learn that Wormwood has indeed tried, though unsuccessfully, to undermine Screwtape by reporting this incident to the secret police. And when, at the end, Wormwood loses his patient to the Enemy and comes whimpering for assurance to Screwtape, there is none to be found. Instead there is only Screwtape's desire that Wormwood now be given to him—a dainty morsel for him to devour (p. 145). The damned prey even upon one another.

The image of "devouring" pervades *The Screwtape Letters*. It is a highly successful attempt to portray a condition completely opposed to love. But Lewis also makes use of other images. For him the collective is closely related to (and in some ways the reverse side of) the competitive individualism of isolated selves seeking to devour one another. The collective is no closer than competitive individualism to genuine community. When Weston has given himself over to possession by an evil spirit in *Perelandra,* there comes a point when Ransom can no longer be certain whether Weston or the spirit possessing him is speaking.

> Indeed, it made little difference. There was, no doubt, a confusion of persons in damnation: what Pantheists falsely hoped of Heaven bad men really received in Hell. They were melted down into their Master. . . . (p. 173)

In this way the image of the collective is tied to that of devouring. What each isolated self finally desires is that the personality of every other self be drawn into his own and submerged within it.

The "grey town" of *The Great Divorce* is one last image of the kind of association in which no true city is possible. The bus which is taking travelers to heaven (though most will decide to return) leaves from this grey town. We learn from conversation among the travelers that no real city exists here. People keep quarreling and moving further and further apart (pp. 18f.). One of the men hopes to correct this. What is needed, he believes, is an economic basis for society. Indeed, this is his purpose in taking the bus ride. He hopes to bring back commodities which will be scarce in the grey town and to use these to build a society based on mutual need. He expects that people would still quarrel, but at least they might stay together. Of course, he adds, it would certainly be necessary to build up a police force (pp. 21f.). According to Lewis, this kind of association is no true community. Such an association would be based on precisely the opposite of a shared good. It would be built on the principle of competition for scarce goods which could not be shared and would inevitably have to be held together not by love but by fear and force. There, just as much as in Screwtape's hell, men would be conjoined but not reconciled.

Pride: The Great Sin

Hell, we have said, is withdrawal into the self combined with the attempt to submerge all other personality within oneself. The same point can be made in terms of love. It is through love that persons are able to overcome isolation and enter into community. Therefore, a "being which can still love is not yet a devil" (SL, p. x). Love is willing to accept the need for community; it can delight in the otherness of a partner in fellowship.

> The direct opposite of love, therefore, is pride, the movement whereby a creature (that is, an essentially dependent being whose principle of existence lies not in itself but in another) tries to set up on its own, to exist for itself. (PP, p. 75)

Hence, whereas human love acknowledges its dependence upon God and its created bond with other human beings, pride denies both. For that reason, in *Mere Christianity* Lewis entitles the chapter dealing with pride "The Great Sin." To be fully human a person must exist in harmonious relation with God and other persons. But within us there are two "other selves" competing with that "true self": the animal self (expressed in purely sensual sins) and the diabolical self (expressed in pride) (MC, p. 80). Lewis clearly regards the latter as the more dangerous.

Unlike other vices, pride is a denial of community. Pride is by its very nature competitive (MC, p. 95). Other vices may accidentally bring persons into competition—as when ambition leads two men to focus on the same job or desire leads them to vie for the attentions of the same woman. That is sinful but not in the same way that pride is sinful, for pride is competitive not accidentally but intrinsically. The crux of pride lies in comparison and competition.

Precisely because this is true, pride can be used to control the vices of the animal self. One man may refuse to compete for the job or try for the woman because he convinces himself that it would be beneath his dignity to do so (*MC*, p. 97). In this sense pride can help one to accomplish much that is good. It may lead one to be brave, chaste, and self-controlled—which shows only that pride struggles to copy the work of love. Nevertheless, it is finally a refusal to give oneself genuinely to the other person, and as such it is vastly different from love.

We can see the essentially competitive nature of pride when we realize that the other vices can sometimes create a genuine bond between people, whereas pride cannot. The other vices need not be competitive. In *Surprised by Joy*, the autobiographical account of his early years, Lewis provides an example of what he means. He is harshly critical of most of his public school life (far more critical, many have said, than the reality deserved). Indeed, it can be said that many of Lewis' images for hell were shaped by his school life. He gives an account of the homosexuality which prevailed, but he is far more critical of the fact that it was "a life almost wholly dominated by the social struggle; to get on, to arrive, or, having reached the top, to remain there, was the absorbing preoccupation" (*SJ*, p. 89). When Lewis compares these two aspects of school life, the homosexuality not only seems the lesser evil but becomes the source of considerable good.

> If those of us who have known a school like Wyvern dared to speak the truth, we should have to say that pederasty, however great an evil in itself, was, in that time and place, the only foothold or cranny left for certain good things. It was the only counterpoise to the social struggle; the one oasis (though green only with weeds and moist only with fetid water) in the burning desert of competitive ambition. In his unnatural love affairs, and perhaps only there, the Blood went a little out of himself. . . . A perversion was the only chink left through

which something spontaneous and uncalculating could creep in. Plato was right after all. Eros, turned upside down, blackened, distorted, filthy, still bore the traces of his divinity. (*SJ*, pp. 109–10)

Although fellowship with God cannot finally coexist with any sort of vice, pride is by far the most dangerous. A person controlled by the sensual vices may come to realize that they do not really bring the joy they seem to offer, and he may then be led to seek the One in whom true joy is to be found. Such vices need only to be re-directed. Pride, on the other hand, must be broken. Since the proud man refuses to look outside himself at all, something more than a mere re-direction of desire is necessary.

This is, in large measure, the theme of Lewis' two autobiographical works—*Surprised by Joy* and *The Pilgrim's Regress*. He attempts to show how a romantic longing— "sweet desire" in *Regress* and *Sehnsucht* in *Surprised by Joy*—led him on until, like Augustine, he found that one could rest only in God. But at the same time he stresses— most clearly in *Surprised by Joy,* the later work—the way in which his pride and desire for autonomy had to be broken. Lewis had always wanted at least some small area of his life over which to hang the "no admittance" sign. What he wanted above all was not to be "interfered with" (*SJ*, pp. 172, 228). The pride within him fought against the conclusion toward which romantic longing was leading. "The reality with which no treaty can be made was upon me" (*SJ*, p. 228). And so, when he begins the description of the moment when he finally gave in and got down on his knees to pray, he writes:

> You must picture me, alone in that room at Magdalen, night after night, feeling, whenever my mind lifted even for a second from my work, the steady, unrelenting approach of Him whom I so earnestly desired not to meet. (*SJ*, p. 228)

Pride had to be broken in surrender, and in that surrender his longings could be re-directed. The longings were re-directed, but the man himself had to be re-created so that pride might give place to love.

The Inner Ring

Lewis' concept of the "Inner Ring" illustrates a kind of perversion of genuine hierarchical authority. He develops the idea primarily in three places: the address called simply "The Inner Ring," his essay on "Kipling's World," and *That Hideous Strength*.[61] The desire to belong to an Inner Ring is, Lewis thinks, "one of the great permanent mainsprings of human action" (*WG*, p. 61). It cannot be explained in terms of economic or erotic motives, nor is it simply to be equated with ambition. Beyond anything those motives may provide, one who desires entrance into an Inner Ring is moved by lust for "the delicious sense of secret intimacy" (*WG*, p. 61). The Inner Ring is never a formally organized secret society. Yet, it exists as a kind of competing hierarchy. We can scarcely do better than let Lewis describe it.

> You are never formally and explicitly admitted by anyone. You discover gradually, in almost indefinable ways, that it exists and that you are outside it; and then later, perhaps, that you are inside it. . . . It is not easy, even at a given moment, to say who is inside and who is outside. . . . People think they are in it after they have in fact been pushed out of it, or before they have been allowed in: this provides great amusement for those who are really inside. (*WG*, pp. 56–57)

Lewis believes Kipling to have been the first to present "the magic of the Inner Ring in all its manifold workings."[62] If Kipling celebrates professional brotherhoods of workingmen, it is not for the sake of the work. He loves the work only for the sake of the professional brotherhood. "To belong, to be inside, to be in the know, to be snugly together against the outsiders—that is what really matters. . . ."[63] We can see here a fact of great importance about the Inner Ring. It exists for the sake of exclusion. As such, it is the opposite of friendship. Friends gravitate to the company of one another because they find that they share mutual interests; that is, real interest in almost anything will sooner

---

[61]The first can be found in *WG*, pp. 55–66; the second in *Selected Literary Essays*, pp. 232–50.

[62]"Kipling's World," *Selected Literary Essays*, p. 247.

[63]*Ibid.*, p. 246.

or later bring one (quite possibly, unconsciously) into a special, select group. But a group of friends does not exist for the sake of exclusion; its exclusions are, so to speak, accidental. Hence, as Lewis says in his discussion of friendship in *The Four Loves*, "true friendship is the least jealous of loves" (p. 92). Not so the Inner Ring. In it exclusion is necessary by definition, not simply because a limited number of people can converse at the same time about a shared interest. Exclusion is the very principle of existence of an Inner Ring. "There'd be no fun if there were no outsiders" (*WG*, pp. 64–65).

Lewis says, on several occasions, that the existence of Inner Rings is itself morally neutral and, even, that their existence helps many people to heights of diligence or courage which they might otherwise not have reached. He condemns the desire to enter Inner Rings, not their existence.[64] One understands his point, but it is not clear that Lewis can or should say this. If an Inner Ring exists for the sake of exclusion, for the sake of a good which its members do not wish to share, it stands in opposition to true community. The union even with other members of the Inner Ring is desired not for its own sake but as a means to isolating and excluding others. This need not mean that Inner Rings never foster anything praiseworthy. Lewis could say of them just what he said of vices such as pederasty: that, though a great evil, they may at certain times and places provide "the only foothold or cranny left for certain good things." This sort of judgment would cohere better with Lewis' general perspective than the judgment that the Inner Ring is itself morally neutral.

Regardless of that, however, Lewis can still drive home the point which concerns him: the way in which the desire to enter an Inner Ring can make a person do great evil. Here again it is impossible to improve upon Lewis' description.

> To nine out of ten of you the choice which could lead to scoundrelism will come, when it does come, in no very dra-

---

[64]*Ibid.*, p. 248. See also *WG*, pp. 59–60.

matic colours. Obviously bad men, obviously threatening or
bribing, will almost certainly not appear. Over a drink or a cup
of coffee, disguised as a triviality and sandwiched between two
jokes, from the lips of a man, or woman, whom you have
recently been getting to know rather better and whom you
hope to know better still—just at the moment when you are
most anxious not to appear crude, or naif, or a prig—the hint
will come. It will be the hint of something which is not quite in
accordance with the technical rules of fair play; something
which the public, the ignorant, romantic public, would never
understand: something which even the outsiders in your own
profession are apt to make a fuss about: but something, says
your new friend, which "we"—and at the word "we" you try
not to blush for mere pleasure—something "we always do."
And you will be drawn in, if you are drawn in, not by desire for
gain or ease, but simply because at that moment, when the cup
was so near your lips, you cannot bear to be thrust back again
into the cold outer world. (WG, pp. 62–63)

If Lewis was wrong to term the Inner Ring morally neutral,
he has more than made up for it with this description of the
desire to get inside.

With this description in mind we can sketch the way in
which Lewis gives fictional development to this theme in
That Hideous Strength. The driving motivation of Mark
Studdock is this desire to be part of an Inner Ring, which
Lewis once wrote was the chief theme of *That Hideous
Strength*.[65] Only six months after her marriage to Mark, Jane
finds herself lonely. He leaves her more and more alone as he
struggles to get inside the progressive element at Bracton
College (p. 13). As he walks to the college one day, Mark
meets Curry, the sub-warden, and they begin to talk about
the business of the college. Mark's efforts seem to be re-
warded; for Curry treats him as one of the insiders. "You
would never have guessed from the tone of Studdock's
reply what intense pleasure he derived from Curry's use
of the pronoun 'we' " (p. 17). Yet, Mark is still clearheaded
enough to recognize that much of the time he does not
really like Curry. "His pleasure in being with him was not
that sort of pleasure" (p. 18).

Mark has come to believe that the real insiders at the

[65]"A Reply to Professor Haldane," *Of Other Worlds*, p. 79.

college are Curry and Busby, the Bursar. However, one evening while dining with them and Feverstone, he realizes that there is another Inner Ring to be penetrated. Feverstone obviously holds Curry and Busby in contempt. He mocks them, "not exactly glancing, much less winking, at Mark, but making him feel that he was somehow being included in the fun" (p. 35). Mark, ever desirous of getting further inside, has a "giddy sensation of being suddenly whirled up from one plane of secrecy to another" (p. 40). Already we can see that the desire to be in an Inner Ring is a never-ending one, for it always finds new levels of secret intimacy to be penetrated.

Mark's first associations with the N.I.C.E. and his unsuccessful attempts to determine the nature of his position leave him feeling unhappy and disgruntled—an outsider. Hence, he is pleased to get attention even from Fairy Hardcastle, whom he finds very disagreeable. There is a "deliciously esoteric" character to their conversation together, and while they talk Mark once again has the feeling that he is getting inside (p. 69). Nevertheless, he speaks of leaving the N.I.C.E. unless he can receive definite information about the position for which he is supposedly being considered. Fairy Hardcastle warns against a decision to leave, and this time the conversation takes on a rather different tone. She seems to be threatening Mark with the loss of his career if he leaves.

> The citizen and the honest man which had been awakened in Mark by the conversation, quailed a little; his other and far stronger self, the self that was anxious at all costs not to be placed among the outsiders, leaped up, fully alarmed. (p. 100)

Mark has been sufficiently cowed and, for the time being, stops protesting and threatening to leave. Then, quite suddenly, he finds that he is allowed into the library, to gather with the real Inner Ring at Belbury. We are not surprised to find that this gives him great pleasure. Having gotten this far inside, Mark learns that the N.I.C.E. plans to use its private police force to engineer demonstrations in Edgestow (where Bracton College is located). The N.I.C.E.

will then claim that the local police are unable to handle the disruptions and that, for the good of all, the N.I.C.E. police should be given "temporary" authority in the area. Newspaper articles espousing this viewpoint will be needed. Mark is to write these articles—the N.I.C.E. evidently being more interested in his literary than his sociological talents.

> This was the first thing Mark had been asked to do which he himself, before he did it, clearly knew to be criminal. But the moment of his consent almost escaped his notice; certainly there was no struggle, no sense of turning a corner. . . . For him, it all slipped past in a chatter of laughter, of that intimate laughter between fellow professionals, which of all earthly powers is strongest to make men do very bad things before they are yet, individually, very bad men. (p. 130)

While at Belbury Mark gradually recognizes that Frost, a seemingly innocuous man, is a key figure in the Inner Ring of the N.I.C.E. As had been the case with Curry and Fairy Hardcastle, there is something about Frost which Mark does not like. Yet, he finds it delightful to talk with him. "The pleasures of conversation were coming, for Mark, to have less and less connection with his spontaneous liking or disliking of the people he talked to" (p. 170). Genuine delight is, in fact, being killed by the passion to penetrate ever further into the Inner Ring.

Later, when Mark is imprisoned by the N.I.C.E. police force and faces possible death, he begins to see the whole of his life in a different perspective. Why had he come to Belbury? Because Feverstone had brought him and he thought it "in" to be with Feverstone. Why had he trusted Feverstone? Because he was a friend of Curry and Busby, the progressive element at Bracton College with which Mark had hoped to ingratiate himself. Why had he desired that?

> He had a picture of himself, the odious little outsider who wanted to be an insider, the infantile gull, drinking in the busy and unimportant confidences, as if he were being admitted to the government of the planet. (p. 245)

He remembers now that the same had been true of his earlier years; how, as a little boy, he had hidden in the shrubbery trying to overhear his sister's conversation with a friend; how he had given up the old walks with his friend Pearson for the sake of afternoons spent with the athletic heroes pretending to enjoy their company; how in his teens he had spent hours "reading rubbishy grown-up novels and drinking beer when he really enjoyed John Buchan and stone ginger"; how, indeed, his whole life could be read as the story of one attempt after another to enter an Inner Ring (p. 246). "When had he ever done what he wanted? Mixed with the people whom he liked? Or even eaten and drunk what took his fancy? The concentrated insipidity of it all filled him with self-pity" (pp. 246–47).

Near the end of the novel something very strange happens to Mark. He finds himself placed in the same room with a tramp whom the N.I.C.E. people have mistaken for Merlin. The tramp is uneducated but no fool, and by judiciously keeping his mouth shut he has managed to deceive Frost and Wither while dining sumptuously at their expense. Mark shares his secret, and the two of them enjoy a kind of continual picnic together. Without realizing or intending it, Mark finds himself enjoying the pleasures of being a member of a circle "as secret and as strongly fenced against outsiders as any that he had dreamed of" (p. 313). This, however, was no Inner Ring; for here there was no desire for power or security, no room for vanity, and no desire for exclusivity for its own sake. Here was only the pleasure of companionship.

In his treatment of the Inner Ring Lewis is doing more than showing us a kind of perversion of hierarchy. He is also driving home once again the truth about community. Human beings are made for fellowship with God and, in him, with one another. Therefore, one who refuses to admit his need for such fellowship or perverts the nature of this community cannot, in the end, find joy. Entrance into an Inner Ring gives birth only to the desire to get still further inside. The longing that possesses us cannot finally be satisfied by entrance to any Inner Ring. "The quest of the Inner Ring will break your hearts unless you break it" (*WG,* p. 65). When that quest is broken; when pride is killed within a man who is created anew; when such a man no longer seeks to get in but simply to give himself in love; only then he will find that, without realizing it, he has gotten in. In losing his life, he will save it. Only fellowship with God will give him understanding of that lifelong quest to get inside, and he will learn that joy comes only to those who cease to grasp for it.

The Place of Animals

Charles Moorman has written of *That Hideous Strength:*

> That Lewis means the contrast of St. Anne's and Belbury to be taken seriously is seen in the fact that he provides a point of comparison by which we may judge the groups by similar standards. Both households keep animals and in the treatment of those animals by each group we are intended to see their basic dissimilarity. At Belbury, the animals are caged awaiting vivisection; at St. Anne's they are treated as 'jesters, servants, and playfellows.'[66]

Vivisection is one of the two ways Lewis pictures a distorted relation to the animal creation, the other being that of the pampered and over-domesticated pet. Vivisection is part of the program of the N.I.C.E., as Moorman notes. In *Perelandra* Ransom discovers Weston walking along the shore and for no reason ripping open the backs of frogs and damaging them in such a way that they can no longer leap (pp. 108–10).

Lewis discusses the topic of vivisection in a short essay.[67] He himself was a confirmed opponent of the practice because of his beliefs about the proper relation of the human and animal creation. A Christian could, he admitted, defend vivisection on the grounds that the superiority of

[66]Charles Moorman, *Arthurian Triptych: Mythic Materials in Charles Williams, C. S. Lewis, and T. S. Eliot* (Berkeley: University of California, 1960), p. 119.

[67]In *God in the Dock,* pp. 224–28. The citations that follow are from this essay.

man to beast had been divinely revealed. Lewis grants that there is indeed a difference in kind; a hierarchical order. He suggests, however, that man's superiority "ought partly to *consist in* not behaving like a vivisector."

Lewis is even more concerned when vivisection is justified on non-Christian grounds. How, he asks, will one who believes there is no difference in kind between man and beast justify vivisection? "All the grounds on which a Christian might defend vivisection are thus cut from under our feet. We sacrifice other species to our own not because our own has any objective metaphysical privilege over others, but simply because it is ours." And, he maintains, any arguments for vivisection not based on a difference in kind will also be arguments for experiments on inferior men. Lewis offers this, however, only as a further argument against the practice. His own opposition is based not only on a fear of where the practice may lead but also on the belief that it is incompatible with man's position as priest of the animal creation.

Another way in which we may fail to respect the proper place of animals is by pampering and over-domesticating them. We noted earlier that Lewis' vision of the properly tamed animal retains something of the animal's wildness. The lion may frolic before man, but he retains the aweful character of his leonine self. Lewis notes in *The Four Loves* that the tyrannous need to be needed, when not satisfied with fawning attention of other persons, may express itself in one's relation to a pet. "You can keep it all its life in need of you" (p. 79). The animal can be cut off from any genuine animal well-being and made dependent on the "countless little indulgences which only you can grant" (p. 79). Lewis also has an antipathy toward zoos, as becomes clear in the first stanza of his poem "The Condemned."

> There is a wildness still in England that will not feed
> In cages; it shrinks away from the touch of the trainer's hand,
> Easy to kill, not easy to tame. It will never breed
> In a zoo for the public pleasure. It will not be planned.[68]

[68]*Poems*, p. 63.

The animal, too, Lewis seems to be saying, is (through its relation to man) to share in community. To deny the animal its proper measure of freedom or to use it simply as a means to the advancement of human aims is to distort the proper relationship. Human beings come from the dust of the ground, and those who cease to view the animals as, in some sense, their fellows may never learn to appreciate the full meaning of human community.

LOGRES VS. BRITAIN

The pictures of genuine community and its perversion are not merely pictures. Neither is perfectly realized in this world, but such a perfect realization is the end which each seeks. The life we presently live can only be described as a continual movement between these two possibilities. In the life of every human being one must finally triumph. There is no neutral ground. Human life is an arena of conflict, and throughout a person's life he is turning "either into a creature that is in harmony with God, and with other creatures, and with itself, or else into one that is in a state of war and hatred with God, and with its fellow-creatures, and with itself" (*MC*, p. 72).

It takes no great insight to see in this the Augustinian theme of the two cities which are forever opposed, and critics have certainly recognized this.[69] Lewis has written that his debts to Augustine are "incalculable" (*FL*, p. 167). In *That Hideous Strength* the conflict between the two cities is obviously imaged in the conflict between St. Anne's and Belbury. This is accentuated by the elements of Arthurian legend which Lewis weaves into the story.[70] The

[69]See, for example, Moorman, *Arthurian Triptych*, p. 116. See also the subtitle of another book by Moorman, *The Precincts of Felicity: The Augustinian City of the Oxford Christians* (Gainesville: University of Florida, 1966). Also, Richard Purtill, *Lord of the Elves and Eldils: Fantasy and Philosophy in C. S. Lewis and J. R. R. Tolkien* (Grand Rapids: Zondervan, 1974), p. 94.

[70]For a discussion of the legend and Lewis' use of it, see Moorman, *Arthurian Triptych*, chapters 2 and 4. Also important in Lewis' thinking was Charles Williams' "The Figure of Arthur," which Lewis edited after Williams' death and published with his own commentary on Williams' Arthurian poems in *Arthurian Torso*.

conflict between St. Anne's and Belbury is an instance of the battle between Logres and Britain, a struggle which involves superhuman forces. Lewis has taken from Charles Williams the notion of a perpetual struggle between Logres and Britain—which was Williams' own reading of the significance of the Arthurian legend. This is nothing other than a struggle between *caritas* and *cupiditas.*

According to the tradition, King Arthur was transported to the isle of Avalon to be cured of his wounds. There he stands perpetual guard over England, ready to return when he is needed. Hence, there is always hope that some day Logres (the Arthurian ideal community) will triumph over Britain (the secular reality) and England will be saved. In *That Hideous Strength* we learn that Ransom and Dr. Dimble have made extremely thorough investigations of Arthurian legend. They have discovered, Dimble says, that it is mostly true history.

> "There was a moment in the Sixth Century when something that is always trying to break through into this country nearly succeeded. Logres was our name for it—it will do as well as another. And then . . . gradually we began to see all English history in a new way. We discovered the haunting." (pp. 368–69)

That haunting is the haunting of Britain by Logres.

> "Haven't you noticed that we are two countries? After every Arthur, a Mordred; behind every Milton, a Cromwell: a nation of poets, a nation of shopkeepers; the home of Sidney—and of Cecil Rhodes. Is it any wonder they call us hypocrites? But what they mistake for hypocrisy is really the struggle between Logres and Britain." (p. 369)

England can only be characterized as "this swaying to and fro between Logres and Britain" (p. 370). Logres is the special haunting of England, but each people has its own special haunting. In the life of every people the battle goes on as true community seeks to become incarnate among them.

Because life must finally be described relative to this struggle, commitment becomes necessary. There is no neutral ground on which to stand aloof from the conflict. As Ransom muses to himself in *Perelandra*, there is no road

through human life that does not finally lead to the Beatific
or the Miserific Vision (p. 111). Both Jane and Mark are told
this as they waver indecisively in the struggle between St.
Anne's and Belbury. Jane is consistently hesitant to be
"drawn in." She wants to avoid taking sides and asks
Camilla how she can take sides in something she does not
yet completely understand: " 'But don't you see,' broke in
Camilla, 'that you can't be neutral? If you don't give yourself to us, the enemy will use you' " (p. 115). Dimble says
the same to Mark when he offers him one last chance
to leave the N.I.C.E. and come over to the other side.
Mark is uncertain.

> "I—I'd need to think that over," he mumbled.
> "There is no time," said Dimble. "And there is really noth-
> ing to think about. I am offering you a way back into the human
> family. But you must come at once."
> "It's a question affecting my whole future career."
> "Your career!" said Dimble. "It's a question of damnation
> or—a last chance. But you must come at once."
> "I don't think I understand," said Mark. "You keep on
> suggesting some kind of danger. What is it? And what powers
> have you to protect me—or Jane—if I do bolt?"
> "You must risk that," said Dimble. "I can offer you no
> security. Don't you understand? There is no security for any-
> one now. The battle has started. I'm offering you a place on the
> right side. I don't know which will win." (p. 223)

This is the choice Lewis presents throughout his work.
Our world is not, he says, one in which the roads are like
radii of a circle. If that were the case, all roads, if followed
long enough, would finally converge at the center. A different image is closer to the reality. Ours is a world in which
the roads all fork into two every few miles along the way
and each of these into two more, and so on. And at every
fork a decision must be made (*GD*, pp. 5f.). Ours is a world
dominated by a great either-or: Logres vs. Britain, the conflict between true community and its perversion. Christianity can, Lewis says, come very close to Dualism; for we
are to think of the world as "enemy-occupied territory"
(*MC*, p. 36).

We do not say enough, though, if we think only in terms

of a kind of choice between heaven and hell. What is at stake is a person's very humanity. For here again Lewis' reality principle is operative. Man is created for life in community and cannot be himself apart from it. Man is created to live in love which reaches out to the other, not to be dominated by pride which vaunts and isolates the self. What Dimble offers Mark is "a way back into the human family." Charles Moorman is correct when he says that Belbury "is obviously Augustine's and Williams' Earthly City pushed to its extreme. Here is a City not only without God, but without humanity."[71]

There is, finally, no way to save one's humanity except by giving it in fellowship to others. The gift would not, of course, be a gift if there were any prior assurance of a happy outcome. Lewis is fond of stressing the theme of Norse mythology, which had captivated him in his youth, that it is better to die with the gods than live with the giants. Similarly, Dimble offers Mark a place, not on the winning side, but on the right side. It is only on the other side of that choice—from within—that one can be surprised by joy. But the choice is real and decisive: either the ruthless, unsmiling, and deadly isolation of self; or "the revelry of insatiable love."

[71]Moorman, *The Precincts of Felicity,* p. 77.

CHAPTER III

THE DIVINE SURGEON

"There was a boy called Eustace Clarence Scrubb, and he almost deserved it." With that line Lewis begins *The Voyage of the "Dawn Treader,"* third of the Chronicles of Narnia. Within the opening paragraphs we learn of Eustace that "deep down inside he liked bossing and bullying" (p. 2). When the story ends, some two hundred pages and many adventures later, a great deal has changed. Eustace has been to Narnia with Lucy and Edmund, and "back in our own world everyone soon started saying how Eustace had improved, and how 'You'd never know him for the same boy' " (p. 210).

At first glance *The Voyage of the "Dawn Treader"* would seem to be almost purely picaresque in character. There is less plot outline to it than any of the other Narnia tales. It consists largely of different adventures faced by the children in the company of Caspian and other Narnians as they sail toward the end of the world in search of some vanished nobles. However, once we take note of the way in which the story begins and ends with the character of Eustace, we see that it is not only a series of exciting adventures. The book is also about the transformation of Eustace. This, in turn, means that the two chapters (six and seven) which tell of this transformation are crucial.

The "Dawn Treader" has survived a terrible storm at sea and has dropped anchor off an island. Caspian and the sailors plan to stay there until they can repair the extensive damage to their ship. Eustace, hoping to avoid sharing in the work, decides to steal off and explore the island. Unwit-

tingly, he manages to get himself lost in a fog, and finds
himself in an unknown valley on the island with the sea and
the ship nowhere in sight. By a pool of water Eustace
encounters a dying dragon and is just in time to watch it
breathe its last. When rain begins to fall, Eustace takes
refuge in the dragon's cave. He lies down to rest in the cave
but is puzzled by the way it feels.

> Most of us know what we should expect to find in a dragon's
> lair, but, as I said before, Eustace had read only the wrong
> books. They had a lot to say about exports and imports and
> governments and drains, but they were weak on dragons. That
> is why he was so puzzled at the surface on which he was lying.
> Parts of it were too prickly to be stones and too hard to be
> thorns, and there seemed to be a great many round, flat things,
> and it all clinked when he moved. There was light enough at
> the cave's mouth to examine it by. And of course Eustace found
> it to be what any of us could have told him in advance—
> treasure. (p. 71)

Overcome by greed, Eustace makes plans to carry off as
much of the treasure as he can. He fills his pockets with
diamonds and slips a bracelet on his wrist. It proves to be
too big for his wrist, so he pushes it up above his elbow.
Then he lies down to sleep until the rain ends.

He is awakened by a pain in his arm. The bracelet has
gotten very tight on his arm, and he decides that the arm
must have swollen while he slept.

> He moved his right arm in order to feel his left, but stopped
> before he had moved it an inch and bit his lip in terror. For just
> in front of him, and a little on his right, where the moonlight
> fell clear on the floor of the cave, he saw a hideous shape
> moving. He knew that shape: it was a dragon's claw. It had
> moved as he moved his hand and became still when he
> stopped moving his hand. (p. 73)

He is terrified to think that the dragon's mate must have
returned. He tries to sneak off to his left, but when he turns
in that direction, he finds a dragon's claw there too. Each
time he moves, the dragons on either side of him move and
mimic his motions. Completely terrified he dashes out of
the cave, hoping to jump into the pool of water.

> But just as he reached the edge of the pool two things happened. First of all it came over him like a thunderclap that he had been running on all fours—and why on earth had he been doing that? And secondly, as he bent towards the water, he thought for a second that yet another dragon was staring up at him out of the pool. But in another instant he realised the truth. That dragon face in the pool was his own reflection. There was no doubt of it. It moved as he moved: it opened and shut its mouth as he opened and shut his.
>
> He had turned into a dragon while he was asleep. Sleeping on a dragon's hoard with greedy, dragonish thoughts in his heart, he had become a dragon himself. (pp. 74-75)

Eustace's first thought is that now, as a dragon, he can repay Edmund and Caspian for all the insults he had imagined them to give him. But in almost the same moment he realizes that this is not at all what he wants.

> He wanted to be friends. He wanted to get back among humans and talk and laugh and share things. He realised that he was a monster cut off from the whole human race. An appalling loneliness came over him. He began to see that the others had not really been friends at all. He began to wonder if he himself had been such a nice person as he had always supposed. (p. 75)

There we have the beginning of Eustace's transformation. It has taken this great a shock—finding that he has become a dragon—to begin in him a process of regeneration. This is immediately evident to the others back at the ship. For as soon as Eustace flies back to the ship and manages to let them know who he is, he begins to use his skills as a dragon to help them. It was

> clear to everyone that Eustace's character had been rather improved by becoming a dragon. He was anxious to help. He flew over the whole island and found that it was all mountainous and inhabited only by wild goats and droves of wild swine. Of these he brought back many carcasses for the revictualling of the ship. (p. 83)

Eustace cannot help overhearing snatches of conversation among the others. They do their best to be kind, but as the work on the ship moves toward its conclusion they are faced with a difficult question: What shall they do with Eustace when they are ready to leave? "And poor Eustace realised

more and more that since the first day he came on board he
had been an unmitigated nuisance and that he was now a
greater nuisance still" (p. 85).

One morning the others are surprised to find Eustace
back in camp and once again his normal self. Edmund is the
first to see him, and Eustace tells Edmund his strange
experience of the previous night. A huge lion (Aslan, of
course) had approached and taken him to a well on the top
of a mountain. He thinks that the pain from the bracelet
might ease if he could jump in the water, but the lion tells
him that he must undress first. What this means, evidently,
is that he must take off his dragon scales. So Eustace begins
to scratch at the scales and soon the skin begins to peel. In a
minute he steps out of the skin and gets ready to go into the
water.

> "But just as I was going to put my foot into the water I
> looked down and saw that it was all hard and rough and wrin-
> kled and scaly just as it had been before. Oh, that's all right, said
> I, it only means I had another smaller suit on underneath the
> first one, and I'll have to get out of it too." (p. 89)

Eustace scratches his way out of this skin too, but finds
another inside it. For a third time he peels off his skin only
to find still another beneath it.

> "Then the lion said—but I don't know if it spoke—You will
> have to let me undress you. I was afraid of his claws, I can tell
> you, but I was pretty nearly desperate now. So I just lay flat
> down on my back to let him do it.
> "The very first tear he made was so deep that I thought it had
> gone right into my heart. And when he began pulling the skin
> off, it hurt worse than anything I've ever felt. The only thing
> that made me able to bear it was just the pleasure of feeling the
> stuff peel off." (p. 89)

Then the lion picks Eustace up and throws him into the
water. Splashing around in it Eustace finds that he is no
longer a dragon but is once again a boy. The lion dresses
him in new clothes and sends him back to the others.

> It would be nice, and fairly nearly true, to say that "from
> that time forth Eustace was a different boy." To be strictly
> accurate, he began to be a different boy. He had relapses.

There were still many days when he could be very tiresome. But most of those I shall not notice. The cure had begun. (p. 92)

The baptismal imagery is fairly obvious. More important for our purposes, however, is the function of pain. In his innermost being Eustace had "liked bossing and bullying." He had not really been fit for, nor had he desired, fellowship with others. Becoming a dragon had been no change at all for Eustace; it had only revealed the end of the road he was traveling. "He realised that he was a monster cut off from the whole human race." That is what Eustace finally understands when he becomes a dragon, but it is a fate he had chosen for himself even prior to this transformation. Only as a dragon does he begin to desire human community; only then does he want to "get back among humans and talk and laugh and share things."

Aslan does what Eustace himself cannot do. He transforms Eustace—makes him over into a person fit for community. And the transformation is a painful one. There is no other way for the bossing and bullying self to be changed. For such a self it must be painful for the Lion to peel off the layers which serve as barriers against true community. Eustace's conversion and baptism are the beginning of his cure. The Christian life is for Lewis a pilgrimage—a process of sanctification understood in terms of the Christian story. Throughout this journey pain functions to remind the Christian that the sinful self will have to be killed, completely and totally, before he is fit to share in the community of the regenerate.

PURGATORY

The process of transforming the sinner into a person who desires a life in common with God and other persons—a person who can "talk and laugh and share things"—continues, according to Lewis, after death. Lewis' biographers recount an incident in which a television interviewer asked Lewis whether he planned to become a Roman Catholic since he believed in purgatory. "But not," answered Lewis, "the *Romish* doctrine."[1] Green and Hooper state that in order to eliminate such rumors, Lewis finally explained his belief in purgatory in *Letters to Malcolm.* There were, however, hints of it in earlier writings. In fact, it would not be wrong to say that the belief in purgatory, though seldom explicitly stated, is deeply embedded in Lewis' thought.

Certainly it is striking to find such a strong affirmation of this belief in Lewis, who habitually avoided topics of great theological controversy in his effort to articulate "mere Christianity." Thus, for example, it is almost impossible to find in Lewis any discussion of sacramental theology. Hence, when we find deeply embedded in his work the concept of purgatory, which has been highly controversial, we are entitled to wonder whether it may not be of more than passing importance.

Lewis explicitly tells us only that he believes in purgatory but not in "the Romish doctrine" of purgatory.[2] The easiest way to arrive at some clarity about what he affirms is to learn what he denies. First, we should be clear that belief in purgatory is not to be equated with a kind of second chance after death. Lewis had already made this plain years before he ever affirmed his belief in purgatory. In *The Problem of Pain* he states that any number of second chances would be given if they were likely to do any good (p. 112). In a footnote to that discussion he points out that such a notion of a second chance is distinct from purgatory, which is for souls already saved.

Lewis' rejection of "the Romish doctrine" of purgatory is certainly a reference to Article XXII of the Thirty-Nine Articles of Religion of the Anglican Church. Article XXII states:

> The Romish Doctrine concerning Purgatory, Pardons, Worshipping and Adoration, as well of Images as of Relics, and also

[1]Green and Hooper, p. 234.

[2]*Letters to Malcolm,* p. 108. For another reference to "the Romish doctrine," this one in the context of literary criticism, see "Neoplatonism in Spenser's Poetry," in *Studies in Medieval and Renaissance Literature,* p. 154.

Invocation of Saints is a fond thing, vainly invented, and
grounded upon no warranty of Scripture, but rather repugnant
to the Word of God.

Lewis explains in *Letters to Malcolm* why the Reformers
were correct to condemn the Romish doctrine.

I don't mean merely the commercial scandal. If you turn from
Dante's *Purgatorio* to the sixteenth century you will be ap-
palled by the degradation. In Thomas More's *Supplication of
Souls* Purgatory is simply temporary Hell. In it the souls are
tormented by devils, whose presence is "more horrible and
grievous to us than is the pain itself." Worse still, Fisher, in his
Sermon on Psalm VI, says the tortures are so intense that the
spirit who suffers them cannot, for pain, "remember God as he
ought to do." In fact, the very etymology of the word *purgatory*
has dropped out of sight. Its pains do not bring us nearer to
God, but make us forget Him. It is a place not of purification
but purely of retributive punishment.
    The right view returns magnificently in Newman's *Dream*.
There, if I remember it rightly, the saved soul, at the very foot
of the throne, begs to be taken away and cleansed. It cannot
bear for a moment longer "With its darkness to affront that
light." Religion has reclaimed Purgatory. (p. 108)

Lewis discusses both Fisher and More in his volume in the
Oxford History of English Literature, and there he sheds
more light on the kind of belief in purgatory which he
rejects. He contrasts the views of St. John Fisher (1459–
1535), Bishop of Rochester, with those of Dante. The latter's view is, says Lewis, "profoundly religious." "That
purification must, in its own nature, be painful, we hardly
dare to dispute."[3] But in Fisher, Lewis continues, the pain
cannot really be part of a purifying process since, for as long
as it lasts, it separates the sufferer from God. Lewis notes,
and clearly sympathizes with, Tyndale's charge against
Fisher that such a concept of purgatory, in which one who
has turned against his sin is nevertheless punished on account of it, cannot be purgative but can only be a means for
satisfying the "lust of a tyrant."[4] More's *Supplication of
Souls* "illustrates a further stage in the degradation of the

[3]*English Literature in the Sixteenth Century, Excluding Drama*,
p. 163.
    [4]*Ibid.*, p. 164.

idea of purgatory."[5] By making devils rather than angels inflict the sufferings More cuts the last link between purgatory and heaven. Lewis summarizes:

> Instead of the psalms and litanies which resounded on the sunlit terraces of Dante's mountain from souls 'contented in the flame', out of the black fire which More has imagined, mixed with the howls of unambiguous physical torture, come peals of harsh laughter. All is black, salt, macabre. . . . This sort of thing, among others, was what the old religion had come to mean in the popular imagination during the reign of Henry VIII: this was one of the things a man left behind in becoming a Protestant.[6]

Presumably, it is also what Lewis rejects in rejecting "the Romish doctrine" of purgatory. He simply aligns himself with Article XXII in condemning, not any belief in purgatory, but any belief in this kind of purgatory. He appears to be in agreement with a modern commentator on the Thirty-Nine Articles who says of the late medieval understanding: "The disciplinary aspect of purgatorial suffering had retreated to a secondary position."[7] The article on purgatory in *The Oxford Dictionary of the Christian Church* states that belief in purgatory reentered the Church of England through the teachings of the Tractarians. "The most widely received opinion would seem to be that this state is not so much a process of purification from sin, as in Roman Catholic theology, as one of growth and development."[8] In light of Lewis' reference to Newman's *Dream of Gerontius* it seems probable that Newman and, of course, Dante are the sources for his concept of purgatory as purification without punishment.

It should be clear by now that in rejecting "the Romish doctrine" of purgatory (i.e., what that belief had become in the popular English mind of the sixteenth century) Lewis is not necessarily rejecting the Roman Catholic doctrine of

---

[5]*Ibid.*, p. 172.
[6]*Ibid.*, p. 173.
[7] E. J. Bicknell, *A Theological Introduction to the Thirty-Nine Articles of the Church of England*, third edition revised by H. J. Carpenter (London: Longmans, Green & Co., 1955), p. 282.
[8]"Purgatory," *The Oxford Dictionary of the Christian Church*, ed. F. L. Cross (London: Oxford, 1959), p. 1126.

purgatory. However, his view does differ in many important ways.

Article XXII was drafted in 1553, exactly ten years before the decree of the Council of Trent which treated purgatory. It is interesting to note that when Article XXII was revised, there was a change made in its wording. It had originally spoken not of "the Romish doctrine" but of "the doctrine of the school-authors." The revision in 1563 evidently pointed to a belief that at Trent the Roman Church had made its own the doctrine of the later schoolmen.[9] In Roman Catholic teaching purgatory is defined as

> the state, place, or condition in the next world, which will continue until the last judgment, where the souls of those who die in the state of grace, but not yet free from all imperfection, make expiation for unforgiven venial sins or for the temporal punishment due to venial and mortal sins that have already been forgiven and, by so doing, are purified before they enter heaven.[10]

The article from which this definition is taken goes on to make clear that, even in the midst of their purgatorial sufferings, souls "experience great joy over the certainty of salvation." The experience is without feelings of horror or anguish, and the sufferings are voluntarily accepted as a means to union with God.[11]

For Lewis the process of purification appears to be just that: a continuation of the cure which has already begun in this life when a man puts on Christ and takes up the pilgrim's journey toward complete sanctification. Purgatory, for him, seems to involve neither payment for the guilt of (venial) sin nor suffering the punishment due forgiven sin. Payment for the guilt has been made by Jesus, of whom Lewis says, "He has done vicariously whatever can be so done."[12] With respect to suffering punishment still due forgiven sin, it seems safe to assume that Lewis concurs

---

[9]E. Tyrrell Green, *The Thirty-Nine Articles and the Age of the Reformation* (London: Wells Gardner, Darton & Co., 1896), pp. 146f.

[10]"Purgatory," *New Catholic Encyclopedia*, Vol. 11 (New York: McGraw-Hill, 1967), p. 1034.

[11]*Ibid.*, p. 1037.

[12]*A Grief Observed* (London: Faber & Faber, 1961), pp. 36f.

with Tyndale against Fisher. The purpose of the purgatorial suffering cannot be to punish the soul for sin the soul itself abhors but to purge it of the habits and inclinations toward sin which continue to cling to it. His belief in purgatory rose up to attack Lewis while he grieved the death of his wife.

> How do I know that all her anguish is past? I never believed before—I thought it immensely improbable—that the faithfulest soul could leap straight into perfection and peace the moment death has rattled in the throat. It would be wishful thinking with a vengeance to take up that belief now. H. was a splendid thing; a soul straight, bright, and tempered like a sword. But not a perfected saint. A sinful woman married to a sinful man; two of God's patients, not yet cured. I know there are not only tears to be dried but stains to be scoured. The sword will be made even brighter.[13]

The cure is not over; the process of sanctification is not finished until the sinner has become one who is able with undivided heart to rejoice in fellowship with God.

The article from the *New Catholic Encyclopedia* from which the definition of purgatory was taken states that the purpose of purgatory is to give the soul a threefold freedom: from (1) guilt of venial sin; (2) inclination toward sin; and (3) temporal punishment due to sin. It goes on to state that the second of these—which, interestingly, is not really explicitly mentioned in the definition given—has received more attention in recent years. There is, evidently, an increasing tendency to view purgatory as a process of growth in which the weaknesses due to lifelong habits of sin are overcome.[14] This more recent stress is closer to the concept of purgatory which Lewis espouses.

> Our souls *demand* Purgatory, don't they? Would it not break the heart if God said to us, "It is true, my son, that your breath smells and your rags drip with mud and slime, but we are charitable here and no one will upbraid you with these things, nor draw away from you. Enter into the joy"? Should we not reply, "With submission, sir, and if there is no objec-

[13]*Ibid.*, p. 35.
[14]"Purgatory," *New Catholic Encyclopedia*, Vol. 11, p. 1037.

tion, I'd *rather* be cleansed first." "It may hurt, you know"— "Even so, sir."[15]

Hence, for Lewis, purgatory is almost a requisite for the completion of the cure begun in this life, a process by which the imperfect person can be wholly sanctified and made ready for the enjoyment of the vision of God. It is painful, not because suffering is any part of its purpose, but simply because it will never be pleasant for one who seeks to live out of his own resources to become one who is willing to enter fully into fellowship with God.[16]

The most important elements in Lewis' view of purgatory can be summarized in the following three points: (1) the sufferings of purgatory are the continuation of the process of sanctification which has begun before death; (2) they are voluntarily accepted by the sufferer; and (3) the process is curative rather than retributive. Purgatory is, says Lewis, "a process by which the work of redemption continues, and first perhaps begins to be noticeable after death."[17] In an earlier chapter we noted that Lewis views human nature within the contours of the Christian story of creation, fall, incarnation, redemption, and *eschaton*. His belief in purgatory amounts, therefore, simply to a belief that redemption continues after death before the *eschaton*. It must be admitted that Lewis has taken care to guard against a conception which would be open to criticism on the grounds that it offered a second chance or was simply a doctrine of "works-righteousness." Or, to put the matter differently, if

[15]*Letters to Malcolm*, p. 109.

[16]Cf. Bicknell, p. 284: "When we consider the moral imperfection of so many who die in the faith of Christ and the impossibility of seeing God 'without sanctification' (Heb. 12:14), it is almost impossible not to think that the life beyond the grave includes discipline through which the character is purified. ... Such would, indeed, involve suffering, but it would be suffering voluntarily accepted." One could scarcely ask for a closer parallel to Lewis' view.

[17]*Letters of C. S. Lewis*, pp. 246f. The last part of this citation seems to imply a notion of "anonymous Christians." This would not be out of keeping with other elements in Lewis' thought, but this too should be distinguished from the notion of a second chance. The example of Emeth in *The Last Battle* gives some idea of what Lewis has in mind.

Lewis' understanding of sanctification and his characterization of the Christian life as process and journey are
adequate, there may be little reason to turn a critical eye at
his belief in purgatory. The attack, if one wishes to make it,
will have to come at the more fundamental theological
level, his understanding of sanctification. If Lewis is mistaken on the issue of sanctification, his theology will be inadequate with or without a belief in purgatory; and if he is
right on the more fundamental point, one need scarcely
worry about purgatory as Lewis himself understands it.

When Wormwood's patient has suddenly been killed (in
a state of grace) and is therefore irrevocably lost to
Wormwood, Screwtape writes: "Pains he may still have to
encounter, but they *embrace* those pains" (*SL*, p. 148). It is
important to emphasize that the sufferings of purgatory are
not retributive in character. God makes use of pains not to
punish but to cure—to purge from the soul any lingering
inclinations toward sin, any tendencies to seek only the
good of the self and turn from "the taste for the other."
Suffering is not the purpose of purgation.

> I can well believe that people neither much worse nor much
> better than I will suffer less than I or more. "No nonsense
> about merit." The treatment given will be the one required,
> whether it hurts little or much.[18]

This is an essential element in Lewis' understanding of
purgatory, and we will return to it later to ask whether it can
be reconciled with other aspects of his thought.

THE IMPORTANCE OF A STARTING POINT

Is there any important connection between Lewis' belief in
purgatory and his vision of human community? Perhaps for
one who takes the concept of community as a starting point,
such belief may be an almost inevitable—though certainly
not necessary—conclusion.

Human beings are created for fellowship with God.
That, as we have seen, is at the center of Lewis' thinking.

[18]*Letters to Malcolm*, p. 109.

> The happiness which God designs for his higher creatures is
> the happiness of being freely, voluntarily united to Him and to
> each other in an ecstasy of love and delight compared with
> which the most rapturous love between a man and a woman on
> this earth is mere milk and water. (*MC*, pp. 37f.)

Participation in such fellowship cannot be compelled. It
must be the free response of a willing and undivided heart,
the response of creature to Creator in love. Thus, this description of community is for Lewis only another way to talk
of a fellowship of love. From eternity the fellowship of
self-giving love goes on in the life of God. The Father
generates the being of the Son and the Son offers back in
filial obedience what paternal love has given. Man is
created to take his place within the concrete reciprocities of
love which form this divine fellowship. The divine pattern
of love is to take root in human life. The Creator confers will
upon the creature. That will is to be offered back "in delighted and delighting obedience" (*PP*, p. 91).

Paradisal man, says Lewis, did just this (*PP*, p. 91). He
enacted such self-giving love. But, of course, man fell into
sin as a result of pride, the opposite of love. The vision of
community defines for Lewis the end toward which creation
moves, and the whole Christian story defines the course of
that movement. To bring a fallen creature to the point
where he can willingly live in a community of love involves
pain and suffering. For,

> to render back the will which we have so long claimed for our
> own, is in itself, wherever and however it is done, a grievous
> pain. . . . But to surrender a self-will inflamed and swollen with
> years of usurpation is a kind of death. (*PP*, p. 91)

Here we can see how natural it is for Lewis to believe in
purgatory. To speak of a sinner drawn by love for God is to
speak of a person who must suffer. From this perspective
pain is not so much something God inflicts as it is the
natural consequence of learning self-giving love. Such a
love will, for a time, be painful for anyone who has tried to
stake out his claims to independence. In *Surprised by Joy*
Lewis puts the matter personally when he speaks of his
own struggles toward conversion: how his longing for God

fought against his "deep-seated hatred of authority" and his "monstrous individualism" (p. 172).

It would be a mistake to think of this turn from self and its accompanying purgation as a condition which God requires a person to meet before permitting him to enter the divine fellowship. God is not to be pictured, at least for Lewis, as if he were hard at work setting up requirements which must be met for life in the community of his love. Rather, God is at work building that community, and he may use pains to move some people toward the end he desires for them. The turn from self is not a condition for *getting* in—it is a definition of *being* in.

> Remember, this repentance, this willing submission to humiliation and a kind of death, is not something God demands of you before He will take you back and which He could let you off if He chose: it is simply a description of what going back to Him is like. (*MC*, p. 45)

Once again it is clear: Lewis is describing the path of the pilgrim. In the same context he makes clear that the entire journey is to be understood as the work of grace, something done in and by Christ. For in the description of "going back" he finds something paradoxical. Only a good man could really make this journey. Only a bad man needs to make it. "The worse you are the more you need it and the less you can do it. The only person who could do it perfectly would be a perfect person—and he would not need it" (*MC*, p. 45). Christ therefore walks the path, retracing—this time with perfect obedience—the steps of Adam, and all others do it only with his help. Yet, Lewis is insistent that others must also walk the path and, hence, they too will suffer. In one sense we might pause here to ask whether Lewis has not discerned a deeper problem than his system, including purgatory, can solve. If only a good man can make the journey, how is the process of sanctification ever to be completed in those who are fallen? And if Christ has actually done it, why does Lewis continue to enjoin all to do it? But to ask those questions is to move beyond the purview of Lewis' own thought and toward another system of theological construction. For Lewis the answer to the question lies, evidently, in the fact that Christ's goodness is like a "holy infection" which others gradually catch and make their own.

This much at least is clear: God does not require particular *works* simply for their own sakes. He wants *people* of a particular kind, and it is painful to become that kind of person. Lewis' theme is constant:

> The point is not that God will refuse you admission to His eternal world if you have not got certain qualities of character: the point is that if people have not got at least the beginnings of those qualities inside them, then no possible external conditions could make a "Heaven" for them. . . . (*MC*, p. 63)

In *The Great Divorce* many Ghosts make their way on the bus from the grey town to the realms of heaven, but only one chooses to stay. This is a Ghost who, when first seen, has on his shoulder a little red lizard which is constantly twitching its tail like a whip and whispering things in the Ghost's ear. (We learn in context that the lizard represents the man's lust.) The Ghost decides that he will take the bus back because he does not want to remain there with the lizard on his shoulder. He discusses this with an angel.

> "Yes. I'm off," said the Ghost. "Thanks for all your hospitality. But it's no good, you see. I told this little chap," (here he indicated the lizard), "that he'd have to be quiet if he came—which he insisted on doing. Of course his stuff won't do here: I realise that. But he won't stop. I shall just have to go home."
> "Would you like me to make him quiet?" said the flaming Spirit—an angel, as I now understood.
> "Of course I would," said the Ghost.
> "Then I will kill him," said the Angel, taking a step forward.
> "Oh—ah—look out! You're burning me. Keep away," said the Ghost, retreating.
> "Don't you *want* him killed?"
> "You didn't say anything about *killing* him at first. I hardly meant to bother you with anything so drastic as that."
> "It's the only way," said the Angel. . . . (pp. 98f.)

The Angel cannot kill the lizard without the Ghost's permission, but the Ghost fears the pain. The Angel assures him only that it will not kill him; he admits that the process will hurt. At last the Ghost agrees that even if he should be killed it would be better than continuing to live with the lizard. So once again the Angel requests permission.

> "Then I may?"
> "Damn and blast you! Go on can't you? Get it over. Do what you like," bellowed the Ghost: but ended, whimperingly, "God help me. God help me."
> Next moment the Ghost gave a scream of agony such as I had never heard on Earth. The Burning One closed his crimson grip on the reptile: twisted it, while it bit and writhed, and then flung it, broken backed, on the turf. (p. 101)

Suddenly the Ghost begins to grow more solid, like the solid persons of heaven. Even more surprising, the lizard grows into a white stallion. Horse and master are united and, after falling with thanks at the feet of the angel, the man mounts the horse and begins to ride into the mountains.[19]

We are entitled to ask whether there may not be a bit too much of More and Fisher and not quite enough of Dante in that passage (which is, however, written earlier than Lewis' reflections about More, Fisher, Dante, and purgatory discussed previously). Nevertheless, the passage does show clearly with what harmony the belief in purgatory flows from Lewis' basic social vision. He begins with an image of community. It is a vision of individuals freely united yet remaining themselves—"extreme differentiation of persons in harmonious union" (WG, p. 34). And, as we have seen, only love can overcome the recalcitrant claims of selves and make such a union possible. In this context purgatory functions quite naturally as a completion of the process by which love draws fallen men out of themselves and evokes in them a desire for a life which is truly shared with others. The purgatorial suffering is, as it were, a by-product of

[19]For a striking similarity in imagery, see the passage from *Miracles* in which Lewis says that our bodies are given to us as ponies are given to schoolboys: "Not that we may some day be free of horses altogether but that some day we may ride bare-back, confident and rejoicing, those greater mounts, those winged, shining and world-shaking horses which perhaps even now expect us with impatience, pawing and snorting in the King's stables" (p. 169).

learning to love—which learning can, for a fallen creature, be experienced only as a kind of self-sacrifice.

We can clarify the point from another angle by using a distinction made by Anders Nygren in *Agape and Eros*. He contrasts the view of Luther with that of medieval Catholicism (and its source, Augustine) in various ways. One of the most illuminating is his contrast in terms of the level on which fellowship with God takes place.

> Quite soon in the Early Church, and still more markedly in the Medieval Church, fellowship with God was conceived as a fellowship on the level of God's holiness; but in Luther a Copernican revolution takes place, and fellowship with God now becomes a fellowship on our human level. In an acutely pointed paradox, Luther's conception might be expressed by the formula, *"Fellowship with God on the basis of sin, not of holiness."*[20]

For Lewis fellowship with God is, to use Nygren's contrast, on the basis of holiness. His view corresponds quite closely to what Nygren describes as Augustine's "caritas synthesis." The union of the creature with God is fully and entirely the work of grace; yet, it is a union in which the deepest desires of the creature are fulfilled and in which he is cleansed and made fit to dwell in the divine presence. In interpreting Lewis in this way, however, we need to guard against an error from which Nygren is not immune. He writes at one point:

> The religion of the natural man consists in this, that he wishes to become good and holy, and by this means to enter into fellowship with God. . . . But the error, the false relation to God, which it is the task of theology to overcome, lies already in this will. For this intention, apparently so good and praiseworthy, has its deepest ground in man's unwillingness to live wholly upon God's "misericordia," in other words, upon God's Agape in Christ.[21]

We need to note carefully the antithesis to Luther's view as Nygren describes it here; for this antithesis does not correspond precisely to Lewis' view (and perhaps not to some

[20]Nygren, *Agape and Eros*, p. 684.
[21]*Ibid.*, p. 685.

of those discussed by Nygren). He describes a person who
wants to become good and holy and *by this means* attain
fellowship with God. We have already seen, however, that
Lewis does not think of the purifying process as a means to
entering the divine fellowship. It is not a condition for
getting in; it is a definition of being in. As long as we are
careful to avoid this danger, however, we can use Nygren's
contrast to illuminate Lewis' thought. Fellowship with
God, though the work of grace, is always on the level of
divine holiness. This belief is characteristic of everything
Lewis writes.

Thus, there are tendencies—which are not immediately
related to dogmatic controversies about purgatory—within
the structure of Lewis' thought which make belief in purgatory an appropriate addition to his viewpoint. Quite simply, it fits. The starting point of community makes certain
conclusions, though not necessary, very apt and almost inevitable. This is worth seeing since, of course, Lewis might
have begun elsewhere than with his vision of community.
He could, for example, have begun with the concept of
love. In his thought love (at least, love defined in terms of
self-giving) functions largely as the means by which community is created. But he might have made love itself central and divorced it from the question of fellowship with
God. He might have justified it simply on the grounds that it
imitates the shape of God's own action. From that starting
point it is possible that no need for purgatory would have
arisen. Or again, he might have begun with a concept of
man, not as created for community, but as justified sinner
who responds in obedient love to the grace of God. In this
kind of ethic too there might have been little internal pres-
sure leading on to an affirmation of purgatory.

These comments will be misunderstood if they are read
as an attempt to criticize Lewis' position (from, no doubt, a
more Protestant perspective). Rather, they are an attempt to
explicate his viewpoint; to sense the direction of its movement. Lewis certainly has a concept of love, and he also has
a concept of the justified sinner (though he does not use that
terminology and, as we have seen, rather carefully cir-

cumscribes its place within his theology), but he begins with neither of these. He begins with a vision of community, and he then uses the Christian story to place each individual in relation to that vision.

Anyone questioning whether his is a good starting point would certainly have to remember the way in which Lewis centers his vision in the Trinitarian life of God. At the least it seems true to say that his starting point is rich with implications for social thought. One of these, no doubt a minor one, is his belief in purgatory. His thought provides, in this way, a good case study of the way in which a basic vision may influence even what seem to be the remote corners of one's viewpoint. Lewis clearly and explicitly affirms his belief in purgatory only in *Letters to Malcolm*, one of his latest works (and a posthumous publication). Yet, no careful reader of Lewis should have needed such an affirmation or been surprised by it. The essentials were there all along.

SOME DIFFICULTIES

Having done what we can to understand the connections within Lewis' thought, we must still say that certain internal problems remain and demand consideration. Austin Farrer has criticized Lewis' treatment of pain and suffering, and his criticism provides a convenient place to begin our reflection.

> Man, to Lewis, is an immortal subject; pains are his moral remedies, salutary disciplines, willing sacrifices, playing their part in a drama of interchange between God and him. But this is not all the truth, nor perhaps half of it. Pain is the sting of death, the foretaste and ultimately the experience of sheer destruction. Pain cannot be related to the will of God as an evil wholly turned into a moral instrument. Pain is the bitter savour of that mortality out of which it is the unimaginable mercy of God to rescue us.[22]

It is only fair to note that Farrer's comment does not take

[22]"The Christian Apologist," in *Light on C. S. Lewis*, p. 40.

full account of what Lewis says about death. Lewis finds in pain the same ambivalence he sees in death.

> It is punishment because Death—that Death of which Martha says to Christ, "But . . . Sir . . . it'll *smell*"—is horror and ignominy. . . . It is mercy because by willing and humble surrender to it Man undoes his act of rebellion and makes even this depraved and monstrous mode of Death an instance of that higher and mystical Death which is eternally good and a necessary ingredient in the highest life.[23]

As with death, so with pain. Pains for Lewis are not merely moral remedies and salutary disciplines. They remain evils, which God nevertheless uses to kill the rebellious pride which lives in sinful human beings. It is true, though, that Lewis tends to look at sufferings in the light of the vision which sees our destiny as persons made for fellowship with God. That vision, he thinks, enables us to accept great evils as salutary disciplines. But Lewis never fully removes the ambivalence from pain and death. "What is unforgivable if judged as an hotel may be very tolerable as a reformatory."[24] That is his comment on life.

Lewis speaks of pain and suffering in two ways. On the one hand, as we have seen in this chapter, it is simply part of the process of putting to death the self with its inordinate loves. As a person is drawn closer to God by love for him, more and more of these inordinate desires will inevitably be choked off and eliminated. But Farrer is certainly correct in saying that it is at least as common for Lewis to think of pain as God's moral remedy by which he brings us into line. Pain, Lewis says, "insists upon being attended to. God whispers to us in our pleasures, speaks in our conscience, but shouts in our pains: it is His megaphone to rouse a deaf world" (*PP*, p. 93). This is the Lewis for whom the dentist becomes a favorite image of God: "What do people mean when they say 'I am not afraid of God because I know He is good?' Have they never been to a dentist?"[25] From this

[23]*Miracles*, p. 134.
[24]"Preface" to *Essays Presented to Charles Williams* (Grand Rapids: Eerdmans, 1966), pp. xii, xiii.
[25]*A Grief Observed*, p. 36.

perspective we are not so much drawn toward God by love for him as we are pushed in his direction by the pains we suffer. It is not hard to see that these two ways of talking about pain correspond fairly closely to Lewis' two ways of describing love. God's love as self-giving is the infinitely attractive love which awakens in us a responsive love and moves us, in turn, to give ourselves to him. This corresponds to Lewis' first way of discussing pain—the way in which our sufferings are seen simply as part of the process by which we turn from Adam's path and journey once again toward fellowship with God. But Lewis also thinks of God's love as a steady determination to devote himself to our good—a devotion which may have to cause great pain along the way. This corresponds to the God who uses sufferings to awaken in us a sense of our insufficiency and push us toward dependence on him. Lewis expands on Jesus' warning to the potential disciple to count the cost.

> Whatever suffering it may cost you in your earthly life, whatever inconceivable purification it may cost you after death, whatever it costs Me, I will never rest, nor let you rest, until you are literally perfect. . . . (MC, p. 158)

When Lewis thinks of God's love in this way, as a love which may cause great pain, he tends to speak of God in terms of certain images: inventor, painter, and so forth (MC, p. 159). The inventor knows what the machine is supposed to become. The painter knows how the picture is supposed to look when finished. And the Creator knows what the creature is meant to be. From these images it is natural to think of a love which causes pain; for as Dorothy Sayers has written,

> a work of creation is a work of love, and that love is the most ruthless of all the passions, sparing neither itself, nor its object, nor the obstacles that stand in its way.[26]

This is quite understandable. Nevertheless, as we noted in our earlier discussion of love, it stands in tension with Lewis' description of love as self-giving. In that description

---

[26]The Mind of the Maker, p. 104.

the image tends to be that of a union between two persons rather than the relation between maker and artifact. God is not so much the ruthless creator as he is the lover whom Screwtape describes: "He cannot ravish. He can only woo" (*SL*, p. 38).

Perhaps, however, we can do a little more here than simply let stand the tension between these two ways of talking about love (and pain). We can draw on some of the themes from chapter one in order to gain some clarity about the tension. Seen from the end of the pilgrim's story—that is, from the divine fellowship for which a person is made and into which he will enter—the purgatorial sufferings are only the inevitable by-product of the turn toward God. They are part of the definition of the way back. But we need to remember that for Lewis purgatory is, in one way, nothing special; it is a continuation of the process of sanctification which begins in this life. And, to draw on an earlier distinction, the Christian (even, presumably, in purgatory) cannot fully experience his pains only as a by-product of his growth in love for God. He is not yet at the end of his journey, and the story is not yet complete. The pilgrim will, as often as not, experience God as Divine Surgeon rather than Wooing Lover. What can be seen to be true from the end of the story cannot necessarily be fully experienced here and now. Hence, though the Christian may tell himself that God is only the Lover who woos him, his sufferings speak another language. They speak of God as the Divine Surgeon who must cut in order to heal, and they may even in a moment of testing tempt him to believe that the final truth about the world requires still another image: the Cosmic Sadist or Eternal Vivisector who wields the knife without pity.[27] Hence, the tension between the two ways of talking about love and pain, though it cannot be resolved in one's experience, can be understood as part of what it means to be a pilgrim for whom the end of the story has not yet come. There is no way for us, in our present pilgrim condition, to overcome the tension between the two images

[27]*A Grief Observed*, p. 32.

of God or to think of his love in only one way. Therefore, it
will also be true that our action as it is shaped by the pattern
of God's action will have to reflect both concepts of love.
Attempting to surmount the tension between them would
be, from this point of view, an attempt to leap out of the
limits the story places upon us. It would be an unwillingness to accept our status as creatures and pilgrims.

We can also recall what was said in the first chapter
about the role of faith as trust in Lewis' thought. It is not the
foundation of his theological construction. That place is
reserved for the Christian story which depicts life as growth
in sanctification toward community with God. But faith has
an important role to play in the face of temptation, in the
face of experiences which seem to make the whole story
questionable. Faith will be needed precisely in those moments when it is impossible to experience suffering as part
of the way back, when it seems simply to be torture. Faith's
task will be to find in the Eternal Vivisector not the Wooing
Lover—that would be asking too much—but at least the
Divine Surgeon. In *A Grief Observed*, when Lewis is
wrestling with his own bereavement, he considers the possibility that the truth about life might be expressed in three
short words: "God always vivisects." What, he asks, have
we to set against that? And responds, "We set Christ against
it."[28] This is part of that obstinacy in belief which Lewis
believes to be involved in "the logic of personal
relations"—a part of what it means, not simply to believe a
proposition, but to be loyal to a person.[29] Once again, the
tension is not fully resolved, but it is to some extent
understood.

All this has been, in a sense, a different approach (from
the vantage point of our discussion of purgatory) to a problem we met earlier. We turn now to a second, and new,
difficulty which Lewis' treatment of purgatory raises. This
is largely a question of internal consistency in his thought.
We can state it fairly simply: Lewis strongly advocates a
retributive theory of punishment; yet the sufferings of pur-

[28]*Ibid.*, p. 26.
[29]"On Obstinacy in Belief," in *The World's Last Night* . . . , p. 30.

gatory are expressly interpreted as therapeutic rather than retributive. The full force of the difficulty will become clear when we discuss Lewis' argument in defense of a retributive theory; for it involves not only argument for that theory but also argument against a purely therapeutic understanding of the infliction of suffering.

Lewis advocates a retributive theory of punishment not primarily in the interests of society but in the interests of the criminal.[30] No other theory, he believes, seriously considers the humanity of the criminal. His arguments against a deterrent theory do not particularly concern us here, and they are fairly standard: It makes a person nothing more than a means to an end and does not even require that the person punished be the person who has committed the crime. It is his arguments against the curative or therapeutic theory which concern us here, for from this viewpoint the person is not a criminal to be punished but rather a patient to be cured. Lewis notes that

> it appears at first sight that we have passed from the harsh and self-righteous notion of giving the wicked their deserts to the charitable and enlightened one of tending the psychologically sick.[31]

But there is, he thinks, a catch or two. The cure will still be compulsory just as the punishment was. And one does not ask whether a cure is just but whether it gets the job done. Hence, in place of a definite sentence reflecting a moral judgment about the nature of the crime, the therapeutic theory substitutes an indefinite sentence which can be terminated only when the experts in rehabilitation decide that the cure is complete.

This is the heart of Lewis' description of the theory he opposes. He believes such a theory to be dangerous in the hands, not just of bad men, but of good men as well. Indeed, the danger might be even greater if the therapists were particularly good men.

> Of all tyrannies a tyranny sincerely exercised for the good of its victims may be the most oppressive. It may be better to live

[30]*God in the Dock*, p. 287.
[31]*Ibid.*, p. 288.

under robber barons than under omnipotent moral busybodies.
The robber baron's cruelty may sometimes sleep, his cupidity
may be satiated; but those who torment us for our own good
will torment us without end for they do so with the approval of
their own conscience.[32]

It is in many ways a powerful argument. At the moment,
however, our task is not to assess the merits of his argument
but to remember that Lewis does not consider purgatory a
place of punishment for sin. Instead, it is the completion
of the process by which inordinate desires are killed and the
individual made holy. It is a time not of punishment but of
growth and development through suffering.

I can well believe that people neither much worse nor much
better than I will suffer less than I or more. "No nonsense
about merit." The treatment given will be the one required,
whether it hurts little or much.[33]

To juxtapose that description of purgatory with his criticism
of punishment as cure is at once to encounter difficulties.
For Lewis, the God of purgatory is a therapist. That this is
no imagined difficulty can be seen in the fact that Lewis
himself encountered it in facing his grief after the death of
his wife. In *A Grief Observed* he accepts the fact that sufferings even beyond death still await her and, whether correct
or not, writes:

But oh God, tenderly, tenderly. Already month by month
and week by week you broke her body on the wheel whilst she
still wore it. Is it not yet enough?
The terrible thing is that a perfectly good God is in this
matter hardly less formidable than a Cosmic Sadist. The more
we believe that God hurts only to heal, the less we can believe
that there is any use in begging for tenderness. A cruel man
might be bribed—might grow tired of his vile sport—might
have a temporary fit of mercy, as alcoholics have fits of sobriety.
But suppose that what you are up against is a surgeon whose
intentions are wholly good. The kinder and more conscientious he is, the more inexorably he will go on cutting. (pp. 35f.)

In one sense this passage is a marvelous achievement: to
have faced with such clarity the implications of one's theory

[32]*Ibid.*, p. 292.
[33]*Letters to Malcolm*, p. 109.

even in a time of intense grief. But admiration for that will
not solve the problem of consistency. If a therapeutic theory
of punishment does not take our humanity seriously, what
are we to say of Lewis' purgatory?

Still more, what can Lewis himself say? There are a
number of options one might take, and we can look at
several before considering what might be done to save the
theory as it stands. It would be possible to take refuge in the
idea that this is simply one of those puzzles which cannot
be solved until the story is complete. But in this case that is
not a very good solution. What we face here is not a temptation to be met by faith or a tension between what we can
experience and what we can, from the point of view of the
end of the story, believe to be the case. Rather, what we
encounter here is, quite simply, a question of consistency.
Lewis never counsels turning to faith in order to meet that
sort of difficulty. The theory which in human hands Lewis
rejects, and rejects forcefully, is precisely the one which he
places in God's hands.

Nevertheless, this very fact—that there is a difference
between placing the theory in human hands and placing
it in God's hands—might be offered in Lewis' defense.
There are at least these differences, that the believer might
trust God's goodness more than that of even the best man,
and that (presumably) the Divine Surgeon would know
without error exactly how much suffering was required to
complete the cure. Are these differences sufficient to justify
advocating a retributive theory of *human* punishment and,
at the same time, a therapeutic theory of purgatorial suffering under *divine* governance? Perhaps they are; yet, one is
uneasy trying to place this suggestion in Lewis' mouth. On
some views it would be quite possible to think of the purgatorial sufferings as retribution which is also therapeutic.
However, Lewis' purgatory seems so clearly to be a place
for growth in sanctification rather than retribution that one
is hesitant to make this move. And if we appeal only to the
difference between human and divine therapists, we are
left with Lewis ascribing to God activity which he finds
iniquitous when practiced by men. Lewis is willing, as any

believer no doubt must be, to grant that what seems evil to
us may not always be evil in God's wiser judgment. Yet, he
also insists that

> if God's moral judgement differs from ours so that our "black"
> may be His "white," we can mean nothing by calling Him
> good; for to say "God is good," while asserting that His good-
> ness is wholly other than ours, is really only to say "God is we
> know not what." (*PP*, p. 37)

We may want to ask whether one who says that and who
argues powerfully against a therapeutic theory of punishment can rest content simply because the therapist on a
given occasion happens to be divine.

Another possible way to resolve the difficulty would be
to give up one of the two conflicting views. To take this
course Lewis would either have to modify his view of purgatory or give up his advocacy of a retributive theory of
punishment. In some ways it might be easier to do the
former. He could not very well give up belief in purgatory
entirely, since that would be more than a minor change in
his theological system. But he might, without returning to
Fisher and More, move in the direction of a less Anglican
and more Catholic view which would give more scope to
the element of punishment in the purgatorial sufferings.

If none of these is particularly appealing as a way out of
the difficulty, we may try to save the theory by pointing to
two important differences between Lewis' conception of
purgatory and his characterization of a therapeutic theory of
punishment. The pains inflicted by the therapist when he
functions as society's replacement for the jailer are still
compulsory. One is given no choice in the matter. That is
not exactly true of purgatory; for there the pains are, according to Lewis, voluntarily embraced. It is always possible—
to put the matter starkly—to choose hell in preference to
purgatory. Lewis believes that some may do that. This points
to the other important difference. The therapist may torture
without end. He may wield the knife forever. That is not
true of the sufferings of purgatory. These are only one part
of a story destined to come to a conclusion. Furthermore,
there seems to be in Lewis' thought an idea that, however

horrible hell may be, it will not involve this sort of suffering.
The man who chooses hell in preference to purgatory might,
in other words, escape a good bit of suffering. However
difficult it may be to grasp completely, something like that
seems to be in Lewis' mind.

> God in His mercy made
> The fixèd pains of Hell.
> That misery might be stayed,
> God in His mercy made
> Eternal bounds and bade
> Its waves no further swell.
> God in His mercy made
> The fixèd pains of Hell.[34]

We need to take Lewis seriously when he writes that "tribu-
lations cannot cease until God either sees us remade *or sees
that our remaking is now hopeless*" (*PP*, p. 107; italics added). The sufferings of purgatory, though painful, are not a
horror precisely because they are accepted. And the horror
of hell does not primarily consist in suffering. Rather, it
consists in the fact that a creature made for fellowship with
God has preferred "the ruthless, sleepless, unsmiling concentration upon self which is the mark of Hell" (*SL*, p. ix).
Thus, purgatory with suffering is not a horror; hell even
without suffering is.

> Thomas Aquinas said of suffering, as Aristotle had said of
> shame, that it was a thing not good in itself, but a thing which
> might have a certain goodness in particular circumstances.
> That is to say, if evil is present, pain at recognition of the evil,
> being a kind of knowledge, is relatively good; for the alterna-
> tive is that the soul should be ignorant of the evil, or ignorant
> that the evil is contrary to its nature, "either of which," says the
> philosopher, "is *manifestly* bad." And I think, though we
> tremble, we agree. (*PP*, p. 122)

It may be that these differences between Lewis' characterization of the therapeutic theory of punishment and his
belief about purgatory are sufficient to answer the difficulty.
If not, we are left with the other alternatives outlined
above. What does seem clear, however, is that purgatory,

[34]*The Pilgrim's Regress*, p. 180.

though seldom explicitly affirmed, is an integral part of Lewis' vision. Men are made for community with God and, in order to bring them to their journey's end, God must for a time appear to be the Divine Surgeon. Only in that way can the sinner learn as Eustace did to want once more "to get back among humans and talk and laugh and share things."

CHAPTER IV

THE TETHER AND PANG OF THE PARTICULAR

If it is true to say that Lewis thinks of human beings as creatures made for fellowship with God, it is just as true to say that he lays great stress upon the earthly ties that bind one human being to another in a particular time and place. And it is characteristic of Lewis' vision to discern a constant tension between the loyalties we have to our earthly loves and the loyalty called for by God. Devotion to God may seem to undermine the claims of the earthly loves. Lewis shared a sense for this tension with Charles Williams, and he puts the point unforgettably in commenting on Williams' Arthurian poems. The saint, he says, inevitably causes great suffering.

> Christians naturally think more often of what the world has inflicted on the saints; but the saints also inflict much on the world. Mixed with the cry of martyrs, the cry of nature wounded by Grace also ascends—and presumably to heaven. That cry has indeed been legitimized for all believers by the words of the Virgin Mother herself—'Son, why hast thou thus dealt with us? Behold, thy father and I have sought thee sorrowing.'[1]

Nature wounded by grace. The ultimate goal of this chapter will be to explore that theme and thereby seek some reconciliation between earthly and divine love.

How can the earthly loves survive when they are drawn into a fellowship which includes God? This theme makes its appearance in *The Magician's Nephew* of the Chronicles of Narnia when Digory is faced with an excruciating choice.

[1]"Williams and the Arthuriad," *Arthurian Torso*, p. 175.

It is largely due to him that evil (in the person of the Witch, the former Queen of Charn) has entered Narnia. Aslan asks him, therefore, if he is ready to undo the wrong he has done to Narnia on the day of its birth. Digory is filled with concern for his mother who is dying and toys momentarily with the idea of striking a bargain with Aslan, until he realizes that the Lion cannot be bargained with. So he agrees to do whatever Aslan requires but, thinking of his mother, blurts out:

> "But please, please—won't you—can't you give me something that will cure Mother?" Up till then he had been looking at the Lion's great front feet and the huge claws on them; now, in his despair, he looked up at its face. What he saw surprised him as much as anything in his whole life. For the tawny face was bent down near his own and (wonder of wonders) great shining tears stood in the Lion's eyes. . . .
> "My son, my son," said Aslan. "I know. Grief is great. Only you and I in this land know that yet. Let us be good to one another." (p. 127)

Aslan knows the meaning of grief and knows that because of his own love he will one day have to suffer at the hands of the Witch (as he does in *The Lion, the Witch and the Wardrobe*). He knows too the price that a self-giving love will exact.

For the moment, however, he sends Digory on a quest. Digory must journey to a special garden where apple trees grow and bring back an apple from which a magic tree can be planted, a tree which will protect Narnia from the Witch for many years. The journey is the easy part of Digory's task. The difficult part is resisting the temptations of the Witch, whom he meets at the Garden. She tells him that the fruit is the apple of life, and then strikes him where the wound will be felt most deeply.

> "But what about this Mother of yours whom you pretend to love so?"
> "What's she got to do with it?" said Digory.
> "Do you not see, Fool, that one bite of that apple would heal her? You have it in your pocket. We are here by ourselves and the Lion is far away. Use your Magic and go back to your own world. A minute later you can be at your Mother's bedside, giving her the fruit. Five minutes later you will see the

colour coming back to her face. She will tell you the pain is
gone. Soon she will tell you she feels stronger. Then she will
fall asleep—think of that; hours of sweet natural sleep, without
pain, without drugs. Next day everyone will be saying how
wonderfully she has recovered. Soon she will be quite well
again. All will be well again. Your home will be happy again.
You will be like other boys."

"Oh!" gasped Digory as if he had been hurt, and put his
hand to his head. For he now knew that the most terrible
choice lay before him. (p. 145)

Digory finally resists the temptation, but the price is high.
He is sustained in his decision by one memory.

Digory never spoke on the way back, and the others were shy
of speaking to him. He was very sad and he wasn't even sure
all the time that he had done the right thing: but whenever he
remembered the shining tears in Aslan's eyes he became sure.
(p. 147)

Significantly, it is not any lack of love for his mother which
leads to Digory's decision; rather, it is the overpowering
character of his love for Aslan that guides and sustains him.

The wound inflicted by grace on nature is a terrible one.
But it is also true that the natural love cannot come to its
fruition apart from grace. Digory and Polly mention to Aslan
that the Witch had already eaten one of the apples. They
suppose, therefore, that Aslan must have made some mistake in thinking the Witch would be afraid of the tree and
would stay away when it was planted in Narnia.

"Child," he replied, "that is why all the rest are now a
horror to her. That is what happens to those who pluck and eat
fruits at the wrong time and in the wrong way. The fruit is
good, but they loathe it ever after." (p. 157)

Aslan tells Digory that the fruit would certainly have healed
his mother, but it would not, finally, have brought joy. "The
day would have come when both you and she would have
looked back and said it would have been better to die in
that illness" (p. 158). And Digory can say nothing in reply;
for

tears choked him and he gave up all hopes of saving his
Mother's life; but at the same time he knew that the lion knew
what would have happened, and that there might be things

more terrible even than losing someone you love by death. But now Aslan was speaking again:

"That is what *would* have happened, child, with a stolen apple. It is not what will happen now. What I give you now will bring joy. It will not, in your world, give endless life, but it will heal. Go. Pluck her an apple from the tree." (p. 158)[2]

Digory receives his mother back as a very chastened and changed young boy. He has stood on the brink of an inordinate love and turned back to Aslan. He is, therefore, ready to receive his mother back and to cherish her as one given him by Aslan.

Another example is found in *Prince Caspian*, when Lucy is faced with a decision as painful as that which confronted Digory. The children have been called back to Narnia by the magic horn and have been met by Trumpkin the Dwarf. They are trying now to make their way to Caspian's camp without falling into the hands of Miraz and his Telmarine soldiers. Early in the day they are faced with a decision about their direction of travel—either downstream (as seemed reasonable to them) or upstream. Only Lucy has seen Aslan beckoning them to go upstream. Finally, they vote and decide to go downstream. And so they do, with Lucy coming along last and crying bitterly.

It proves to be a bad decision. They encounter Miraz's soldiers and are forced to retrace their steps. When they lie down to sleep that night they are tired, hungry, and no nearer than they had been to Caspian's camp. Lucy wakes from a deep sleep with a feeling that someone has been calling her name. As she begins to walk through the trees she sees Aslan. Their reunion is a joyful one, but Aslan has come on serious business. He seems to indicate that the day's wasted effort has been Lucy's fault.

[2]Digory's tears are important. He is ready to admit "that there might be things more terrible even than losing someone you love by death." He is not ready to admit that the loss is anything other than a great evil. This is different from an attitude such as that expressed by Kierkegaard when he writes in *Works of Love*: "That a man dies is, eternally understood, no misfortune ..." (New York: Harper, 1962), p. 302. See also *Miracles*, pp. 129-35, where Lewis discusses the ambivalence of death, and also Ransom's concern with the teaching of the *felix peccatum Adae* in *Perelandra* (pp. 120-21).

"Oh Aslan," said Lucy. "You don't mean it was? How could I—I couldn't have left the others and come up to you alone, how could I? Don't look at me like that . . . oh well, I suppose I *could*. Yes, and it wouldn't have been alone, I know, not if I was with you. But what would have been the good?"

Aslan said nothing.

"You mean," said Lucy rather faintly, "that it would have turned out all right—somehow? But how? Please Aslan! Am I not to know?"

"To know what *would* have happened, child?" said Aslan. "No. Nobody is ever told that."

"Oh dear," said Lucy.

"But anyone can find out what *will* happen," said Aslan. "If you go back to the others now, and wake them up; and tell them you have seen me again; and that you must all get up at once and follow me—what will happen? There is only one way of finding out."

"Do you mean that is what you want me to do?" gasped Lucy.

"Yes, little one," said Aslan.

"Will the others see you too?" asked Lucy.

"Certainly not at first," said Aslan. "Later on, it depends."

"But they won't believe me!" said Lucy.

"It doesn't matter," said Aslan.

"Oh dear, oh dear," said Lucy. "And I was so pleased at finding you again. And I thought you'd let me stay. And I thought you'd come roaring in and frighten all the enemies away—like last time. And now everything is going to be horrid." (pp. 117–18)

Lucy does as Aslan wants. She wakes the others, sleepy and tired, and tells them that they must follow Aslan at once.

"And I do hope," said Lucy in a tremulous voice, "that you will all come with me. Because—because I'll have to go with him whether anyone else does or not." (p. 122)

There once again is the wound inflicted on the natural loves. Aslan's request is simple but stern. If the others will not listen, Lucy must leave them—despite the fact that they are her siblings as well as her friends and comrades—and follow him alone.

That is what life is like in Narnia and elsewhere. For the task Aslan lays upon Lucy is nothing special. Lewis believes it is the task laid upon every Christian, a task both harder and easier than one might think.

Christ says "Give me All. I don't want so much of your time and so much of your money and so much of your work: I want You. I have not come to torment your natural self, but to kill it. No half-measures are any good. I don't want to cut off a branch here and a branch there, I want to have the whole tree down. I don't want to drill the tooth, or crown it, or stop it, but to have it out. Hand over the whole natural self, all the desires which you think innocent as well as the ones you think wicked—the whole outfit." (*MC*, p. 153)

One could not ask for anything harder. Yet, Lewis believes, it is also easier than our evasions. For the reality principle is operative here too. To evade the claim is to evade the one possibility for life. To cling to the natural loves in defiance of the claim is to lose them. The wound inflicted on nature can be healed, but it must first be endured.

EROS AND MARRIAGE

How can the earthly loves survive when they are drawn into fellowship with God? Lewis approaches this issue from several directions in his discussion of the "natural loves"—family affection, friendship, and erotic love. He has most to say about eros, and, therefore, we will concentrate on it. Our ultimate aim, though, is to deal with one basic problem: the relation of the natural loves to divine love and the community it creates. However, we will begin by examining what Lewis has to say about eros, since it is a topic of great interest to him and since it has always played an important role in Christian reflection.

Love is that mode of relationship which unites persons. This is a continual theme in Lewis' work. "As there is no other way of enjoying beer but by drinking it, or of enjoying colour but by looking at it, so there is no other way of enjoying personality but by loving it."[3] Lewis wrote of his own short but fulfilling marriage that "the most precious gift that marriage gave me was this constant impact of something very close and intimate yet all the time unmistakably other, resistant—in a word, real."[4] This is true of all the

[3]"Open Letter to Dr. Tillyard," *Essays and Studies* . . . , p. 166.
[4]*A Grief Observed*, p. 18.

natural loves, each in its own way. Each unites even while it retains the separate identities of those bound together in love.

Much of what Lewis has to say about eros can be comprehended under two headings: Eros personalizes sexual appetite, and marriage makes eros faithful. In *Surprised by Joy* Lewis writes about the lust he felt as an adolescent for the dancing mistress at school. This was, he says, not a romantic passion; it was sheer appetite: "the prose and not the poetry of the Flesh. I did not feel at all like a knight devoting himself to a lady; I was much more like a Turk looking at a Circassian whom he could not afford to buy. I knew quite well what I wanted" (p. 69). This is similar to the distinction he makes in *The Four Loves* between Eros and Venus. The latter is the sexual appetite which man shares in common with the beasts. It can but need not be a part of "being in love." Eros is, in the first instance, "simply a delighted pre-occupation with the Beloved—a general, unspecified pre-occupation with her in her totality" (*FL*, p. 133). Venus can be or become a part of eros, but it can also remain quite separate. "Sexual desire, without Eros, wants *it, the thing in itself*; Eros wants the Beloved" (*FL*, p. 134).[5]

Sexual appetite needs to be domesticated and personalized. It must be personalized in order to raise it to the level of a fully human relationship. It must be domesticated because appetite has been distorted and perverted by sin. In one of his radio broadcasts Lewis deals with the distortion sin brings in a simple, direct way not likely to be forgotten by the "plain man" to whom the talks were addressed.

> You can get a large audience together for a strip-tease act—that is, to watch a girl undress on the stage. Now suppose you came to a country where you could fill a theatre by simply bringing a covered plate on to the stage and then slowly lifting the cover

[5]In his essay, "Edmund Spenser, 1552–99," Lewis mentions a distinction in medieval allegory between Cupid (love) and Venus (sexual appetite). Cf. *Studies in Medieval and Renaissance Literature*, p. 142. Undoubtedly, Lewis' distinction reflects this one. Thus, he can say in *The Four Loves*, "The carnal or animally sexual element within Eros, I intend (following an old usage) to call Venus" (p. 131). For another use of a similar distinction by Screwtape, cf. *SL*, p. 93.

so as to let everyone see, just before the lights went out, that it contained a mutton chop or a bit of bacon, would you not think that in that country something had gone wrong with the appetite for food? (*MC*, p. 75)

In such circumstances people's attempts to satisfy their sexual appetites could cause great harm—harm which would, Lewis thinks, fall disproportionately on women.

A society in which conjugal infidelity is tolerated must always be in the long run a society adverse to women. Women, whatever a few male songs and satires may say to the contrary, are more naturally monogamous than men; it is a biological necessity. Where promiscuity prevails, they will therefore always be more often the victims than the culprits. . . . And the quality by which they most easily hold a man, their beauty, decreases every year after they have come to maturity, but this does not happen to those qualities of personality . . . by which we hold women. Thus in the ruthless war of promiscuity women are at a double disadvantage. They play for higher stakes and are also more likely to lose.[6]

More often Lewis concerns himself not with the distortion brought by sin but simply with the claim that appetite alone is not yet fully human. It must be personalized. He suggests that our talk itself reveals this; as when, for example, one speaks of "wanting sex." It is an apt idiom. It is inaccurate,

[6]*God in the Dock*, pp. 321-22. For a similar statement of the view that women are more naturally monogamous than men, cf. Helmut Thielicke, *The Ethics of Sex* (New York: Harper & Row, 1964), pp. 87-98. Note also an interesting, if controversial, article by George Gilder, "In Defense of Monogamy," in *Commentary* (November, 1974), pp. 31-36. Gilder argues that the result of sexual liberation in the United States has been a vast intensification of sexual competition—and that this will especially benefit older men: "Unlike divorced men, most of whom find wives within a few years, women over forty only rarely remarry. The median age for these divorced women was approximately forty, while the median age for the women whom the men took as their second wives was about thirty. A woman divorced after forty—after her child-bearing years—is most likely to spend the rest of her life unmarried" (p. 34). "The chief beneficiaries of the 'sexual revolution,' therefore, are older, married men with exceptional appeals and powers. They can leave their older wives and marry younger ones" (p. 35). "Sexual appeal is distributed with an unevenness more inexorable and irreversible than almost any other human advantage. . . . Monogamy is designed to minimize the effect of such inequalities—to prevent the powerful of either sex from disrupting the familial order" (p. 36).

Lewis says, to think that a man prowling the streets wants a woman. "Strictly speaking, a woman is just what he does not want. He wants a pleasure for which a woman happens to be the necessary piece of apparatus" (*FL*, p. 135).

But "love is the great conqueror of lust" (*MC*, p. 84). Sexual appetite, though not wrong in itself, needs to be personalized if it is not to cause great harm and suffering. This is, in the first instance, the work of eros. "In some mysterious but quite indisputable fashion the lover desires the Beloved herself, not the pleasure she can give" (*FL*, p. 135). Venus, brought into contact with eros, is curbed and controlled. Screwtape sees this all too clearly.

> His [the Enemy's] real motive for fixing on sex as the method of reproduction among humans is only too apparent from the use He has made of it. Sex might have been, from our point of view, quite innocent. It might have been merely one more mode in which a stronger self preyed upon a weaker—as it is, indeed, among the spiders where the bride concludes her nuptials by eating her groom. But in the humans the Enemy has gratuitously associated affection between the parties with sexual desire. ... The whole thing, in fact, turns out to be simply one more device for dragging in Love. (*SL*, p. 82)

This is the task and glory of eros. It overpowers the lover and raises his sexual appetite so that it becomes a part of something quite different—a truly human relationship between two persons in which each finds in the other the "constant impact of something very close and intimate yet all the time unmistakably other, resistant—in a word, real."

One might imagine that the story could end here, but Lewis thinks more must be said. In order for the relationship between lover and beloved to be perfected more than the personalizing of appetite is required. Eros itself must be made faithful in marriage—a complete sharing and lifelong union between a man and a woman. This is not, for Lewis, something contrary or foreign to eros; it is simply what eros cannot on its own achieve. Lovers are forever promising fidelity. "As Chesterton pointed out, those who are in love have a natural inclination to bind themselves by promises. Love songs all over the world are full of vows of eternal constancy" (*MC*, p. 83). Lovers also seek the kind of total sharing in which each completes and fulfills the other. "It is not," Corbin Carnell writes, "simply on whim that illicit lovers like to make breakfast for each other or in some way play at keeping house."[7]

Eros promises permanence, and permanence is what a full union requires, but (as the love poetry of mankind forever laments) eros is itself fickle (*FL*, p. 158). Therefore, eros alone—the state of "being in love"—is not the ground of marriage. Instead, Lewis interprets the institution of marriage in terms of the "one flesh" union of which the Bible speaks (*MC*, p. 81). This is, in the first place, a physical union, but its character is not taken seriously if the act of intercourse is isolated from all the other kinds of union which enter into a complete sharing of life with life (*MC*, p. 81). Hence, prohibitions of divorce and adultery are not for Lewis simply isolated commands. They flow naturally out of the character of the sexual union of a man and a woman. He recognizes that Christians have disagreed on matters like divorce, but he points out that the area of agreement is still great.

> They all regard divorce as something like cutting up a living body, as a kind of surgical operation. Some of them think the operation so violent that it cannot be done at all; others admit it as a desperate remedy in extreme cases. They are all agreed that it is more like having both your legs cut off than it is like dissolving a business partnership or even deserting a regiment. What they all disagree with is the modern view that it is a simple readjustment of partners, to be made whenever people feel they are no longer in love with one another, or when either of them falls in love with someone else. (*MC*, p. 82)

In Lewis' eyes the state of "being in love" will not by itself ensure a perfected human relationship. Eros does delight in the beloved, to be sure, and that is something far better than simply desiring a passing pleasure. However, more will be needed to build a complete relationship. For

---

[7]"C. S. Lewis on Eros as a Means of Grace," *Imagination and the Spirit: Essays in Literature and the Christian Faith Presented to Clyde S. Kilby* (Grand Rapids: Eerdmans, 1971), p. 347.

his understanding of what is involved in a one flesh union Lewis turns to the three ends of marriage cited in the marriage service: fidelity, fertility, and goodwill (*SL*, p. 83). Screwtape counsels Wormwood: "Don't neglect to make your man think the marriage service very offensive" (*SL*, p. 84). It *will* be offensive for a person who wants only Venus or Eros. But a complete union—one which unites two people in a one flesh sharing of all that they are—will involve lifelong loyalty to a partnership for mutual help (goodwill), preservation of chastity (fidelity), and transmission of life (fertility). In this Lewis breaks no new ground. He simply makes clear the way in which Christian teaching on marriage relates to his own analysis of Venus and Eros. In marriage, appetite is personalized and eros is made faithful by being helped to perform what it has promised.

There is no discussing Lewis' view of marriage without treating one more theme: the question of hierarchy between husband and wife. There is some ambiguity in Lewis' view, but that ambiguity cannot conceal the fact that he often speaks of the husband as "head" of the wife and tends to think of this as a fixed hierarchy; that is, a hierarchy of function. In *Mere Christianity* Lewis argues briefly for the headship of the husband. His argument there is built partly on the need for permanence in marriage, which, as we have seen, he considers essential in a one flesh union. The argument is brief and rather wooden, but not without interest. If marriage is actually to be permanent, Lewis says, there will have to be some recognized authority in cases of dispute. For in a union of two people real disagreement must lead either to separation or to acceptance of someone's voice as decisive (*MC*, p. 87). Hence, there must be a head.

But why should it be the husband? At this point the argument builds on factors other than permanence. Lewis asks first whether women themselves want it otherwise, and he thinks they do not normally want to be considered "head" in their homes (*MC*, p. 88). That is, of course, a purely empirical question, and it is possible that the opinions of women might undergo changes in this regard;

might, in fact, have changed since Lewis wrote those lines. In fairness to him, however, we must note that it would not be enough to argue that women want not to be head but to be equal; for the premise from which he begins is that some head will be required if permanence is to be ensured. Lewis also suggests that the husband will normally be more just to outsiders. His picture is that of a woman who exerts herself primarily in defense of her children and husband against the rest of the world. The husband, Lewis believes, must have the last word in order to protect others from "the intense family patriotism of the wife" (MC, p. 88). We must understand, of course, that Lewis intends by this no criticism of such family patriotism. The woman quite legitimately permits the claims of husband and children a very special place. "She is the special trustee of their interests" (MC, p. 88).

Before proceeding to Lewis' later treatments of this question, we should note certain aspects of the argument in Mere Christianity. The argument, as summarized, falls into two parts. On the one hand, Lewis argues that hierarchy is necessary on the grounds that permanence requires it. Then he argues that, if there must be headship, it should be exercised by the husband. His reason at this point is that women themselves do not wish to be head and that the husband's headship is more likely to assure justice to outsiders. (And, whether correct or not, the materia of that argument ought to be noted by anyone disagreeing with Lewis.) When evaluating Lewis' argument here, we should keep separate the parts into which it falls. The argument that permanence may, at some point, require hierarchy carries force, and Lewis is certainly not the only one to enunciate it.[8] About the headship of the husband in particular,

---

[8]Cf., for example, Helmut Thielicke's rather agonized wrestling with the same issue in his Ethics of Sex, pp. 154–62. He considers the possibility of a conflict in opinion between husband and wife—after serious attempt on their part to seek a common will—in some area where a decision must be made. (He thinks especially of matters arising in the course of raising children.) At such a point, Thielicke thinks, simply to speak about equal rights for husband and wife must suggest that the conflict can be resolved in only one way if the two are to remain together at all; namely, by

however, it is more difficult to know what to say. Lewis' arguments are at least partially dependent upon social conditions, which are certainly subject to change. It is quite possible to argue that the "intense family patriotism" of the wife is a result of certain social conditions rather than a reason for advocating them and, in this sense, there is an element of circularity in Lewis' argument. However, a more fundamental difficulty is present. The hierarchy between husband and wife is a hierarchy of function, and, on Lewis' own account, it is essential that such hierarchies remain somewhat opaque and mysterious. No reason can be given to explain why a particular person ought to exercise headship, precisely because such a reason might suggest that greater merit is possessed by this person. Yet, considerations of merit are ruled out by definition. It is still possible to interpret Lewis' argument as a suggestion designed to help us partially understand the husband's headship without thinking that the argument provides any full explanation or defense of it. Nevertheless, I think Lewis elsewhere is clearer that reasons of this sort cannot be given to justify a hierarchy of function.

More commonly Lewis argues for hierarchy in marriage, not from the need for permanence, but from the nature of the one flesh union. He considers both the fact that it is a union in the *flesh*—as, for example, when he discusses what he calls the pagan sacrament in sex—and the fact that it is a *union*, with all that implies for him. We can begin with the latter, picking up the theme of community from the second chapter. Husband and wife are in no sense interchangeable members of a class. They are organically united in a relation of love in which the pleasures of obedience and admiration

---

the intervention of a third party such as the state. Thielicke believes that such intervention in the marital relationship is dangerous and, even more, destructive of the character of the relationship. He concludes, therefore, that in borderline cases "it would be inevitable that one of the parents should have the right to make the final decision. . . . At this point where a choice simply has to be made and where the exceptional character of a borderline situation prevails, a theological ethics cannot abstain from declaring, in line with the tradition of Christendom based upon the Holy Scriptures, that the father holds the final decision" (p. 158).

are all important. To concentrate attention on claims to
equality is almost certain to destroy the kind of pleasure
peculiar to such a union. That is Lewis' constant theme.

The suggestion that "obedience is an erotic necessity" is
a prominent motif in *That Hideous Strength*. Indeed, one
could make a case for saying that marriage itself is central in
this work, which begins by citing words of the Prayer Book
on the estate of matrimony and ends with the descent of
Venus on St. Anne's and a feast of love-making by animals
and humans (including, centrally, Jane and Mark, now re-
stored to one another). By following the relationship of Jane
and Mark Studdock through *That Hideous Strength* we can
learn a great deal about the meaning of community in
marriage.

> "Matrimony was ordained, thirdly," said Jane Studdock to
> herself, "for the mutual society, help, and comfort that the one
> ought to have of the other." She had not been to church since
> her schooldays until she went there six months ago to be
> married, and the words of the service had stuck in her mind.
> (p. 13)

That is the book's opening paragraph. Jane has found, however, that marriage has seemed more like solitary confine-
ment than like a society for mutual help and comfort. She
has seen little of Mark, since he is almost always preoccupied with his work.

But Jane is not left without resources. She is trying to
finish her doctoral thesis on Donne—hoping to stress his
"triumphant vindication of the body" (p. 14). "She had always intended to continue her own career as a scholar after
she was married; that was one of the reasons why they were
to have no children, at any rate for a long time yet" (p. 14).
That is the state of the Studdocks' marriage as the book
opens: Mark, caught up in his work coming home tired at
night and, at best, simply "wanting sex" before dozing off
immediately. Jane, intellectually concerned with a celebra-
tion of the body but herself concerned primarily to maintain
her independence even within marriage. When Jane is resisting the idea of being "drawn in" to the company at St.
Anne's, she cannot help connecting this to her marriage.

One had to live one's own life. To avoid entanglements and interferences had long been one of her first principles. Even when she had discovered that she was going to marry Mark if he asked her, the thought, "But I must still keep my own life," had arisen at once and had never for more than a few minutes at a stretch been absent from her mind. Some resentment against love itself, and therefore against Mark, for thus invading her life, remained. She was at least very vividly aware how much a woman gives up in getting married. Mark seemed to her insufficiently aware of this. Though she did not formulate it, this fear of being invaded and entangled was the deepest ground of her determination not to have a child—or not for a long time yet. One had one's own life to live. (pp. 72–73)

One night Mark comes home from the college to find Jane huddled and sobbing on the doormat. She has seen another of the visions which so frighten her and is now almost out of control.

He found himself, on the doormat, embracing a frightened, half-sobbing Jane—even a humble Jane—who was saying, "Oh Mark, I've been so frightened."

There was a quality in the very muscles of his wife's body which took him by surprise. A certain indefinable defensiveness had momentarily deserted her. He had known such occasions before, but they were rare. They were already becoming rarer. And they tended, in his experience, to be followed next day by inexplicable quarrels. (p. 44)

However, Mark is not equal to the occasion: "It was a pity, he thought, that this should have happened on a night when he was so late and so tired and, to tell the truth, not perfectly sober" (p. 46).

Clearly, if Mark and Jane are to be truly united in their marriage, a great deal is going to have to happen to each of them. And it does. For Jane, the new vision results from her association with the company at St. Anne's and its Director (Ransom). The first time Jane seriously considers joining the company it is the Director himself who places a stumbling block in her way. He is hesitant to accept Jane without her husband's permission.

"But is it really necessary?" she began. "I don't think I look on marriage quite as you do. It seems to me extraordinary that

everything should hang on what Mark says . . . about something he doesn't understand."

"Child," said the Director, "it is not a question of how you
or I look on marriage but how my Masters look on it."

"Someone said they were very old fashioned. But—"

"That was a joke. They are not old fashioned; but they are
very, very old."

"They would never think of finding out first whether Mark
and I believed in their ideas of marriage?"

"Well—no," said the Director with a curious smile. "No.
Quite definitely they wouldn't think of doing that." (pp. 146–
47)

Jane ventures the opinion that it might make a difference if
the marriage had not proved successful. She blames neither
Mark nor herself but simply suggests that the marriage has
been a mistake from the outset.

"What would you—what would the people you are talking
of—say about a case like that?"

"I will tell you if you really want to know," said the
Director.

"Please," said Jane reluctantly.

"They would say," he answered, "that you do not fail in
obedience through lack of love, but have lost love because you
never attempted obedience." (p. 147)

Jane cannot quite rid herself of the opinion that love means
equality and free companionship. The Director's response
is Lewis' view which we have already met. Equality is
needed to protect us from one another because we are
fallen, but it is not the deepest truth about our nature
(p. 148). Jane has never been taught the truth about eros.
"No one has ever told you that obedience—humility—is an
erotic necessity" (p. 148). Before Jane leaves the Director
gives her a strange demonstration of his meaning. He tips
the crumbs from his plate onto the floor, draws a little silver
whistle from his pocket, and blows a note on it. Three mice
scurry across the carpet and set busily to work until not a
crumb is left. Then, after another blow on the silver whistle,
they vanish behind the coal box.

The Director looked at her with laughter in his eyes. . . .
"There," he said, "a very simple adjustment. Humans want

crumbs removed; mice are anxious to remove them. It ought
never to have been a cause of war. But you see that obedience
and rule are more like a dance than a drill—specially between
man and woman where the roles are always changing." (p. 149)

Some of the ambiguity in Lewis' view is already evident. Is it obedience or humility which is an erotic necessity? They are conflated in the words of the Director to
Jane. In addition, we can see here some of the tension
between various images of community, a tension noted in
an earlier chapter. The relation between a man and a
woman is here said to be like that in a dance, "where the
roles are always changing." It would be incorrect to take
one passage such as this and claim that Lewis did not think
the hierarchy in marriage to be a fixed one. But it is not
wrong to turn to this passage as evidence for ambiguity
(and, perhaps, uncertainty) in his development of the meaning and implications of that hierarchy.

Jane learns that there is more than she had thought in
her fierce struggle to retain her independence even within
marriage. She is fighting not just against the nature of marriage. Jane had always considered the spiritual world as a
kind of "democratic vacuum" where differences were taken
away. But now she comes to see that there may be differences all the way up the scale of being. What she had
objected to in marriage and considered a mere relic of
patriarchal barbarism may actually be "the lowest, the first,
and the easiest form of some shocking contact with reality
which would have to be repeated—but in ever larger and
more disturbing modes—on the highest levels of all"
(p. 315).

> "Yes," said the Director. "There is no escape. If it were a
> virginal rejection of the male, He would allow it. Such souls
> can bypass the male and go on to meet something far more
> masculine, higher up, to which they must make a yet deeper
> surrender. But your trouble has been what the old poets called
> *Daungier*. We call it Pride. You are offended by the masculine
> itself: the loud, irruptive, possessive thing—the gold lion, the
> bearded bull—which breaks through hedges and scatters the
> little kingdom of your primness as the dwarfs scattered the
> carefully made bed. The male you could have escaped, for it

exists only on the biological level. But the masculine none of us can escape. What is above and beyond all things is so masculine that we are all feminine in relation to it." (pp. 315–16)

Here we meet Lewis' belief that gender is a more fundamental reality than sex.

Jane is not the only one who must be changed; the same is true of Mark. We do not find his transformation quite so obviously detailed (his story is more that of the "inner ring"), but we see clearly enough that he becomes a changed man in relation to Jane. Part of his new self-knowledge turns on precisely that relationship. When he comes to see himself as the odious little outsider forever trying to get inside, he realizes that he has badly misused Jane in the process. And, after Belbury has been destroyed and Mark is sent to meet Jane at St. Anne's, he feels a "sort of shyness." He had chosen the wrong circle to enter, but Jane has found her proper world (p. 360). He might now be admitted to her world, but that would be "only out of kindness, because Jane had been fool enough to marry him" (p. 360). And so, Mark determines that he must give Jane her freedom.

> When she first crossed the dry and dusty world which his mind inhabited she had been like a spring shower; in opening himself to it he had not been mistaken. He had gone wrong only in assuming that marriage, by itself, gave him either power or title to appropriate that freshness. As he now saw, one might as well have thought one could buy a sunset by buying the field from which one had seen it. (p. 360)

Mark has learned what union with Jane means. He has learned to see her as a person and not just as a physical convenience.[9] And in seeing her as a person he has run up against something "unmistakably other, resistant—in a word, real." Although he has floundered on the brink of hell, he has come in the end to recapture that "taste for the *other*" which is the very antithesis of hell (*PP*, p. 123). This did not come about by a simple change in his view of

[9]Eugene Warren, "Venus Redeemed," *Orcrist*, 6 (1971–72), p. 15.

marriage. Mark is now moved by a self-giving love which desires only good for Jane, and it is no accident that only when he is so moved does community become a possibility for them.

The truth is now clear: In very different ways both Mark and Jane have been troubled by the same problem—an inability to give of themselves.

> That same laboratory outlook upon love which had forestalled in Jane the humility of a wife, had equally forestalled in him, during what passed for courtship, the humility of a lover. (p. 380)

As Venus descends on St. Anne's and the animals begin to seek their mates, the Director sends Jane to Mark.

> "You are waited for."
> "Me, Sir?"
> "Yes. Your husband is waiting for you in the Lodge. It was your own marriage chamber that you prepared. Should you not go to him?"
> "Must I go *now*?"
> "If you leave the decision with me, it is now that I would send you."
> "Then I will go, Sir. But—but—am I a bear or a hedgehog?"
> "More. But not less. Go in obedience and you will find love. You will have no more dreams. Have children instead." (pp. 379–80)

Jane leaves in obedience to the Director's words, and on that note the book ends.

> And Jane went out of the big house with the Director's kiss upon her lips and his words in her ears, into the liquid light and supernatural warmth of the garden and across the wet lawn (birds were everywhere) and past the see-saw and the greenhouse and the piggeries, *going down all the time*, down to the lodge, *descending the ladder of humility*. . . . When she came to the lodge she was surprised to see it all dark and the door shut. . . . Then she noticed that the window, the bedroom window, was open. Clothes were piled on a chair inside the room so carelessly that they lay over the sill: the sleeve of a shirt—Mark's shirt—even hung over down the outside wall. And in all this damp too. How exactly like Mark! Obviously it was high time she went in. (p. 382, italics added)

If we can for the moment set to one side the ambiguities noted earlier, the general thrust seems clear. Lewis suggests that the union of husband and wife, because it is a union in love, must be hierarchical. This alone, however, shows at best that hierarchy is necessary. It does not indicate why headship should always belong to the husband, why in this case the rules should not be "constantly changing." Lewis' earlier argument for hierarchy on the basis of permanence had a certain force, but the move from that to permanent headship of the husband was less obvious. Here the argument for hierarchy proceeds from the nature of the marital union as a genuine community of love, but we must again cast around for reasons in support of the husband's headship.

It is fair to remember that we have, in a sense, been forewarned. We are to expect something opaque about hierarchies of function. Lewis' major reason for believing that headship belongs to the husband is that he understands this to be the teaching of the biblical revelation as it has been understood in the tradition of the church. This is the explanation most in keeping with his general belief regarding the opacity of hierarchies of function. But he is also impressed with the fact that the union of husband and wife is a union in the flesh. In the act of love a man and a woman participate in what Lewis calls the "Pagan sacrament" in sex. They become representatives of forces older than they.

> In us all the masculinity and femininity of the world, all that is assailant and responsive, are momentarily focused. The man does play the Sky-Father and the woman the Earth-Mother; he does play Form and she Matter. (*FL*, p. 145)

We are to think of the sun as masculine in relation to the earth. The earth is full of potential life which the sun draws out and actualizes. In reproduction the flow of potential life from the female is "arrested, determined, actualized by the male seed."[10] Lewis is quick to stress that the man and woman must remember that these are roles they are *playing*. The woman cannot literally surrender herself com-

[10]"Williams and the Arthuriad," *Arthurian Torso*, p. 147.

pletely to any man without becoming an idolatress; nor can any man claim as his own the kind of sovereignty he enacts in the act of intercourse; "But what cannot lawfully be yielded or claimed can be lawfully enacted" (FL, p. 146). Every man who lies with a woman participates, Lewis thinks, in this pagan sacrament. It is inherent in the nature of the fleshly act itself. If the act of love is to bring pleasure; if each is to delight in the other as male or female, the lovers will have to play their roles. It is in that sense, first of all, that the woman's obedience is an erotic necessity.

This is, Lewis thinks, a clue to the nature of reality. He does not isolate the sexual act from the whole of life. One has to learn, as Jane Studdock did, that hierarchy is the truth about life. The sexual hierarchy is only one instance of this truth, and there are other, deeper, levels at which surrender is required. Lewis suggests that gender is a more fundamental reality than sex. The point is made not only in *That Hideous Strength* but also in *Perelandra*. When Ransom has accomplished his task of purging Perelandra of the UnMan, the Oyarsa of Malacandra and Perelandra appear to him in human form. Both bodies are naked and lack any of the secondary sexual characteristics; they are not, in other words, male and female. Nevertheless, Ransom perceives that the one is masculine and the other feminine. They have gender but not sex.

> The Oyarsa of Mars shone with cold and morning colours, a little metallic—pure, hard, and bracing. The Oyarsa of Venus glowed with a warm splendour, full of the suggestion of a teeming vegetable life. (p. 199)

For Lewis the masculine is martial and austere, connected with associations of reaching out, penetrating, and possessing. The feminine is warm and sensuous, associated with welcoming and receptivity.[11] This is the vision revealed to Ransom.

[11]Rosemary Katherine Ziegler, *The Roles of Women in the Life and Fiction of C. S. Lewis* (University of Florida: Unpublished M.A. Thesis, 1973), p. 27. Ziegler says that Lewis' understanding of gender as a more fundamental reality than sex echoes Jung.

> What Ransom saw at that moment was the real meaning of
> gender. . . . Gender is a reality, and a more fundamental reality
> than sex. Sex is, in fact, merely the adaptation to organic life of
> a fundamental polarity which divides all created beings. . . .
> Masculine and Feminine meet us on planes of reality where
> male and female would be simply meaningless. (p. 200)

Lewis suggests that it might be better to speak of God as
transcorporeal rather than incorporeal. He is too definite for
the vagueness of our language, and even our sexuality
should be considered "the transposition into a minor key of
that creative joy which in Him is unceasing and irresisti-
ble."[12]

Lewis believes that the mystery of the headship of the
husband, though it might suggest itself to natural reason, is
clearly enunciated in the biblical revelation. Though he
seldom discusses this, its influence on him seems certain.
He consistently points out that this headship is to be
Christ-like. It consists, first of all, in loving and delighted
condescension; and it becomes, in a sinful world, a crown of
thorns (*FL*, p. 149).

In general, it would be a mistake to forget that serious-
ness with which Lewis considers sin. His attempt to do it
justice is, no doubt, part of the explanation for what ambiguity there is in his view. When we speak of his advocacy
of hierarchy, we must immediately say of him what he said
of Milton: "We shall be in constant danger of supposing that
the poet was inculcating a rule when in fact he was
enamoured of a perfection."[13] The ideal could be fully
enacted only in a perfect community where the whole of
life had been taken up into the divine life of love. We do
well here to remember what Charles Williams wrote of
Milton, in an essay praised by Lewis.

> He has been blamed, not without justice, for his continual
> insistence on the subordination of women to men. We have
> changed all that. Yet even in that the subordination is to be
> within Love—and love. Eve's submission is but part of her
> passion. When she is not in love she loses the submission;
> when she recovers passion she recovers obedience. Milton

[12]*Miracles*, p. 94.
[13]*A Preface to Paradise Lost*, p. 81.

may have erred, as we all err, by formulating for everyday life laws only tolerable in rare paradisal states. But it was the passion of Paradise. . . .[14]

Lewis sees that the ideal may not be completely realized in a fallen world. The implication remains that equality is only a compromise we make with ourselves, and that implication alone might make Lewis' view unacceptable to many. He recognizes the humor of this in his volume in the Oxford History of English Literature when he discusses John Knox's *First Blast of the Trumpet Against the Monstrous Regiment of Women*. The theologians, Lewis says, found Knox's work "embarrassing." It was embarrassing not because it was wrong—nearly everyone agreed that according to divine law women should not rule men—but because it came during the reign of Elizabeth. In order to answer Knox and defend Elizabeth's rule, any responsible theologian of the day would have had to appeal, not to a supposed natural equality of women with men, but to the fallen state of the world, which makes any return to a Golden Age impossible.

> No book more calculated to damage the Protestant cause could have been written. . . . No one wanted the thing to be said, yet no conscientious doctor could answer it in the resounding style which alone would satisfy Queen Elizabeth. No woman likes to have her social position defended as one of the inevitable results of the Fall.[15]

What should be evident by now is that Lewis does not begin with marriage in his treatment of hierarchy. His defense of subordination of wives to husbands is simply part and parcel of his general understanding of community. His belief that the marital relation, in particular, should be hierarchical is grounded in its need for permanence and, more centrally, in its character as a genuine community of love. The husband's headship is grounded in the biblical revelation as well as in the character of human sexuality. No merit or worthiness is involved. His headship is simply an

[14]Charles Williams, "The New Milton," *The Image of the City* . . . , p. 25.
[15]*English Literature in the Sixteenth Century, Excluding Drama*, pp. 199f.

instance of the hierarchical principle—making of marriage a school in which we learn the requirements of self-giving love and practice the steps required by the dance of obedience. Though this hierarchy will not (in accord with Jesus' words) last in heaven, Lewis believes that hierarchy will remain; and those who have not come to terms with it will not yet be ready for the kingdom.

This is, it is necessary to remember, part of Lewis' vision of ideal community—a vision of "the revelry of insatiable love." He makes no argument for a general subordination of women to men. Indeed, the most obvious way to deal with the ambiguities in his view is to make a distinction of levels. Between men and women the roles of super- and subordination are always changing. In the marital union, however, the husband exercises a permanent headship. And yet, since the more general considerations also pervade the husband-wife relationship, many hierarchies of merit will be present in any marital union. This accounts for some of the ambiguity and makes for a rather complex picture. But it remains true that the marriage relationship itself ought, in Lewis' judgment, to image a deeper truth. It ought to provide an opportunity to begin to enter into the pattern of the divine life. This will require, in different ways, humility and self-giving love on the part of both husband and wife—as Mark and Jane came to learn. It would not be wrong to characterize Lewis' view in words another author has used: "Marriage is a hierarchical game played by coequal persons."[16] Unless it is that, Lewis thinks, it will not image the hierarchy that is present "all the way up." Persons will never learn to find their identities in the functions for which they were created; and husband and wife may never learn to reverence the ultimate Father before whom all are feminine.[17] To repeat: Lewis does not

[16]Robert Farrar Capon, *Bed and Board: Plain Talk About Marriage* (New York: Simon and Schuster, 1965), p. 54.

[17]For similar reasons Lewis opposes the idea of female priests in the church. It too is a body—an organic union—in which the parts are not interchangeable. See his essay, "Priestesses in the Church?" in *God in the Dock*, pp. 234–39. He contends that a woman cannot properly represent God to the congregation in the worship of the church. For, "image and

think that such a community is always possible for sinful human beings, but it is the perfection of which he is enamored.

THE LIMITS OF THE NATURAL LOVES

Several important problems have been, as it were, submerged in our discussion of eros and marriage. To them we now turn. Our discussion of eros has tended to stress two people: lover and beloved. But the world is a much larger place than that, however true it may be that lovers as lovers seek to be alone. We must now consider lover and beloved in relation to others. Is it not likely that eros may lead lovers to act unjustly toward others; to neglect their parents, to cheat a business partner, to fail to help someone in great need? Lewis agrees that all this is very likely indeed (*FL*, p. 157). The same is true of the other natural loves. Family affection—tinged as it so often is with jealousy—may resent the new acquaintance who threatens the intimate structure of the family simply by his presence (*FL*, pp. 70f.). Despite his high praise of friendship Lewis writes that the ancients did not always see that it could be a school of vice as well as virtue (*FL*, p. 115). The sort of unplanned exclusivity which naturally characterizes any circle of friends may lead to something quite different. Those who were quite properly regarded as outsiders for a particular purpose may be simply discounted as generally inferior.

> To discount the voice of the peasant where it really ought to be discounted makes it easier to discount his voice when he cries for justice or mercy. The partial deafness which is noble and necessary encourages the wholesale deafness which is arrogant and inhuman. (*FL*, p. 117)

---

apprehension cleave closer together than common sense is here prepared to admit," and Christianity would be a very different religion if God were conceived as a female goddess (p. 237). Advocates of a female priesthood tend to think, Lewis believes, that sexuality is something superficial and irrelevant to the spiritual life. That, however, is unacceptable to Lewis, who thinks of it as a representation on the biological level of the still more fundamental reality of gender, which permeates all that is. Lewis' hope was that the church might remain an area of life in which courtesy, reverence, and obedience might still find a place.

The love of home or place—quite legitimate in itself as an
innocent element in patriotism—may be transmuted into
the belief that one's country has the duties of a superior
toward all others (*FL*, pp. 41ff.).

In short, the natural loves are not in themselves the
whole of our humanity. Taken by themselves they could
lead to great injustice. Having granted this, however, Lewis
will not turn in the other direction and question the legitimacy or importance of the bonds between people created
by these natural loves. They may conflict with more universal claims, but the very possibility of such conflict depends on the fact that the natural loves themselves have a
genuine claim on us. We do not, in other words, have to
begin with the command to love each neighbor or a duty to
esteem the dignity of every man and deduce from that our
obligations to spouse, parent, child, friend, or fellow-
townsman. Rather, the natural loves have their own independent legitimacy—grounded, for Lewis, in his belief that
God as Creator has implanted them in our nature (*FL*, pp.
177f.).

In fact, Lewis seems to recommend that we begin with
the natural loves toward those who stand in special relation
to us and "work outward."

> Those who do not love the fellow-villagers or fellow-
> townsmen whom they *have* seen are not likely to have got very
> far towards loving "Man" whom they have not. (*FL*, p. 41)

This corresponds to the advice Screwtape gives Wormwood
regarding the benevolence and malice which co-exist in his
patient. Wormwood is told to

> direct the malice to his immediate neighbours whom he meets
> every day and to thrust his benevolence out to the remote
> circumference, the people he does not know. The malice thus
> becomes wholly real and the benevolence largely imaginary.
> (*SL*, p. 31)

Lewis has no intent of equating the natural loves with the
love of charity, but he does insist that, as the work of the
Creator, they retain their identity and not simply be absorbed into charity. This is in keeping with his contention
that grace perfects but does not destroy nature. The natural

loves have no need to be justified as instances of a more universally other-regarding love, nor, Lewis thinks, can any justification of that sort be convincing. He gives an example in his discussion of patriotism (love of place and heritage).

> Good men needed to be convinced that their country's cause was just; but it was still their country's cause, not the cause of justice as such. The difference seems to me important. I may without self-righteousness or hypocrisy think it just to defend my house by force against a burglar; but if I start pretending that I blacked his eye purely on moral grounds—wholly indifferent to the fact that the house in question was mine—I become insufferable. (*FL*, pp. 47f.)

Having said this, however, we must recall that Lewis says only that we *begin* with the particular bonds created by the natural loves. He recognizes that this is something other than pure charity or *agape*: "it involves love of our neighbours in the local, not of our Neighbour, in the Dominical sense" (*FL*, p. 41). These loves may on any occasion find themselves to be competitors with more universal claims, and they will sometimes have to be renounced. Lewis insists only that there is no renunciation without prior commitment. Normally, he thinks of such renunciation taking place for the sake of one's commitment to God, but the same could be true of competition between the claims of the natural loves and the requirements of justice. Lewis pictures a Christian son rebuking his mother. This, he says, may be edifying, though tragic, but only so long as we are certain that

> in his rebuke, spiritual zeal is triumphing, not without agony, over strong natural affection. The moment there is reason to suspect that he *enjoys* rebuking her—that he believes himself to be rising above the natural level while he is still, in reality, grovelling below it in the unnatural—the spectacle becomes merely disgusting. The hard sayings of our Lord are wholesome only to those who find them hard. There is a terrible chapter in M. Mauriac's *Vie de Jésus*. When the Lord spoke of brother and child against parent, the other disciples were horrified. Not so Judas. He took to it as a duck takes to water. . . .[18]

As we will see in the next chapter, Lewis seldom concerns

[18]*God in the Dock*, pp. 191–92.

himself with specifying rules of priority by which to resolve such conflicts of obligations. His central concern is to uphold the legitimacy and worth of the natural loves.

However, he does more. The natural loves are schools of virtue. By taking the natural loves seriously we may, Lewis thinks, come to learn something of what it means to love the neighbor (in the Dominical sense), for each of the natural loves images the divine love in some way. This is especially true of eros. The glory (as well as the danger) of eros lies in the fact that it claims to be honored and obeyed unconditionally. It demands of the lover a kind of total commitment which can serve as "a paradigm or example, built into our natures, of the love we ought to exercise towards God and Man" (*FL*, p. 153). Eros gives content to our understanding of charity, content which we might never find if we did not begin with the natural love. "It is as if Christ said to us through Eros, 'Thus—just like this—with this prodigality —not counting the cost—you are to love me and the least of my brethren'" (*FL*, p. 154). Hence, Lewis has no wish to denigrate the requirement that we love any neighbor whom we meet. He does not start with that general requirement for several reasons. On the one hand, he wants to do justice to our character as creatures in whom the natural loves have been instilled. But also, he believes that by beginning with the concrete character of love as we know it we can achieve some understanding of what love will have to mean in more universal relationships.

Opinions about the wisdom of this approach will vary, but it would be difficult to deny that Lewis is successful in using the natural loves to provide content for the word 'charity.' Consider, for example, what he says of eros.

> In one high bound it has overleaped the massive wall of our selfhood; it has made appetite itself altruistic, tossed personal happiness aside as a triviality and planted the interests of another in the centre of our being. Spontaneously and without effort we have fulfilled the law (towards one person) by loving our neighbour as ourselves. It is an image, a foretaste, of what we must become to all if Love Himself rules in us without a rival. It is even (well used) a preparation for that. (*FL*, p. 158)

The self-giving commitment of the lover is paradigmatic of the kind of self-giving love which ought to pervade and inform every relationship of life. Still more, it is a preparation for those other relationships. To live out what eros promises will require such an attack on our self-centeredness that we will be training ourselves to exercise love toward others for whom we feel no eros. The natural love becomes, in that sense, a school of virtue.

The other natural loves also image divine love. Friendship, for example, is almost wholly without jealousy: friends are eager to be joined by any newcomer who shares their interests (FL, pp. 92f.). Then, too, this love is almost wholly free from the need to be needed—another way in which it, more than affection or eros, images divine love. Even affection, in some ways the least exalted of the natural loves, images divine love in its own distinctive manner. For, "almost anyone can become an object of Affection; the ugly, the stupid, even the exasperating. There need be no apparent fitness between those whom it unites" (FL, p. 54). Affection, in other words, is an appreciative rather than a discriminating love. In all these ways, then, the natural loves deepen our understanding of Christ's command to love the neighbor.

This is as much as Lewis has to say about one important problem: the relation between the special bonds of the natural loves and the more universal claims which tie us to all mankind. Other difficulties still remain. In chapter two we saw that the natural loves were insufficient, needing to be perfected by divine love itself. Our discussion of eros and marriage has, in effect, provided us with a case study of how this perfecting works. To bring eros into marriage and thereby make it faithful means, for Lewis, to bring it into the sphere where divine love operates.

When Lewis writes of the insufficiency of the natural loves, he suggests that they need to be transformed so that, while retaining their identity as natural loves, they become "modes of Charity" (FL, p. 184). The natural loves are "taken up" into divine love, into the life of charity itself. Nothing is too trivial to be thus transformed: "A game, a

joke, a drink together, idle chat, a walk, the act of Venus—
all these can be modes in which we 'seek not our own'"
(FL, p. 184). When taken up in this way, the natural loves
are not destroyed, for in a paradoxical way, "natural loves
that are allowed to become gods do not remain loves" (FL,
p. 20). In the case of eros, Lewis says that *eros, left to itself,
cannot be itself*. It is a natural, an earthly, love. To honor it
as more than that or to isolate it from its Creator is to destroy
it.

Because we are fallen creatures some combination of sin
and selfishness must always infect our natural loves. We can
think, for example, of what may happen in the case of eros.
The great danger is that the lover may come to live for or
idolize the passion itself (FL, p. 155). The result can be
predicted and is well known: eros becomes notoriously
fickle. When the passion of eros is idolized and made the
object of one's desire, the self has turned back in upon
itself. Eros leaps that massive wall of our selfhood, but we
invariably turn back. Eros places the beloved in the center
of the lover's concern, but such forgetfulness of self cannot
be maintained. Something more than eros will be needed if
the bond between lover and beloved is to be sustained. And
if that something more is absent—if eros is left to itself—
the lover will soon have to be off again in search of new
experiences of passion, forgetful of his promise of fidelity.

Left to itself eros cannot ensure fidelity. Yet, fidelity *is*
what eros promises. Hence, Lewis' conclusion: Left to itself, eros cannot be itself.

> He cannot of himself be what, nevertheless, he must be if he is
> to remain Eros. He needs help; therefore needs to be ruled.
> The god dies or becomes a demon unless he obeys God. (FL,
> p. 160)

The same is true of affection and friendship. They too
cannot be themselves if left to themselves. A favorite example of Lewis' is that of maternal affection, which is in itself a
good and wholesome love. In this affection there is a
natural gift-love; it is not by any means all need. Yet, just
here the paradox arises. Maternal affection also seems to
hold out a promise of more than it can by itself deliver.

The proper aim of giving is to put the recipient in a state where he no longer needs our gift. . . . Thus a heavy task is laid upon this Gift-love. It must work toward its own abdication. We must aim at making ourselves superfluous. The hour when we can say "They need me no longer" should be our reward. But the instinct, simply in its own nature, has no power to fulfill this law. The instinct desires the good of its object, but not simply; only the good it can itself give. (FL, p. 76)

If this affection is not transformed by divine love, it is subject to terrible perversion. It too can turn back in upon the self. Lewis is a master at picturing a person who, under the guise of living for others, manages to make their lives miserable. In a playful but serious epitaph he makes the case clear.

> Erected by her sorrowing brothers
> In memory of Martha Clay.
> Here lies one who lived for others;
> Now she has peace. And so have they.[19]

Another instance of natural affection becoming demonic is given us in *Till We Have Faces*. Lewis writes that Orual is an example of

human affection in its natural condition, true, tender, suffering, but in the long run tyrannically possessive and ready to turn to hatred when the beloved ceases to be its possession.[20]

In Lewis' myth Orual comes to recognize the truth about her love: that her love for Psyche, for the Fox, for Bardia, and no doubt for many others was a "gnawing greed." She comes to see that "Glome was a web—I the swollen spider, squat at its center, gorged with men's stolen lives" (p. 276). Yet, of her love Lewis quite genuinely means what he says: it is "true, tender, suffering."

We badly misunderstand him if we think of Lewis as seeking to denigrate any natural affection. On the contrary, he believes that the inadequacy of the natural loves reveals itself when they are at their highest and best. For in that condition they really are most godlike and, therefore, most

[19]*Poems*, p. 134.
[20]In a letter to Clyde Kilby, dated February 10, 1957, in *Letters of C. S. Lewis*, p. 274.

dangerous. The natural love at its best can image the divine love and, even, serve as a means of approach to the divine love precisely because it is then, to some extent, a self-giving love. Yet, there is the danger that a natural love at its best *can* image the divine love. It is godlike and, therefore, can easily become a demon. Here again Lewis strikes a chord in harmony with Charles Williams, who wrote in a different context:

> Deep, deeper than we believe, lie the roots of sin; it is in the good that they exist; it is in the good that they thrive and send up sap and produce the black fruit of hell.[21]

The roots of sin can thrive just as much in the love of friendship as in eros or affection. We saw before that, in its freedom from jealousy and its willingness to welcome a stranger who shares the interests of the circle, friendship images divine love. Yet, every circle of friends excludes some people, not intentionally but accidentally. Founded as it is on shared interests, the love of friendship will inevitably exclude those who are not absorbed by the same vision. This is the other side of its lack of jealousy. Lewis finds no fault in this, viewing it simply as an aspect of friendship as a natural love. It is friendship's glory—and its danger; for this love too can turn back in upon itself. The line between excluding some and developing a spirit of exclusiveness is simply too fine for sinful creatures to manage (*FL*, p. 122). True friendship must be full of mutual admiration; yet it must not become a "mutual admiration society" (*FL*, p. 124). It is meant by the Creator as an opportunity for us to glory in the beauties of another; it can become an occasion for us to pride ourselves upon the circle of friends we have "chosen" (*FL*, p. 125). Here again the paradox: Left to itself, friendship cannot be itself.

THE TRANSFORMATION OF THE NATURAL LOVES

Eros promises fidelity but cannot perform what it promises. Affection wants to liberate the loved one but may end in an

---

[21]Charles Williams, *The Descent of the Dove*, p. 108.

oppressive tyranny. Friendship holds out the promise of a circle wholly free from exclusiveness and may become nothing more than an "inner ring." The natural loves at their very best are insufficient and in need of transformation. If we ask why this should be true, the answer seems to lie both in the character of the loves themselves and in the fallen nature of the lovers. In themselves the natural loves are perfectly good, but they were never meant to be by themselves. To isolate and separate them from the context of divine love is to remove them from the environment in which they flourish. Even in such isolation a trace of their origin will remain and manifest itself in the ways they image the divine love, but such isolation will also subject them to the possibility of terrible perversion and distortion. The problem lies, therefore, not so much in the loves as in the way human beings isolate and idolize them. It is our refusal to recognize that these are *creaturely* loves which causes them to turn back in upon themselves. And when we allow that to happen, we pay the price: we lose the natural loves themselves. That is the burden of Lewis' message. If we want the natural loves by themselves we will find that we cannot have them. They cannot flourish in that environment. Left to themselves they cannot be themselves.

Thus, the experienced transformation of the natural loves is a transformation of what fallen people have made of them. We could with equal justification say that it is a restoration of them to the condition in which they were meant to be and, as such, it is not only a restoration but a liberation. To bring the natural loves back into living contact with the divine love of charity is to let them be in reality what they can now only image in passing moments. In a way it has been treacherous to speak throughout this chapter of these loves as "natural" loves, for in the condition we find them they can image but not fully realize their natural or uncorrupted state. It is their fallen condition that is the "nature" which is wounded by grace. Only the work of divine love permeating and transforming them could make them fully natural; for it is a distortion of their nature to separate them from that divine love.

What Lewis has given us here is the old, old theme of inordinate love.[22] The natural loves are good in themselves, but isolated from divine love they cannot flourish. Hence, the corollary to saying that the natural loves cannot be themselves when left to themselves is—the Augustinian theme—that while we were meant to enjoy these loves we were not meant to rest in them. The natural loves all image divine love, the love which we are to have toward God and all men. And each in its own way urges us to press on. Thus, to stop with the natural loves is to have missed the message.

This theme was of great interest to both Lewis and Charles Williams, and they have been called "romantic theologians." Lewis defines a romantic theologian as "one who considers the theological implications of those experiences which are called romantic."[23] Williams concentrated his attention in particular upon what he called the "Beatrician moment." In such a moment one almost adores the beloved and achieves a state of humility and pure love. The goal toward which one is to press on is this: to make that state habitual toward all.[24] There are rather obvious dangers in talk about adoring the beloved, but there are also built-in safeguards in the understanding Lewis and Williams share. One is always to press on toward love for God. Lewis describes Williams' concept in this way:

> The Beatrician experience may be defined as the recovery (in respect to one human being) of that vision of reality which would have been common to all men in respect to all things if Man had never fallen. The lover sees the Lady as the Adam saw all things. . . . The great danger is lest he should mistake the vision which is really a starting point for a goal. . . .[25]

It is for this reason that Williams (and Lewis) combine the "Way of Affirmation" and the "Way of Negation." Every natural love can be affirmed as an image of divine love and, rightly followed, a way to approach it. Yet, at the same time,

[22]He can, in fact, use the terminology. Cf., for example, *FL*, p. 167 and *Letters to Malcolm*, p. 22.
[23]In his "Preface" to *Essays Presented to Charles Williams*, p. vi.
[24]Charles Williams, *He Came Down From Heaven* and *The Forgiveness of Sins* (London: Faber & Faber, 1950), p. 73.
[25]"Williams and the Arthuriad," *Arthurian Torso*, pp. 116f.

any natural love understood as an independent rival to divine love must be rejected; for it then leads only to damnation.

In one sense Lewis is painting a picture of harmony between grace and nature. The picture of the natural loves achieving their fruition when they are transformed and permeated by charity is a picture of a community in which love for our fellow human beings and love for God exist in harmony and right order. This picture is, so to speak, what one sees from "the inside"—in those moments when we gain a vision of true community. But for the most part we live on "the outside," and what we can see we cannot often experience. All that is "far away in 'the land of the Trinity',," and we remain pilgrims (*FL*, p. 191).

Existentially, therefore, we experience not a harmony but a rivalry between our love for God and our natural loves. We *are* idolaters. We *do* try to isolate the natural loves from the transforming power of grace. We *do* set them up as rival objects of our love. We cannot very often manage the intricate simultaneities of loving man *in* God. Therefore, Lewis believes that, for the most part, we will be able to believe but not experience the harmony of natural and divine loves.

The deficiency of the natural loves has been described in two ways. On the one hand, they tend to turn back in upon the self. On the other hand, the natural loves tend to rest in the creature and thereby treat the creature as an idol. From this perspective God becomes the great rival to the natural loves. The descriptions merge in this way: It is the self's refusal to permit the natural loves to be transformed by self-giving love (because of the self's tendency to cling to the creature) which turns God into a rival object of love. Therefore, self-sacrifice and renunciation may be required to help the self give up its inordinate claims. Once again we come upon a theme we met earlier: A self-giving love incarnate in a fallen world may become a self-sacrificing love. There may be no other way to break the power of inordinate love. Hence, the picture of a harmonious transformation of the natural loves may have to give way to a picture of tension between rival claimants for our love—the creature and the Creator.

In the preceding paragraphs it has been suggested that nature is wounded by grace and that God is experienced as rival to the natural loves primarily because of human sinfulness. However, there are certain ambiguities in Lewis' thought on this point. We might put the issue this way: What is the source of the insufficiency of the earthly loves? Is it simply that they are earthly, or is it that we are inordinate lovers? Is it simply that what is creaturely is (ontologically) insufficient? Or that sinners have perverted the creaturely?

Lewis tends to locate the problem in sin rather than in our finite condition; nevertheless, there are aspects of his thought which might lead in the other direction. In *Surprised by Joy* Lewis tells how Owen Barfield was instrumental in arguing him from philosophical realism into philosophical idealism, and how from there he moved to theism (and, thence, to Christianity). Barfield explains Lewis' movement from idealism to theism in that Lewis came to believe that we can live not a sameness with God but an otherness which we experience when we call him "Thou."[26] One might intellectually see or affirm identity with God, but in the will there could be no such experience. This was the beginning of Lewis' turn from idealism, and it is the germ of his belief that much of the time we will experience God not simply as the perfecter of our natural loves but as their great rival.

Facts such as these might lead us to suspect that for Lewis the experience of God as rival is grounded in our creaturely condition. His specifically Christian writings do place great emphasis upon the fact of sin; yet even in these one can find passages which suggest that what the creature truly needs is not merely a restoration of his unfallen status

[26]This information is taken from an address by Barfield titled simply, "C. S. Lewis." The address was delivered by Barfield at Wheaton College in Wheaton, Illinois, on October 16, 1964. I have had access to the copy which resides among the manuscripts in the Wade Collection at Wheaton College, and I refer to it here by permission of Dr. Clyde S. Kilby, Curator of the Wade Collection.

but an elevation to a more-than-human condition. Thus, in one of his last works Lewis could write:

> The Eternal may meet us in what is, by our present measurements, a day, or (more likely) a minute or a second: but we have touched what is not in any way commensurable with lengths of time, whether long or short. Hence our hope finally to emerge, if not altogether from time (that might not suit our humanity) at any rate from the tyranny, the unilinear poverty, of time, to ride it not to be ridden by it, and so to cure that always aching wound ("the wound man was born for") which mere succession and mutability inflict on us. . . .[27]

Ambiguities enter into this very passage. Human nature is elevated; yet is to remain human. The central thrust, however, is surely that which finds our nature wounded by the constraints of mere finitude.

Lewis' clearest treatment of the question comes in *Mere Christianity*. There Lewis distinguishes the life which we have as creatures from the kind of life God has. The former he calls *Bios*; the latter *Zoe* (pp. 122f.). According to Lewis, creatures exist to be taken into the divine life (p. 126). He can even use the well-known formulation of the Eastern Fathers: "The Son of God became a man to enable men to become sons of God" (p. 139). In this sense the final state of the redeemed might be said to be more than a restoration of true creatureliness. Had the human race not sinned, this elevation would still have taken place.

> Perhaps every man would have been "in Christ," would have shared the life of the Son of God, from the moment he was born. Perhaps the *Bios* or natural life would have been drawn up into the *Zoe*, the uncreated life, at once and as a matter of course. But that is guesswork. (p. 139)

But at any rate—and this is what justifies interpreting the experience of God as rival as a consequence of sin—apart from sin the two kinds of life would have been different but harmonious. It is because of the Fall into sin that they are not only different but also opposed (p. 139). "The process of being turned from a creature into a son would not have

---

[27]*Reflections on the Psalms* (New York: Harcourt, Brace & World, 1958), pp. 137f.

been difficult or painful if the human race had not turned away from God centuries ago" (p. 143).

Thus, the need of the natural loves for transformation by divine love lies both in the character of the loves themselves and in their distortion by human sin. However, the experience of this transformation as a painful wound and the sense of God as rival are the direct result of sin. Talk of elevation or even transformation cannot now stand alone. It is necessary to talk also of killing the natural self and replacing it with a new one (*MC*, p. 149), for that is the only way the transformation can be experienced.

Lewis provides an example of such an experience in *The Great Divorce*. In one of the scenes the Ghost of a woman named Pam has made the trip in the bus from the grey town. She meets now a "solid person"—a spirit who in his earthly life has been her brother Reginald (pp. 90ff.). But it was not Reginald whom she hoped to see. She has come in search of her son, Michael. Reginald tells her that she will not be able to see Michael until she becomes "more solid."

> You will become solid enough for Michael to perceive you when you learn to want someone else besides Michael. I don't say 'more than Michael,' not as a beginning. That will come later. It's only the little germ of a desire for God that we need to start the process. (p. 91)

Pam berates him on the ground that he is not a mother and has no appreciation for the bonds of maternal affection. But, says Reginald, "there is no such thing as being only a mother. You exist as Michael's mother only because you first exist as God's creature. That relation is older and closer" (p. 92). She has tried to isolate the love of affection, to make it a god, by depriving it of its place within divine love. Therefore, she has ended with a demon. For some, maternal affection might have been a way to approach God, but not for her. For her there is no way to self-giving love except through self-sacrifice.

> You cannot love a fellow-creature fully till you love God. Sometimes this conversion can be done while the instinctive

love is still gratified. But there was, it seems, no chance of that in your case. (p. 92)

But she will not listen. Her experience of the loves as rivals is too intense, and so she lashes out at Reginald.

> How dare you laugh about it? Give me my boy. Do you hear? I don't care about all your rules and regulations. I don't believe in a God who keeps mother and son apart. I believe in a God of Love. No one has a right to come between me and my son. Not even God. (p. 95)

There we have the cry of nature wounded by grace, and again we recognize how deeply Lewis feels the wound. When wrestling with his own grief after the death of his wife, Lewis returned to the theme of maternal affection wounded by the claims of God.

> If a mother is mourning not for what she has lost but for what her dead child has lost, it is a comfort to believe that the child has not lost the end for which it was created. . . . A comfort to the God-aimed, eternal spirit within her. But not to her motherhood. The specifically maternal happiness must be written off. Never, in any place or time, will she have her son on her knees, or bathe him, or tell him a story, or plan for his future, or see her grandchild.[28]

In other moments Lewis can, as we will see, be more hopeful. Here, though, he is attempting to be true to what we can experience, and what we often experience is God as the great rival to all our earthly loves. We may be able to *trust* that the natural loves can dwell harmoniously in divine love, but we can seldom *experience* it. We are inordinate lovers, and there is no cure for that except death and rebirth. Lewis states this very succinctly and bleakly.

> We find thus by experience that there is no good applying to Heaven for earthly comfort. Heaven can give heavenly comfort; no other kind. And earth cannot give earthly comfort either. There is no earthly comfort in the long run. (*FL*, p. 190)

That is Lewis' picture of the life to which the sinner has condemned himself. No purely earthly comfort is available;

[28]*A Grief Observed*, p. 24.

to isolate the natural loves is to destroy them. And heavenly comfort may seem a bitter pill to swallow; for it will often appear to require renunciation. Hence the cry of nature wounded by grace—the cry "legitimized for all believers by the words of the Virgin Mother—'Son, why hast thou thus dealt with us? Behold, thy father and I have sought thee sorrowing'."[29]

Lewis' most haunting presentation of the theme of nature wounded by grace must certainly be *Till We Have Faces*. In that story, Orual's love for Psyche and others is not mere selfishness. It is natural affection at its best. As we saw before, Lewis describes it as "true, tender, suffering." Yet, there is something in that love which cannot co-exist with the gods who sit in judgment upon Orual. Almost inevitably she finds herself thinking of the gods as her great rival for the love of Psyche. She can only tell what she has experienced: "the Divine Nature wounds and perhaps destroys us merely by being what it is" (p. 284).[30] Even more revealing is the passage when Orual comes before the gods to have her complaint heard. As she stands stark naked venting her rage, we see what Lewis means when he says that the cry of nature wounded by grace ascends to heaven. Why is it, Orual asks, that the gods had to steal Psyche's love from her? Why could they not simply have been honest and admitted that they were Orual's rival in love? But no, they claim to be very different from Ungit, that possessive, devouring womb. They make that claim, and then steal the hearts of those we love.

> You'll leave us nothing; nothing that's worth our keeping or your taking. Those we love best—whoever's most worth loving—those are the very ones you'll pick out. . . . The son turning his back on the mother and the bride on her groom, stolen away by this everlasting calling, calling, calling of the

---

[29]"Williams and the Arthuriad," *Arthurian Torso*, p. 175.

[30]In *Bright Shadow of Reality* (p. 114) Corbin Carnell points to the relationship between this theme and the ongoing interest of Lewis and Charles Williams in the Grail legend. Galahad's quest for the Grail destroys the unity and harmony in Arthur's kingdom. As Lewis writes in *Arthurian Torso*, "Who can seek the Grail without damaging the Round Table?" (p. 176).

gods. Taken where we can't follow. It would be far better for us
if you were foul and ravening. We'd rather you drank their
blood than stole their hearts. We'd rather they were ours and
dead than yours and made immortal. ... That's why I say it
makes no difference whether you're fair or foul. That there
should be gods at all, there's our misery and bitter wrong.
There's no room for you and us in the same world. (pp. 290f.)

All true in a way—or, at least, a true account of Orual's
experience. Yet, Orual is claiming for herself an independence which no creature has. That claim, which goes to
the very heart of her being, must be crushed, broken, and
destroyed. That is what she finally realizes. In claiming
independence she has been making war on the great reality
principle of the universe. She has been striving to make
herself into what she is not. And so, she asks the question
from which the book takes its title:

"How can they [the gods] meet us face to face till we have
faces?" (p. 294)

This means more than that Orual's life has involved hypoc-
risy and pretense. Striving for independence, she did not
wear the human countenance. She was one who had to be
broken in order to be reborn.

But her anguish was real, and Lewis will not let us
forget this. The picture of the natural loves harmoniously
perfected by divine love must never blind our eyes to what
this may mean in any person's experience. It may mean
conflict, rivalry, renunciation, and grief. Rightly used, the
natural loves can become means of approach to God, images
of the love that must abide in us and move us in every
relation. So often, however, they are not rightly used. If the
lover is not healthy, neither is the love; they are not easily
separated. The only cure is the drastic one of death and
rebirth.[31]

[31]In the second half of this chapter we have seen Lewis struggling with
one of the deepest and knottiest of problems faced in Christian social
ethics—a problem greatly illuminated by H. Richard Niebuhr in *Christ
and Culture* (New York: Harper Torchbook Edition, 1956). Here, tucked
safely away in a footnote where it cannot disturb the flow of exposition, I
want to speculate where we ought to place Lewis in Niebuhr's typology.
Lewis' terminology on occasion might tempt us to consider him a synthesist

Even here, however, Lewis does not intend to demean the natural loves. After all, one way to deal with the problem of inordinate love would be to turn away completely from the earthly loves to love of God. If we cannot manage the intricate simultaneities of loving man in God, perhaps we ought simply to turn away from the creature. Lewis will have none of this—as we might expect of a "romantic theologian." He will not approve it because this solution cannot do justice to the needs and character of human nature.

When at the end of *The Pilgrim's Regress* John and

(like St. Thomas), placing Christ above culture. He can certainly speak of nature and supernature. More probably, however, his understanding of the way in which charity must permeate the natural loves—and the way in which they are insufficient by themselves and cannot truly be themselves in isolation—ought to lead us to place him in the camp of those whom Niebuhr calls "conversionists" or "transformists." Nevertheless, I think there is also something to be said for classifying Lewis as a dualist—one who holds Christ and culture in a kind of tension. If we see how this is true, we may also begin to see how some peace can be made between dualists and transformists. Of the dualistic motif Niebuhr writes: "It mirrors the actual struggles of the Christian who lives 'between the times'. . . . It is a report of experience rather than a plan of campaign" (p. 185). Further, the dualist "likes to point out that the will to live as gods, hence without God, appears in man's noblest endeavors" (p. 155)—a theme reminiscent of Lewis' treatment of the demonic possibilities in all the natural loves (especially) at their best. Yet, of course, Lewis is no pure dualist. He is surely more positive about the natural (created) loves than most dualists would be, and it is not likely that many from that camp would join him in believing that the natural loves can sometimes be a means of approach to the divine love. It seems to be the case that Lewis, like the transformist, takes creation very much into account in constructing his position. He permits the harmony which can exist (and, in a perfect world or a wholly redeemed one, would exist) between the natural loves and divine love to come through in his treatment. Yet, at the same time, he admits with the dualist that we often cannot truly experience the truth of that picture. What we experience is the opposition of God; the one whom we call "Thou" is seen as a rival. Hence, there is a continual movement between that experience of rivalry and a re-affirmation of the truth of the picture of harmony. The picture gives hope and some guidance; the experience drives one back in search of hope. As Niebuhr says of the dualist position: "It sounds paradoxical, because the effort is being made to state in a monologue a meaning that is clear only in the dramatic encounters and re-encounters of God and the souls of men" (p. 158). Perhaps that is why Lewis' greatest success at expressing his sense of the rivalry comes in *Till We Have Faces*, where we see Orual in her "encounters and re-encounters" with the gods who are both terror and delight.

Vertue have been made what neither of them is separately—a whole man—and virtue has become a passion, we meet the other side of the Lewis who said that heaven offers no earthly comfort. Even at the point of death virtue can seek no reward or desire any resurrection, but—as Lewis tells us in the running headline he provides for the allegory—"Faith, being humbler, asks more." And so John says, "Be sure it is not for nothing that the Landlord has knit our hearts so closely to time and place—to one friend rather than another and one shire more than all the land" (p. 198). He then sings a song about "the tether and pang of the particular."

> Passing to-day by a cottage, I shed tears
> When I remembered how once I had dwelled there
> With my mortal friends who are dead. Years
> Little had healed the wound that was laid bare.
>
> Out, little spear that stabs, I, fool, believed
> I had outgrown the local, unique sting,
> I had transmuted away (I was deceived)
> Into love universal the lov'd thing.
>
> But Thou, Lord, surely knewest Thine own plan
> When the angelic indifferences with no bar
> Universally loved but Thou gav'st man
> The tether and pang of the particular;
>
> Which, like a chemic drop, infinitesimal,
> Plashed into pure water, changing the whole,
> Embodies and embitters and turns all
> Spirit's sweet water to astringent soul.
>
> That we, though small, may quiver with fire's same
> Substantial form as Thou—not reflect merely,
> As lunar angel, back to thee, cold flame.
> Gods we are, Thou hast said: and we pay dearly. (p. 198)

Part of the reality of being human is, for Lewis, legitimately to feel "the local, unique sting." Hence, there can be no principled rejection of particular ties forged by the natural loves.

The sense of competition and rivalry may come, and the day for renunciation may come, but that will not happen unless we have given ourselves to the natural loves and have pressed on to where they lead. As Charles Williams put it in a memorable though characteristically esoteric phrase,

> unless devotion is given to a thing which must prove false in the end, the thing that is true in the end cannot enter. . . . Usually the way must be made ready for heaven, and then it will come by some other; the sacrifice must be made ready, and the fire will strike on another altar.[32]

We should realize, therefore, what Lewis is asking of us. We are to give ourselves to the earthly loves, to feel deeply the tether and pang of the particular. That is the way to fellowship with God. Yet, of course, even as we give ourselves over to "the local, unique sting," to the particular bonds of life with life, we do so as inordinate lovers; as those who may well one day have to go the way of negation and renunciation. Each must, at least, risk that much. The gods cannot meet us face to face until we have faces, and that may be more reality than we can presently bear. It is a risky way, this way of love which Lewis recommends, but he does not believe there is any other.

> To love at all is to be vulnerable. . . . The alternative to tragedy, or at least to the risk of tragedy, is damnation. The only place outside Heaven where you can be perfectly safe from all the dangers and perturbations of love is Hell. (*FL*, p. 169)

Not all will suffer tragedy but each must risk it. We must feel "the tether and pang of the particular"; we must lay our natures open to be wounded by grace, for to do anything less is to lose our humanity.

---

[32]Charles Williams, *He Came Down From Heaven* . . . , p. 25.

CHAPTER V

THE PRIMEVAL MORAL PLATITUDES

In *The Magician's Nephew* the story of Aslan's creation of Narnia is recounted. When Narnia has been created, Aslan selects some of the animals to be Talking Beasts. To them he says:

> "I give to you forever this land of Narnia. I give you the stars and I give you myself. The Dumb Beasts whom I have not chosen are yours also. Treat them gently and cherish them but do not go back to their ways lest you cease to be Talking Beasts." (p. 105)

It is possible, in other words, for the Talking Beasts to give up their privileged position and cease to view themselves as anything other than Dumb Beasts. They can view themselves "from below" and see their kinship with the Dumb Beasts. That is part and parcel of the freedom bestowed on them at their creation.

They *can* do that; however, in so doing they turn from the nature that is theirs. That is why, at the great scene of judgment at the end of Narnia, the Talking Beasts who look on the face of Aslan with hatred rather than love cease in that moment to be Talking Beasts and become just ordinary animals.[1] A freely chosen abolition of their nature occurs.

The judgment only confirms and finalizes what has happened in life. When the powers of evil enter Narnia, some Talking Beasts begin to go bad. In *Prince Caspian* Lucy is attacked by a bear. After Trumpkin the Dwarf kills the bear

---

[1] *The Last Battle*, p. 146.

the children speculate about whether at one time it might
have been a talking bear.

> "That's the trouble of it," said Trumpkin, "when most of the
> beasts have gone enemy and gone dumb, but there are still
> some of the other kind left. You never know, and you daren't
> wait to see." (p. 100)

Later, Lucy speculates to Susan about the possibility of a
similar process taking place back in their world.

> "Wouldn't it be dreadful if some day in our own world at
> home, men started going wild inside, like the animals here,
> and still looked like men, so that you'd never know which
> were which?" (p. 101)

Lucy is speculating about an "abolition of man." If, by
relinquishing their inheritance, Talking Beasts can become
Dumb Beasts without changing their external appearance,
it is also possible for a human being to become a "trousered
ape."[2]

The abolition of one's nature in Narnia manifests itself
in a search for power. The creature who turns from his
nature turns from Aslan who endowed him with that nature.
In so doing he takes upon himself a burden which he is not
intended to bear: responsibility for all the consequences of
his action. A case in point is the action of the dwarf Nikabrik
in *Prince Caspian*. Like Trumpkin, Trufflehunter, and the
Pevensie children, Nikabrik wants to drive the oppressor
out of Narnia. But he differs from them in the means he
uses to achieve that end. He disbelieves in Aslan, but he
suggests seeking the help of an Ogre or two and a Hag.
Succinctly he states his creed.

> "I'll believe in anyone or anything," said Nikabrik, "that'll
> batter these cursed Telmarine barbarians to pieces or drive
> them out of Narnia. Anyone or anything. Aslan *or* the White
> Witch, do you understand?" (p. 63)

[2]*The Abolition of Man: Reflections on Education with Special Reference to the Teaching of English in the Upper Forms of Schools* (New York:
Macmillan, 1947), p. 20. Hereafter this volume will be referred to with the
abbreviation *AM*.

And he is as good as his word. Later, when hope for their cause seems well-nigh lost, Nikabrik brings a Hag and a Wer-Wolf and suggests using them to call on "other powers" besides Aslan of which the ancient stories tell.

> "Whom do you mean?" said Caspian at last.
> "I mean a power so much greater than Aslan's that it held Narnia spellbound for years and years, if the stories are true."
> "The White Witch!" cried three voices all at once, and from the noise Peter guessed that three people had leaped to their feet.
> "Yes," said Nikabrik very slowly and distinctly, "I mean the Witch. . . . We want power: and we want a power that will be on our side." (p. 140)

Willingness to die, if need be, in a good cause is the ultimate test of one's character. We can compare Nikabrik, who wants his cause to triumph even at the cost of defiling it, with Tirian, the last king of Narnia, and his beloved friend Jewel the Unicorn. In *The Last Battle* Tirian and Jewel encounter some Calormenes driving and whipping talking horses of Narnia in a way that even Dumb Beasts ought not be treated. Enraged at what they see, they fall upon the Calormenes without warning and kill them. As they gallop away in search of reinforcements, Tirian suddenly stops.

> "Hold hard, friend," said Tirian. "Let me off." He slid off the Unicorn's back and faced him.
> "Jewel," said the King. "We have done a dreadful deed."
> "We were sorely provoked," said Jewel.
> "But to leap on them unawares—without defying them—while they were unarmed—faugh! We are two murderers, Jewel. I am dishonoured forever." (p. 25)

But not only have they violated the laws of courtesy in warfare. One of the talking horses tells them that the Calormenes were supposedly acting under the orders of Aslan. Tirian determines to go back and give himself up.

> "You will go to your death, then," said Jewel.
> "Do you think I care if Aslan dooms me to death?" said the King. "That would be nothing, nothing at all. Would it not be better to be dead than to have this horrible fear that Aslan has

come and is not like the Aslan we have believed in and longed
for? It is as if the sun rose one day and were a black sun."
(p. 25).

It is love for the Aslan in whom he believes that enables
Tirian to defy the orders of the one who now claims to be
Aslan. He will not do evil even if it be the command of
Aslan himself. For he seeks not merely to survive with a
powerful Aslan but to live with the Lion who is Goodness
itself. It is not survival but the way in which one lives that
counts. That is the meaning of the message Roonwit the
Centaur, lying with a Calormene arrow in his side, sends to
Tirian: "to remember that all worlds draw to an end and that
noble death is a treasure which no one is too poor to buy"
(p. 86).

We can see here a relation between the morality of loyal
Narnians and their faith. In other chapters we have discussed the nature of Narnian community—a community
built on steadfast love for Aslan. But that is a love for the
Aslan of old Narnian stories. It is love for the Aslan who was
willing to go to death in a good cause: the ransoming of
Edmund from the claim of the White Witch. The Aslan who
is loved and remembered is recognized as good. Also powerful, to be sure, but it is the power of one who is unmistakably good. Suppose Aslan should turn out to be evil? That is
an hypothesis almost beyond the grasp of any faithful Narnian. But if, in some unthinkable way, it should turn out to
be true, then he would have to be opposed—opposed for
the sake of the Aslan of the stories, for the sake of goodness
itself.

THE NATURE OF MORALITY

In what is one of the best discussions of Lewis' fiction, John
Haigh writes that in his stories about Narnia Lewis "pays
the child the compliment of sharing with him his deepest
intuitions."[3] That is true. The short discussion at the beginning of this chapter isolated some of the material from the

[3]John D. Haigh, *The Fiction of C. S. Lewis* (University of Leeds:
Unpublished Ph.D. Dissertation, 1962), p. 296.

Chronicles of Narnia which dealt with Lewis' understanding of morality and the normative moral views he accepts. These were no late addition to Lewis' thought. Lewis had originally hoped to get a teaching position in philosophy, and his movement from philosophical idealism to theism was motivated largely by the decision that idealism could be believed but not lived.[4] It seems fair to say that he was, from the outset, a moralist.

Lewis makes a distinction similar to that now made between normative ethics and meta-ethics.[5] He points out that we can speak of ethical systems and mean either (1) a body of ethical injunctions; or (2) systematic analyses and explanations of our moral experience.[6] He believes that the two will be related in anyone's thought and that there will be far more disagreement about (2) than (1). "The number of actions about whose ethical quality a Stoic, an Aristotelian, a Thomist, a Kantian, and a Utilitarian would agree is, after all, very large."[7]

In this section on the nature of morality we will concentrate not on Lewis' normative position but on his defense of objectivity in moral judgments. He holds both that there is objective moral knowledge (and that, hence, moral judgments can be true or false) and that no practical conclusion (i.e., no "ought") can be derived from propositions about fact alone.[8] Thus, for example, Lewis maintains that the

[4]In *C. S. Lewis: A Biography,* Green and Hooper note that while trying to get a fellowship to teach in philosophy Lewis had submitted for consideration an essay titled, "The Promethean Fallacy in Ethics" (p. 78). Walter Hooper also writes, in his preface to *Selected Literary Essays* (p. xiv, n.1) that in the years before his appointment to the English position at Magdalen Lewis had been at work on a paper titled, "Hegemony of Moral Values." The paper was submitted to *Mind,* never published, and is evidently lost.

[5]Cf., for example, William K. Frankena, *Ethics* (Englewood Cliffs, N.J.: Prentice-Hall, 1963), pp. 78f. Normative ethics is concerned to arrive at "acceptable principles of obligation and general judgments of value in the light of which to determine what is morally right, wrong, or obligatory, and what or who is morally good, bad, or responsible." Meta-ethics is, for the most part, concerned with the meaning of ethical terms and the justification of ethical judgments.

[6]"On Ethics," *Christian Reflections,* pp. 44f.

[7]*Ibid.,* p. 45.

[8]Cf. *AM,* pp. 43–44, 52–53.

judgment that society ought to be preserved is a part of our moral knowledge, and nor merely an attitude we express or a position we choose to adopt. But, at the same time, he holds that from the premise 'this will preserve society' we cannot conclude, 'do this.' To reach that conclusion we need the additional premise, 'society ought to be preserved'—a premise which cannot itself be claimed to be a statement of fact alone (*AM*, p. 43). To understand the way in which Lewis holds these views together we will investigate first his discussions of the meaning of the word 'natural.' Nevill Coghill recounts a conversation which occurred when he and Lewis were dining with Rector Marett of Exeter College. A part of the conversation, according to Coghill, went something like this as Marett spoke to Lewis:

> "I saw in the papers this morning that there is some scientist-fellah in Vienna, called Voronoff—some name like that—who has invented a way of splicing the glands of young apes onto old gentlemen, thereby renewing their generative powers! Remarkable, isn't it?"
> Lewis thought.
> "I would say 'unnatural'."
> "Come, come! 'Unnatural'! What do you mean, *'unnatural'*? Voronoff is a part of Nature, isn't he? What happens in Nature must surely be natural? Speaking as a philosopher, don't you know"—(Marett taught Philosophy)—"I can attach no meaning to your objection; I don't understand you!"
> "I am sorry, Rector; but I think any philosopher from Aristotle to—say—Jeremy Bentham, would have understood me."
> "Oh well, we've got beyond Bentham by now, I hope. If Aristotle or he had known about Voronoff, they might have changed their ideas. Think of the possibilities he opens up! You'll be an old man yourself one day."
> *"I would rather be an old man than a young monkey."*[9]

That conversation over lunch is not, of course, a rigorous argument, but it does express well and amusingly the position which Lewis elsewhere seriously defends. Only in some senses of 'natural' does the word refer to whatever exists. Lewis cites Aristotle: "To find out what is natural, we must study specimens which retain their nature and not those which have been corrupted" (*PP*, p. 129). 'Nature' can

[9]Gibb, *Light on C. S. Lewis*, p. 61.

mean various things depending on the antithesis given it. The characteristically modern use, Lewis believes, is to oppose the civil to the natural and to think of nature as the brutal, the unimproved, the primitive, the original. In discussing Spenser's concept of nature Lewis says that Spenser knows this meaning well, but that it is not central to his thought.

> Most commonly he understands Nature as Aristotle did—the 'nature' of anything being its unimpeded growth from within to perfection, neither checked by accident nor sophisticated by art. To this 'nature' his allegiance never falters. . . .[10]

Nor, we might add, does Lewis'.

If we mean by nature "the whole show"—everything that is—it can, of course, have no opposite.[11] This is the sense in which an external observer would have to consider nature, and it is one way in which it is possible for men to perceive nature (including themselves). It is, in fact, the concept of the natural which Rector Marett was using in the conversation Coghill recounts. But, as Lewis notes, the word 'natural' is used in many other ways in which it has a whole series of opposites. By examining one of these we can better understand Lewis' concept of morality.

The natural may be opposed to the unnatural (SW, p. 43). Anything which has changed from its kind can be unnatural, though, in fact, this is only said if the change is for the worse. We do not say of the timid man who forces himself to be brave that he has acted unnaturally (SW, p. 43). It is obvious that this sense of 'natural' cannot be derived from the sense in which the natural includes everything that is; for in that sense the natural includes perversion just as well as everything else (SW, p. 44). We can see, then, that Lewis' response to Rector Marett was based on rejecting Marett's use of 'natural' (referring to everything that is) and substituting instead a meaning of 'natural' which refers to the kind of thing under consideration; a meaning in which the natural can have a opposite. We can

---

[10]The Allegory of Love, p. 330.
[11]Studies in Words (Cambridge, 1960), p. 43. Hereafter, this work will be referred to with the abbreviation SW.

also see the sense in which Lewis can say that value judgments cannot be derived from propositions about fact alone.
He means that factual statements, as they are commonly
understood, depend on the sense in which nature has no
opposite—that is, nature as perceived by an external observer who seeks only to describe what he finds there.
Lewis' position is that there is no logical way to move from
that meaning of 'natural' to one in which 'natural' may have
'unnatural' for its opposite.

Judgments of value cannot, Lewis thinks, be reduced to
propositions of fact. By this he means that there is no ethical
knowledge available to the external observer—to one who
insists on knowing even himself as a natural object. No
moral knowledge will be found in nature; we will find it
there only if we bring it to our experience. Lewis explains
his position in *The Abolition of Man*. To treat something as
natural is (1) to suspend our judgments of value about it; (2)
to ignore its final cause (if any); and (3) to treat it in terms of
quantity (*AM*, p. 81). The history of man's conquest of nature is a history of coming to view objects in this way.
Hence, it is true, though paradoxical, to say that every
conquest of nature increases nature's domain (*AM*, p. 83).

This conquest does not always come easily. Elements in
what would otherwise be our total reaction to an object
have to be repressed if it is to be possible.

> Something has to be overcome before we can cut up a dead
> man or a live animal in a dissecting room. These objects *resist*
> the movement of the mind whereby we thrust them into the
> world of mere Nature. But in other instances too, a similar
> price is exacted for our analytical knowledge and manipulative
> power, even if we have ceased to count it. We do not look at
> trees either as Dryads or as beautiful objects while we cut
> them into beams: the first man who did so may have felt the
> price keenly, and the bleeding trees in Virgil and Spenser may
> be far-off echoes of that primeval sense of impiety.[12]

[12]*AM*, pp. 81–82. Lewis recaptures that "primeval sense of impiety"
in *The Last Battle* when the Calormenes enter Narnia and begin cutting
down the talking trees. Tirian, Jewel, and Roonwit hear a wailing sound
approaching in the distance.

"Woe, woe, woe!" called the voice. "Woe for my brothers and
sisters! Woe for the holy trees! The woods are laid waste. The axe is

Lewis does not deny that man's conquest of nature has been in many ways beneficial. But how, he asks, are we to decide where this process should stop? Shall we make of man a natural object? Shall we adopt the posture of the external observer and eliminate from consideration our knowledge of ourselves as moral agents?

That we *can* do this Lewis does not doubt. But to do so would, he thinks, constitute an abolition of our humanity. "There are progressions in which the last step is *sui generis* . . . and in which to go the whole way is to undo all the labour of your previous journey" (*AM*, p. 91). It is, Lewis says, "like the famous Irishman who found that a certain kind of stove reduced his fuel bill by half and thence concluded that two stoves of the same kind would enable him to warm his house with no fuel at all" (*AM*, p. 83). If we begin outside the sphere of inherited values which we bring to experience, we will never work our way back into the realm of values. We will never discover genuine moral knowledge by studying man as a physiological or psychological object. Either we bring value to experience or we find none. Lewis believes that in the history of Western thought there has been a "single one-way progression" in the processes by which man has come to know the universe. Qualities of objects and, then, objects themselves

---

loosed against us. We are being felled. Great trees are falling, falling, falling." With the last "falling," the speaker came in sight. She was like a woman but so tall that her head was on a level with the Centaur's; yet she was like a tree too. It is hard to explain if you have never seen a Dryad but quite unmistakable once you have—something different in the colour, the voice, and the hair. King Tirian and the Two Beasts knew at once that she was the nymph of a beech-tree.

"Justice, Lord King!" she cried. "Come to our aid. Protect your people. They are felling us in Lantern Waste. Forty great trunks of my brothers and sisters are already on the ground."

"What, Lady! Felling Lantern Waste? Murdering the talking trees?" cried the King leaping to his feet and drawing his sword. "How dare they? And who dares it? Now by the Mane of Aslan - - -"

"A-a-a-h," grasped the Dryad shuddering as if in pain—shuddering time after time as if under repeated blows. Then all at once she fell sideways as suddenly as if both her feet had been cut from under her. For a second they saw her lying dead on the grass and then she vanished. They knew what had happened. Her tree, miles away, had been cut down (pp. 16–17).

have been taken out of the objective world and transferred to the subject. When, however, the process is applied to the subject himself—to human beings—

> we arrive at a result uncommonly like zero. While we were reducing the world to almost nothing we deceived ourselves with the fancy that all its lost qualities were being kept safe (if in a somewhat humbled condition) as 'things in our own mind'. Apparently we had no mind of the sort required. The Subject is as empty as the Object. Almost nobody has been making linguistic mistakes about almost nothing. By and large, this is the only thing that has ever happened.[13]

In *That Hideous Strength* the scientist Hingest expresses Lewis' view quite succinctly: "I happen to believe that you can't study men; you can only get to know them, which is quite a different thing" (p. 71).

This is what Lewis means by saying that no "ought" can be derived from propositions about fact. If we insist on understanding reality in a particular way (the way of the external observer), ethical knowledge will be impossible because it will be in principle excluded. If we study man as we study cabbages, no moral knowledge will be forthcoming (*MC*, p. 19). That is, if for methodological reasons we eliminate moral knowledge from our analysis of human nature, it will not be surprising if our analysis uncovers no possibility for such knowledge. What alternatives does Lewis offer? He concerns himself, for the most part, with the justification of ethical judgments rather than with the meaning of ethical terms.[14] Stated simply, we can say that he maintains that we have objective moral knowledge which we bring to our experience.[15] We can begin by asking *what* moral knowledge Lewis thinks we have and then ask *how* he thinks we acquire it.

[13]"Preface" to *The Hierarchy of Heaven and Earth*, by D. E. Harding (London: Faber and Faber, 1952), p. 10.

[14]For the distinction cf., again, Frankena, pp. 78f. Also, Glenn C. Graber, "A Critical Bibliography of Recent Discussions of Religious Ethics by Philosophers," *The Journal of Religious Ethics*, 2 (1974), p. 57. This means that Lewis concerns himself with only a part of what philosophers mean by meta-ethics.

[15]If we try to classify Lewis' meta-ethical position we encounter some difficulties. I believe he is closest to what Richard T. Garner and Bernard

A moral argument or quarrel is something quite different from a fight. In a moral argument we try to show the other person that he is wrong (*MC*, p. 3). This presupposes some area of agreement. Appeals to fairness, for example, crop up constantly in moral arguments (*MC*, p. 5). In *The Abolition of Man* Lewis isolates this area of agreement and speaks of a conception which is, he thinks, common to classical, Christian, and Oriental thought. It is the conception of objective value, "the belief that certain attitudes are really true, and others really false, to the kind of thing the universe is and the kind of things we are" (*AM*, p. 29). This conception he calls, for the sake of brevity, 'the *Tao*.' The *Tao* contains principles which must inevitably enter into any moral argument. Such principles are (1) the law of general beneficence (i.e., that we try to avoid harming others and seek to help them); (2) the law of special beneficence (i.e., special concern for those who have claims of kinship upon us); (3) duties to parents, elders, and ances-

---

Rosen call a cognitivist nondefinist in their book *Moral Philosophy: A Systematic Introduction to Normative Ethics and Meta-ethics* (New York: Macmillan, 1967). That somewhat ungainly title is bestowed by them on those who at one time were called rational intuitionists. According to Garner and Rosen (pp. 270ff.) this position is characterized by three tenets: (1) Moral judgments can be objectively true; (2) moral judgments are not reducible to any kind of nonmoral judgments or expressions; (3) moral knowledge is sometimes direct. Lewis seems, in one way or another, to hold all three of these tenets. However, any attempt to classify his position must take account of the following statement in his essay "On Ethics": "You will not suspect me of trying to reintroduce in its full Stoical or medieval rigour the doctrine of Natural Law. Still less am I claiming as the source of this substantial ethical agreement anything like Intuition or Innate Ideas. Nor, Theist though I am, do I here put forward any surreptitious argument for Theism" (*Christian Reflections*, p. 55). This does not mean that our classification of Lewis is simply incorrect. He attacks subjectivist views of moral judgments and, hence, agrees with tenet (1). He criticizes ethical naturalism and, hence, agrees with tenet (2). And he does often speak of moral knowledge as a kind of direct "seeing" and, hence, seems to agree with tenet (3). What is distinctive about his position seems to be an additional (and, evidently, empirical) claim. He does not merely propose to tell us *how* objective moral knowledge is possible. He suggests that meta-ethics cannot be done in isolation from normative ethics. Certain *substantive* principles are embedded in his meta-ethic, and he maintains that moral argument is impossible unless at least some of them are granted from the outset.

tors; (4) duties to children and posterity; (5) the law of justice; (6) the law of good faith and veracity; (7) the law of mercy; (8) the law of magnanimity (i.e., willingness to expend oneself in service of the good).

But what reasons can we give in defense of these principles? Lewis' point is precisely that we cannot give such reasons. We can argue *from* the principles of the *Tao* but not *to* them. They are "to the world of action what axioms are to the world of theory. . . . You cannot reach them as conclusions: they are premisses" (*AM*, p. 53). We may say, in other words, that these principles express truths about human nature (in Aristotle's and Spenser's sense of 'nature').

Much of the support for Lewis' case lies in the examples he provides in defense of it. The *experimentum crucis* is, he says, that of death for a good cause (*AM*, p. 42). What, Lewis asks, was the Roman father doing when he told his son that it was a sweet and seemly thing to die for his country? What justification could be given for the father's moral judgment on the basis of which he sought to instill in his son an emotion appropriate to that belief? Lewis believes that it will be futile to offer any support for the Roman father which begins from factual premises; that part of his argument we have already seen.

How else might we proceed? One can get from propositions about fact to a practical conclusion only through an acknowledged duty or a felt desire (*AM*, p. 43). Under the hypothesis we are considering the former option must for the moment be excluded, since it would constitute a reintroduction of ethical value in the premises. What of the latter? Can we ground a duty to die in a good cause in our felt desires and make that the bridge by which to move from fact to value? Here Lewis discusses a proposal to the effect that we are moved by instinct and desire to seek the preservation of society and the human species. He replies, first, that he doubts whether we do in fact have such an instinct (*AM*, pp. 50ff.). But, more to the point, there are two fundamental problems facing any attempt to reintroduce the ethical by means of instinct or desire.

First, Lewis introduces a variant of Augustine's concept

of the divided will. "Telling us to obey instinct is like telling us to obey 'people.' People say different things: so do instincts. Our instincts are at war" (*AM*, p. 48). In fact, it is plausible that part of the task of morality is the control of our instincts and desires. In *The Pilgrim's Regress* John learns this lesson from Wisdom. It cannot be said that the rules (of morality) simply disguise our desires; for "the rules are frequently denials of these desires" (p. 127). Some instincts will be satisfied while others are denied. To say that some *ought* to be satisfied will obviously not do. To speak of a particular instinct as fundamental also will avail little; for either this refers to its intensity and frequency or else it is a surreptitious smuggling in of an ethical premise (*AM*, p. 49).

Second, suppose even that we are moved strongly by a desire to preserve society or our species. That alone will not tell us whether we ought to act in accord with this desire. It still makes sense to ask why, or whether, we ought to do so.[16]

> Even if it were true that men had a spontaneous, unreflective impulse to sacrifice their own lives for the preservation of their fellows, it remains a quite separate question whether this is an impulse they should control or one they should indulge. (*AM*, pp. 47–48)

When that Roman father told his son that it was a sweet and seemly thing to die for his country, he believed himself to be making a true moral judgment and to be imparting objective moral knowledge. Yet, that precept could not be derived from any propositions of fact, not even propositions about his own physiological or psychological state. It was, rather, a part of the human moral inheritance. That inheri-

---

[16]Is this Lewis' version of G. E. Moore's famous "naturalistic fallacy" argument? Cf. Moore's *Principia Ethica* (Cambridge, 1959), pp. 9ff. Lewis does not say so and, in the absence of such comment, we can only point out that there is some similarity between the arguments. Nowhere to my knowledge does Lewis refer to Moore or acknowledge dependence on his thought. John T. Wilcox offers a short but clear argument that positions such as that defended by Lewis are less than completely convincing. Cf. his "From *Is* to *Ought* Via Psychology," *The Review of Metaphysics*, XVIII (1964–65), pp. 254-66.

tance is what Lewis means by the *Tao*. "In the *Tao* itself, as long as we remain within it, we find the concrete reality in which to participate is to be truly human" (*AM*, p. 86). We can reject that inheritance if we like, but to do so is to cut ourselves off from "the common ground of humanity" (*PP*, p. 25).

In *That Hideous Strength,* Frost gives Mark a systematic training in "objectivity": a training designed to kill in him all specifically human preferences (pp. 296–300). Mark is placed in a room that is ill-proportioned; for example, the point of the arch above the door is not in the center. On the wall there is a portrait of a young woman with her mouth open, and the inside of her mouth is full of hair. There is a picture of the Last Supper, distinguished primarily by the beetles under the table. There is a representation of a giant mantis playing a fiddle while being eaten by another mantis, and another of a man with cork-screws instead of arms. And Mark himself is asked to perform various obscenities, culminating in the command to trample on a crucifix.

> To sit in the room was the first step towards what Frost called objectivity—the process whereby all specifically human reactions were killed in a man. . . .
>   But after an hour or so this long, high coffin of a room began to produce on Mark an effect which his instructor had probably not anticipated. . . . There rose up against this background of the sour and the crooked some kind of vision of the sweet and the straight. Something else—something he vaguely called the 'Normal'—apparently existed. . . . It was all mixed up with Jane and fried eggs and soap and sunlight and the rooks cawing at Cure Hardy and the thought that, somewhere outside, daylight was going on at that moment. He was not thinking in moral terms at all; or else (what is much the same thing) he was having his first deeply moral experience. He was choosing a side: the Normal. (p. 299)

As the training continued, this idea of the Straight or Normal grew stronger in Mark's mind. It was given him, and from it he received strength.

> He had never known before what an Idea meant: he had always thought till now that they were things inside one's head. But now, when his head was continually attacked and

often completely filled with the clinging corruption of the
training, this Idea towered up above him—something which
obviously existed quite independently of himself and had hard
rock surfaces which would not give, surfaces he could cling to.
(p. 310)

That is what one finds in the *Tao:* the human moral
inheritance. It is the arbitrary creation of no one, not even
God. We should think of the *Tao,* Lewis says, as *genitum
non factum*—begotten, not made.[17] Its relation to God is a
difficult question. To say that God obeys the moral law
seems unsatisfactory. However, to say that he creates it may
appear to make it the arbitrary product of his will; even
mere caprice. For Lewis at least, the idea of the Good will
not permit of that. He suggests that we content ourselves
with laying down two negations: "that God neither *obeys*
nor *creates* the moral law."[18] The first negation is necessary
if the ground of our existence is to be not merely a law but a
begetting love. The second is necessary if we are to distinguish our worship of this being from devil worship or worship of power.[19]

If this accurately describes the *Tao,* it is plain that
Screwtape (once again) speaks truly when he says that "all
the great moralists are sent by the Enemy, not to inform
men, but to remind them, to restate the primeval moral
platitudes against our continual concealment of them" (*SL,*
p. 107). This is a common theme in Lewis' writing, crop-
ping up even where we might least expect it. In his famous
Allegory of Love Lewis writes of Langland's *Piers Plowman*
and says that as a moralist Langland has no unique message
to deliver, but he cannot resist adding:

> It is doubtful whether any moralist of unquestioned greatness
> has ever attempted more (or less) than the defence of the
> universally acknowleged; for 'men more frequently require to
> be reminded than informed'.[20]

[17]In a letter to Dr. Clyde Kilby, dated January 11, 1961. This letter is
quoted in part by Dr. Kilby in his book, *The Christian World of C. S. Lewis*
(Grand Rapids: Eerdmans, 1964), p. 190.
[18]"The Poison of Subjectivism," *Christian Reflections,* p. 80.
[19]*Ibid.*
[20]*The Allegory of Love,* pp. 158f. The citation is, I believe, from Dr.
Johnson.

Lewis seems willing to regard this as an empirical question. One should, he says, simply look and see, and in the midst of cultural differences he will find "the same triumphantly monotonous denunciations of oppression, murder, treachery and falsehood, the same injunctions of kindness to the aged, the young, and the weak, of almsgiving and impartiality and honesty."[21] The impression to the contrary comes, he believes, partly from concentrating on those aspects of cultures which are most variable (e.g., sexual practices) and which arouse strong emotions.[22] It comes also from contrasting civilized and savage man. For Lewis the savage is the exceptional man "who in the same number of centuries, either has not learned or has forgotten, what the rest of the human race know."[23] Furthermore, Lewis suggests that even these differences have been exaggerated and that some of them are differences in belief about fact rather than in judgment of value. For example, the fact that we engage neither in human sacrifice nor in persecution of witches does not necessarily demonstrate that our value judgments differ from people's in a society which does engage in these practices. After all, we disbelieve in the existence of witches, and we do not think famine or pestilence can be averted by offering a human sacrifice to the gods.[24]

In describing the *Tao* thus far we have, for the most part, dealt with only one of its principles: enjoining willingness

[21]"The Poison of Subjectivism," *Christian Reflections,* p. 77. We should note that Lewis does not try to prove the validity of the *Tao* by any argument from common consent (and there, I think, parts company from Hooker with whom he so often agrees). He says of the *Tao:* "Its validity cannot be deduced. For those who do not perceive its rationality, even universal consent could not prove it" (*AM,* p. 95).

[22]*Ibid.,* p. 78.

[23]"On Ethics," *Christian Reflections,* p. 54. I am not concerned to ask whether this bespeaks a kind of provincialism in Lewis. For our purposes another question is more important. Can this judgment be reconciled with his epistemological position? If the truths of the *Tao* are simply seen, how is it that some do not see them? Individual exceptions can be explained. (Most of us, after all, see the primary colors; the color-blind do not.) But exceptions of whole societies would be more difficult to account for. Of course, it remains an empirical question whether and how many such societies there are.

[24]"The Poison of Subjectivism," *Christian Reflections,* p. 78.

to die in a good cause. We have seen that by refusing to acknowledge the claim of the *Tao* upon himself, a man abdicates his humanity and steps into an ethical vacuum from which he cannot reenter the ethical sphere. There are, however, distortions of the *Tao* less drastic than simple, radical refusal to recognize its validity. One may abstract a single principle from the *Tao*, absolutize it, use it to reject other principles in the *Tao*, and thus "deprive us of our full humanity."[25] This is, Lewis thinks, illegitimate. The maxims of the *Tao* come down together and are all a part of our human inheritance. None of them is simply to be rejected. Lewis pictures an innovator who wants to hold only to our duty to posterity.

> But then, in every form of the *Tao* which has come down to us, side by side with the duty to children and descendants lies the duty to parents and ancestors. By what right do we reject one and accept the other? Again, the Innovator may place economic value first. To get people fed and clothed is the great end, and in pursuit of it scruples about justice and good faith may be set aside. The *Tao* of course agrees with him about the importance of getting the people fed and clothed. Unless the Innovator were himself using the *Tao* he could never have learned of such a duty. But side by side with it in the *Tao* lie those duties of justice and good faith which he is ready to debunk. What is his warrant? He may be a Jingoist, a Racialist, an extreme nationalist, who maintains that the advancement of his own people is the object to which all else ought to yield. But no kind of factual observation and no appeal to instinct will give him a ground for this opinion. Once more, he is in fact deriving it from the *Tao*: a duty to our own kin, because they are our own kin, is a part of traditional morality. But, side by side with it in the *Tao*, and limiting it, lie the inflexible demands of justice, and the rule that, in the long run, all men are our brothers. Whence comes the Innovator's authority to pick and choose? (*AM*, pp. 54–55)

In *Out of the Silent Planet* Weston can be seen as this sort of innovator. He and Devine have kidnapped Ransom and taken him to the planet of Malacandra (Mars). Devine hopes to bring Malacandra's treasures back to earth, and, significantly, Ransom finds him the more odious of the two (p. 33). Weston does not yet act solely for self-regarding

[25]"On Ethics," *Christian Reflections*, p. 56.

motives. This becomes clear in his interview with the
Oyarsa of Malacandra in which Ransom acts as interpreter.

> "It is well that I have heard you," said Oyarsa. "For though
> your mind is feebler, your will is less bent than I thought. It is
> not for yourself that you would do all this."
> "No," said Weston proudly in Malacandrian. "Me die. Man
> live." (p. 137)

Weston is, in fact, committed to one of the principles of the
Tao. His hope is that as a consequence of his action mankind
may never die out. As life dies on earth, the human species
may be able to hop from planet to planet, in order to maintain life. Thus, at this point Weston retains his humanity,
but it is a truncated humanity. He is willing to sacrifice all
else for the sake of that one principle to which he is committed. On one occasion Ransom can find no other way to
translate Weston's words into Malacandrian except by ascribing to him the view that "the only good thing is that
there should be very many creatures alive" (p. 136). In the
end Oyarsa sizes up Weston's condition as follows:

> "I see now how the lord of the silent world has bent you.
> There are laws that all *hnau* know, of pity and straight dealing
> and shame and the like, and one of these is the love of kindred.
> He has taught you to break all of them except this one, which is
> not one of the greatest laws; this one he has bent till it becomes
> folly and has set it up, thus bent, to be a little, blind Oyarsa in
> your brain. And now you can do nothing but obey it, though if
> we ask you why it is a law you give no other reason for it than
> for all the other and greater laws which it drives you to dis-
> obey." (pp. 138f.)

Thus far, we have been occupied with Lewis' rejection
of ethical naturalism and his defense of objective moral
knowledge (concerning ourselves up till now with *what* we
can know rather than *how* we know it). He begins by rejecting the view that moral knowledge can be derived from
propositions about fact alone. But neither are principles of
morality only hypothetical imperatives founded on our instincts or desires. Hence, our most fundamental moral beliefs cannot be justified by an appeal to facts; not even facts
about what we desire. Such facts as are available to the

external observer systematically exclude our moral knowledge. Furthermore, our desires are divided and in need of
control and guidance. At the same time, however, Lewis
wants to maintain that moral knowledge is truly knowledge.
He opposes (as we have yet to see) the view that we are free
to choose for ourselves whatever moral principles we may
care to adopt. Hence, it is quite correct to say that for Lewis
the basic imperatives of morality are grounded in the structure of reality, but this is a reality in which values are
embedded from the outset. It is the 'natural' not in the
sense of 'everything that is' but in the sense which can be
opposed to the 'unnatural.' In the *Tao* we have objective
moral knowledge; for it expresses truths about human nature, though not the sort of truths available to one who
insists on investigating human beings as if they were cabbages. These truths about human nature provide the first
principles for moral reasoning. Once we see that, we will
see that there is no point in trying to provide some other
justification for them. If we could do that, they would no
longer be first principles.

> It is no use trying to "see through" first principles. If you see
> through everything, then everything is transparent. But a
> wholly transparent world is an invisible world. To "see
> through" all things is the same as not to see. (*AM*, p. 91)

To see through all things is to enter an ethical vacuum
out of which it is impossible to step. It is to make knowledge something which cannot be related to the world of
practice. "On this view, the world of facts, without one
trace of value, and the world of feelings without one trace
of truth or falsehood, justice or injustice, confront one
another, and no *rapprochement* is possible."[26] This, Lewis
thinks, is where such a position must end: unable to relate
reason to the world of activity in which moral problems

[26]*AM*, pp. 30–31. Cf. Josef Pieper, *Reality and the Good*, trans. by
Stella Lange (Chicago: Regnery, 1967), p. 48: "In spite of their being
rooted in a single theoretical-practical 'basic faculty,' Kant makes the
practical reason entirely independent of the theoretical and of all that can
be the object of theoretical activity, that means, independent of all knowledge of reality."

arise. "And, to do him justice, Hume (who is its great
ancestor) warned us not to try. He recommended back-
gammon instead. . . ."[27] Lewis does not mean to say that
people committed to such a theory will act immorally.

> My idea is that sometimes they do forget. That is their
> glory. Holding a philosophy which excludes humanity, they
> yet remain human. At the sight of injustice they throw all their
> Naturalism to the winds and speak like men and like men of
> genius. They know far better than they think they know.[28]

If we ask *what* basic moral knowledge Lewis thinks is
ours, he points us to the *Tao*. An obvious question at this
point, however, is to ask *how* Lewis thinks we acquire this
knowledge—and this is a legitimate question. It is not to
ask for a justification of first principles (which Lewis has
said is impossible to give) but simply to inquire about the
mode by which we know them. Even so, the question is
slightly ambiguous. To ask how we know ethical first principles is different from asking how we become able to know
them. The first is a problem for epistemology; the second
the task of moral education. Lewis is more concerned with
the latter than the former.

> Aristotle says that the aim of education is to make the pupil like
> and dislike what he ought. When the age for reflective thought
> comes, the pupil who has been thus trained in 'ordinate affec-
> tions' or 'just sentiments' will easily find the first principles in
> Ethics: but to the corrupt man they will never be visible at all
> and he can make no progress in that science. Plato before him
> had said the same. . . . In the *Republic*, the well-nurtured
> youth is one 'who would see most clearly whatever was amiss
> in ill-made works of man or ill-grown works of nature, and with
> a just distaste would blame and hate the ugly even from his
> earliest years and would give delighted praise to beauty, re-
> ceiving it into his soul and being nourished by it, so that he
> becomes a man of gentle heart. All this before he is of an age to
> reason: so that when Reason at length comes to him, then, bred
> as he has been, he will hold out his hands in welcome and
> recognize her because of the affinity he bears to her.' (*AM*,
> pp. 26–27)

[27]"Preface" to *The Hierarchy of Heaven and Earth*, p. 11.
[28]*Miracles*, p. 37.

This stress on moral education could be said to be the strongest and most permanent theme of Lewis' ethic. For the moment, however, we will confine our attention to the epistemological problem as it exists apart from the theme of moral education. What is the mode by which a (properly educated) person knows the maxims of the *Tao*? We must, says Lewis, extend the word 'reason' to "include what our ancestors called Practical Reason."[29] The principles of the *Tao* are not mere sentiments; they are rationality itself. In *The Discarded Image* Lewis discusses the place of reason in the Medieval Model. The rational soul was considered to have two faculties: *intellectus* (by which we "see" a self-evident truth) and *ratio* (by which we proceed step by step to uncover a truth which is not self-evident). A cognitive life in which all was *intellectus* would be that of an angel. A cognitive life in which all was *ratio* would be impossible, since nothing could be proved unless something was self-evident.[30] In matters of morality the function of *intellectus* was to grasp the fundamental moral maxims. This view was, Lewis thinks, held by most moralists until the 18th century, when the grasp of moral principles came to be attributed to conscience (as in Butler) or to a moral sentiment.[31]

Without in any way committing himself totally to the Medieval Model, Lewis clearly aligns himself with the view he here attributes to it: the belief that to recognize a duty is to perceive a truth.

> I believe that the primary moral principles on which all others depend are rationally perceived. We "just see" that there is no reason why my neighbour's happiness should be sacrificed to my own, as we "just see" that things which are equal to the same thing are equal to one another. If we cannot prove either axiom, that is not because they are irrational but because they

[29]*AM*, p. 44. Cf. Pieper, *Reality and the Good*, p. 49: "The concept of the practical reason necessarily includes and asserts the theoretical reason as well. The 'basic faculty' is the theoretical reason which 'extends' to become the practical."
[30]*The Discarded Image*, p. 157.
[31]*Ibid.*, pp. 158–61.

are self-evident and all proofs depend on them. Their intrinsic reasonableness shines by its own light.[32]

If we take what seems to be Lewis' most mature expression of this position in *The Abolition of Man*, it will be clear that 'self-evident' does not mean the same as 'obvious.' To claim that the principles of the *Tao* were obvious would undermine the stress on the need for moral education, which is Lewis' chief purpose in *The Abolition of Man*. Lewis intends only to claim that a (properly educated) person will be able to recognize the legitimacy of the primeval moral platitudes and will also recognize that they can be argued *from* but not *to*. That is what he means by referring to them as self-evident.[33] Knowledge of these maxims, for those who acquire it, is direct. However, in the following passage from *Mere Christianity* he says more than this, and we must consider it inconsistent with the position of *The Abolition of Man*.

> This law was called the Law of Nature because people thought that every one knew it by nature and did not need to be taught it. They did not mean, of course, that you might not find an odd individual here and there who did not know it, just as you find a few people who are colour-blind or have no ear for a tune. But taking the race as a whole, they thought that the human idea of decent behaviour was obvious to every one. (*MC*, p. 4)

More often Lewis suggests that the maxims of the *Tao* constitute, in a limited sense, a natural law not because everyone knows them without being taught them, but because they express fundamental truths about human nature.

---

[32]*Miracles*, p. 35.

[33]Lewis' position here is similar to that of St. Thomas, who wrote that "the precepts of the natural law are to the practical reason what the first principles of demonstrations are to the speculative reason, because both are self-evident principles. Now a thing is said to be self-evident in two ways: first, in itself; secondly, in relation to us. Any proposition is said to be self-evident in itself, if its predicate is contained in the notion of the subject; even though it may happen that to one who does not know the definition of the subject, such a proposition is not self-evident. ... But some propositions are self-evident only to the wise, who understand the meaning of the terms of such propositions" (S.T., I/II, q. 94, a.2).

It is still true that those who do know these fundamental truths will directly perceive them. There will be no process of reasoning by which one can arrive at them. Much of Lewis' defense of the possibility of direct moral knowledge consists in his criticism of alternative views, some of which has been discussed above. He also gives us some clues as to why he thinks it impossible to argue to the maxims of the *Tao*. In *Surprised by Joy* he recounts an incident of some importance in his intellectual biography; the reading of Samuel Alexander's *Space, Time and Deity*. From Alexander he took the distinction between "enjoyment" and "contemplation" (*SJ*, p. 217). In his discussion Lewis is concerned with the distinction between enjoying and contemplating objects very much unlike moral truths, such as a table or a beloved woman. However, the point of the distinction may be of some help in understanding what Lewis has to say about moral knowledge.[34]

According to this distinction, to look at a table is to "enjoy" the act of seeing and to "contemplate" the table. If, however, one then studies optics and thinks about seeing, one would be "enjoying" the thought and "contemplating" the seeing (*SJ*, p. 217). More interesting is the case of loving a woman. Part of loving her is thinking of or attending to her. Apart from that, the experience of 'loving the woman' cannot take place. In order to enjoy the experience of loving the woman one must contemplate the woman herself. If, however, I begin to attend not to the woman but to my love—my inner state—I will no longer be experiencing love for the woman. "In other words the enjoyment and contemplation of inner activities are incompatible" (*SJ*, p. 218). To analyze certain experiences is to stop having the experience itself. If the lover tries to introspect and look at what he is experiencing, he will find not the experience of loving the woman but only some mental images and physical sensations. It is an error to confuse these with the activity of

[34]For a helpful discussion of this aspect of Lewis' thought, see Scott Oury, *The Value of Something Other: A Study of C. S. Lewis's Attention to 'The Object Itself'* (Fairleigh Dickinson University: Unpublished M.A. Thesis, 1970).

loving the woman, but that is what one committed to such a procedure of analysis might be tempted to do. By contemplating one's inner state rather than the woman, the enjoyment of the experience is effectively stopped (*SJ*, p. 218).

What Lewis gives us, in effect, is the distinction between having an experience and thinking about that experience. A similar line of thought is developed in his essay "Transposition." There he considers the way in which experiences in our emotional life can be transposed into the life of our sensations. If, as he believes, our emotional life is richer and more varied than our sensations, such transposition will be analogous to the attempt to translate from a language with a large vocabulary into one with a smaller vocabulary: several words will have to be used in more than one sense (*WG*, pp. 20–21). Similarly, if we were to inspect our sensations (flutters in the stomach, tenseness, etc.), there might be little to distinguish love from lust. That does not, however, prove that there is no distinction between the experience of loving a woman and that of lusting after her (*WG*, p. 25). But it does mean, Lewis wants to say, that we can never understand what is going on in the lower medium unless we have experienced the higher. "The brutal man never can by analysis find anything but lust in love. . . . It is no good browbeating the critic who approaches a Transposition from below. On the evidence available to him his conclusion is the only one possible" (*WG*, p. 25).

Similarly, to the external observer—or one who insists on *adopting the viewpoint* of an external observer—there will be no way to find genuine moral knowledge in our experience. It will be like the brutal man trying to understand love. Such a person can rightly claim, from his perspective, to have seen all the facts.

He is, therefore, as regards the matter in hand, in the position of an animal. You will have noticed that most dogs cannot understand *pointing*. You point to a bit of food on the floor: the dog, instead of looking at the floor, sniffs at your finger. A finger is a finger to him, and that is all. His world is all fact and no meaning. And in a period when factual realism is dominant we shall find people deliberately inducing upon themselves this doglike mind. A man who has experienced love from within will deliberately go about to inspect it analytically from outside and regard the results of this analysis as truer than his experience. (*WG*, p. 28)

Although Lewis does not apply this distinction to his discussion of the *Tao*, it helps us to understand what he means when he says that knowledge of the *Tao*'s maxims is self-evident. Those who will not view the matter from within (or, as in transpositions, from above) cannot be convinced of any objective moral values. This also helps us to see why moral education is essential to proper moral understanding. Direct moral exhortation will accomplish little. Addressed to those who do not share belief in the *Tao*, it must fail. Addressed to those who do, it is superfluous. "Only those who are practising the *Tao* will understand it. It is the well-nurtured man, the *cuor gentil*, and he alone, who can recognize Reason when it comes" (*AM*, p. 61). The brutal man who cannot distinguish between love and lust is brutal because he is lacking an essential human response. Similarly, one who thinks the maxims of the *Tao* must be proved has been deprived of his full humanity.

Having said this, we must note what may be an internal difficulty in Lewis' views about the nature of morality. Moral knowledge is, he insists, knowledge of reality—of what is natural for man—even though this knowledge is not available to one who adopts the posture of an external observer of human activity and systematically excludes his own moral experience. However, even if we were to grant the validity of that claim, we might want to ask whether we can be very optimistic about the possibility of human beings attaining such knowledge. And especially when we consider Lewis' Augustinian roots, we may want to ask whether in his discussion of the possibility of moral knowledge he takes seriously enough the corrupting power of self-love.

What we need to ask, in other words, is whether one who is controlled by *cupiditas* can accurately discern reality. Iris Murdoch has stated the issue well:

> By opening our eyes we do not necessarily see what confronts
> us. We are anxiety-ridden animals. Our minds are continually
> active, fabricating an anxious, usually self-preoccupied, often
> falsifying *veil* which partially conceals the world. . . .[35]

As a consequence, Murdoch suggests, the chief enemy in
the moral life is the "fat relentless ego," and the task of
perceiving reality involves at the same time "a suppression
of self."[36] She suggests, therefore, that moralists ought to
discuss this ego and the techniques for its suppression. If
one agrees—as Lewis, to some extent, surely would—with
Murdoch's judgment that the "fat relentless ego" distorts
our perception of reality, one's optimism about the possibility of moral knowledge might be tempered. Further, the
way would be open even to more far-reaching claims
(which neither Murdoch nor Lewis makes) to the effect that
only one controlled by *caritas* rather than *cupiditas* could
attain such moral knowledge. This would, in turn, imply a
position about the relation between religion and morality
different from that espoused by Lewis.

Yet, even if the roots of Lewis' understanding of morality
are more Aristotelian than Augustinian (and, hence, in some
tension with his vision of community), he is not by any
means oblivious to the problem Murdoch raises. In fact, he
lays great emphasis upon one element in the Aristotelian
tradition which is designed to deal precisely with this problem: the element of moral education. Every impulse in our
nature is to be bridled, controlled, and guided. Hence, it
would not be true to suggest that Lewis' understanding of
morality is simply intellectualistic. He can, for example,
write that

> no justification of virtue will enable a man to be virtuous.
> Without the aid of trained emotions the intellect is powerless
> against the animal organism. I had sooner play cards against a
> man who was quite skeptical about ethics, but bred to believe
> that "a gentleman does not cheat," than against an irreproach-
> able moral philosopher who had been brought up among
> sharpers. (*AM*, pp. 33–34)

[35]Iris Murdoch, *The Sovereignty of Good* (London: Routledge &
Kegan Paul, 1970), p. 84.
[36]*Ibid.*, pp. 52, 66.

A right response to the problems of life is not something automatically present in our nature. On the contrary, it involves "a delicate balance of trained habits, laboriously acquired and easily lost."[37]

By inculcating right response, moral education will play an important role in enabling people to act in accord with the maxims of moral knowledge. But Murdoch's suggestion went further than this. She suggested that the intellectual discernment (not just the ability to act in accord with what is discerned) depends on suppression of self-regarding impulses; and it is true that Lewis never seems certain which side of this distinction to opt for. Sometimes (as in the passage about playing cards) intellect and emotion are kept separate. From that perspective moral education enables a man to do what his intellect perceives as right to do. Lewis' tendency to assume sometimes that the primeval moral platitudes will be widely and easily known fits this view also. However, the other view—according to which trained emotions are necessary not only to do but also to know the good—is equally present in Lewis. He says that only the well-nurtured youth can recognize the first principles of ethics upon reaching the age for reflective thought (*AM*, p. 26). Perhaps, then, it would be wrong to think that Lewis' view of human possibilities is overly optimistic. We must, at any rate, permit the serious concern for moral education to qualify the seemingly more optimistic passages about merely seeing moral truths.

Up to this point we have been trying to understand what Lewis means by saying (1) that no practical conclusion (about what we ought morally to do) can be derived from propositions about fact alone, while also maintaining (2) that we do have objective moral knowledge. He holds that moral judgments are not reducible to any kind of nonmoral judgments; yet, they can be true or false. It would not be completely inaccurate to say that Lewis has drawn his distinctions in such a way that he can hold to a kind of natural law theory while at the same time rejecting ethical naturalism.

[37]*A Preface to Paradise Lost*, p. 56.

What we need to consider now is another, and different, option. It could be claimed that Lewis has not gone far enough. He sees, one might say, that moral judgments will not arise from study of the facts alone. But, having seen that, he goes to great lengths to explain how moral *knowledge* is nevertheless possible—how it is possible to have knowledge of human nature against which to measure the truth or falsity of moral judgments. Why not simply acknowledge that moral principles are a matter for decision rather than discovery? Instead of committing us to a difficult thesis about "seeing" truths about human nature, why not recognize that we must decide for ourselves what man is to be? In other words, why not admit that it is misleading to talk about moral knowledge as if moral judgments were capable of being true or false?

Lewis recognizes this as a possible position and one which is not in any way self-contradictory. Nevertheless, he rejects it. It may help us to understand Lewis if we contrast his view with that of R. M. Hare, perhaps the leading contemporary exponent of the view that moral principles are a matter of decision rather than discovery.[38] Hare understands moral principles to be action-guides which we decide upon and which we use to prescribe what ought to be done. He maintains, however, that there are rational constraints upon the action-guides one can espouse (or, perhaps better, upon how one can espouse an action-guide). These constraints flow out of his requirement that we be willing to universalize our chosen action-guides. That is, in making our moral decisions we do not merely prescribe a course of conduct for ourselves. We prescribe universally; we prescribe this course of conduct for anyone similarly situated.[39] Hare's claim that moral language is prescriptive

[38]I will make use of Hare's discussion in *Freedom and Reason* (Oxford, 1965). I must add, of course, that the brief discussion here cannot possibly do justice to Hare's full development of his position. Recognizing that, I have nevertheless decided to accept risks of distortion in order to illuminate certain aspects of Lewis' own thought.

[39]Hare regards the requirement of universalizability as a logical rather than a moral thesis (pp. 32–35). It tells us something about the correct use of language.

is part and parcel of his case for saying that at least certain evaluative terms (good/bad; right/wrong), in their normal uses, do not describe at all. Hence, they are not used to impart truths about human nature. Rather, such language is used to give advice and guide conduct.[40] His further requirement that moral language be universalizable functions then to set certain constraints upon how we may prescribe.

This leads Hare to view moral discourse as a kind of exploration. When we engage in moral reasoning,

> what we are looking for ... is an action to which we can commit ourselves (prescriptivity) but which we are at the same time prepared to accept as exemplifying a principle of action to be prescribed for others in like circumstances (universalizability).[41]

Moral discourse is an attempt to choose action-guides and see whether we can consistently adhere to them. One of the most important ways in which we make this determination is by testing action-guides against our inclinations. Suppose, for example, that person A is owed a sum of money by person B. Now, A might decide that he ought to have B prosecuted if the debt is not paid. That judgment, however, must be universalized. That is, if A wants to adhere to that action-guide he must also be willing to say that he ought to be prosecuted if the situations were reversed and he were

[40]It may be worthwhile to note a way in which Lewis agrees with Hare. He recognizes that at least some evaluative words (what Hare calls "primarily evaluative terms") are used to commend or condemn, and that what Hare calls "secondarily evaluative terms" serve to make our commendations or condemnations more precise. Thus, for example, he writes: "The ultimate, simplest and most abstract [of pejorative words] is *bad* itself. The only good purpose for ever departing from that monosyllable when we condemn anything is to be more specific, to answer the question 'Bad in what way?' Pejorative words are rightly used only when they do this" (*SW*, p. 228). Whether Lewis, like Hare, would consider such use a part of the word's meaning is more doubtful. I think it unlikely, though he does distinguish what he calls a word's meaning from the speaker's meaning (*SW*, pp. 14–17, 103). Lewis has a short but interesting discussion of the way in which the word 'gentleman' began as a purely descriptive term and came to be an evaluative one—so that to call a man a 'gentleman' was no longer to give information about him but simply to praise him (*MC*, pp. ix, x).
[41]Hare, pp. 89f. See also p. 193.

the debtor. He may, therefore, decide to give up the action-guide once he sees what universalizability would entail. If he does give up the principle, we can interpret his action as a statement of what he cannot accept, "his inclinations being what they are."[42] The sense in which moral discourse is seen here as a kind of exploration should be clear. The moral explorer is seeking to determine what principles he can consistently espouse, given the wants and desires which he has.

To view Lewis' position against this background may prove instructive. One of his major objections to any such view must surely be that it cannot make room for moral education as he understands it. We have on several occasions noted his belief that morality is centrally concerned with the development of appropriate emotional responses. We can consider, for example, the case of a man contemplating infidelity to his wife. We can suppose that, for whatever reasons, he is inclined to prefer the pleasures of secret romance to those of lifelong fidelity to the same woman. He desires intense (even if passing) erotic pleasure more than he does a lifelong commitment to mutual support and companionship. Such a man might be quite willing to permit what universalizability requires; namely, that anyone similarly situated (even if it should be his own wife contemplating infidelity to him) would be justified in taking the course of action he prefers. That is a reasonable conclusion for him to draw, "his inclinations being what they are." However, those who speak from within the *Tao* may hold that such a desire should be controlled and that the achievement of such control is part of the function of moral education. The attainment of ethical understanding and the practice of it always means for Lewis the control of some of our self-regarding impulses—quite the opposite of the picture of the explorer considering what positions he can accept, "his inclinations being what they are."

Lewis also believes that a view which grounds moral principle in decision must inevitably misconceive the task

[42]*Ibid.*, p. 109.

of moral education. On the view he espouses, moral education constitutes a kind of initiation: "men transmitting manhood to men" (*AM*, p. 33). The teachers are, in other words,
initiating the young into a view of human nature from
which they themselves claim no liberty to depart (*AM*,
p. 74). The alternative, Lewis thinks, is to regard moral
education not as initiation but as conditioning. One must
either try to inculcate no moral principles at all or he must
inculcate precepts based upon his own decisions of principle but not upon those of the pupil (*AM*, p. 31). One may
still try to instill principles which will be in the interest of
the child and of use to him (and possibly society). Nevertheless, such conditioning for survival, however beneficial, is
not the same as initiation into humanity.

Hare's understanding of moral discourse as a kind of
exploration is his attempt to deal with an antinomy which
he thinks is "the source of nearly all the central controversies of moral philosophy."[43] The antinomy is this: On the
one hand, we think ourselves free to form our own moral
opinions. (Even the *Tao*, Hare might say, must be acknowledged.) On the other hand, we do not want to concede that
the process of forming those moral opinions is mere caprice.
We want to view it as a rational activity. To do justice to both
sides of this antinomy is not easy. One may seriously question whether Hare's view, according to which moral judgments are self-imposed, successfully maintains the rational
character of moral discourse.[44] By the same token, however,
the question to ask of Lewis is whether he purchases objectivity of moral judgments at the price of a loss of the moral
agent's autonomy.

The key to understanding Lewis' answer to such a query
lies in remembering the different senses of the word
'natural' which he isolates. There is no doubt in Lewis'
mind that we not only think ourselves free to form our moral
opinions but, in one sense, are free to do just that. However,
our 'nature' can mean something other than what we do. It

[43]*Ibid.*, p. 3.
[44]Graber, "A Critical Bibliography . . . ," p. 65. Cf. also W. D. Hudson,
Modern Moral Philosophy (Garden City, N.Y.: Doubleday, 1970), pp. 208f.

can mean what is natural to a human being (to a being of that kind) as opposed to what is unnatural. Lewis wants to say: Though we can refuse to accept the maxims of the *Tao* as binding upon us, in so doing we turn against our nature and deprive ourselves of (at least some part of) our humanity. In other words, a person is more than his freedom. This is what Lewis means by writing that those who—standing outside the *Tao*—cannot initiate others into humanity are "men who have sacrificed their own share in traditional humanity in order to devote themselves to the task of deciding what 'Humanity' shall henceforth mean" (*AM*, p. 76). It is logically possible to use our freedom in this way, but it is (so to speak) ontologically disastrous. It is, in fact, the abolition of man. If the *Tao* is the reality within which human life must be lived, it is destructive of one's humanity to claim autonomy over against its maxims. It is, in fact, *self*-destructive. The picture of an intact and whole moral agent deciding what principles to adopt must be given up. The person who tries to stand outside the *Tao* is not whole; his humanity has been shattered by his refusal to see it in any terms but freedom. The resolution of the antinomy does not require an exploration to determine what principles an autonomous agent can accept. Rather, it involves dying to any inclination or impulse which might tempt one to reject the *Tao*—dying, that is, to these impulses so that a free obedience can become possible.

Lewis can envisage a state in which the antinomy between freedom and reason is transcended. If we were truly filled with love, we would with the psalmist delight in the law. But what we find in our present state is that activity in conformity with the *Tao is* impeded. The consequences are three: First, we must still carry out the precepts of the moral law, since "not to practice them is to abandon our humanity."[45] But, second, we cannot do them with spontaneous delight. Hence, third, the category of duty arises. Implicit in the maxims of morality, therefore, is a further command: "You must be born again."[46] The category of duty arises

[45]*Letters to Malcolm*, p. 115.
[46]*Ibid.*

because we are estranged from our nature. To be fully human, therefore, would be to will freely what reason discerns as appropriate for a human being. Virtue must become a passion, as it does for John in *The Pilgrim's Regress*.[47]

What has been said about moral education up to this point may be somewhat deceptive. It might appear as if Lewis recommends adding one more subject to the curriculum. Along with history and literature and physics we might also teach something called 'moral education.' This, in turn, conjures up images of pupils sitting at desks while teachers try to inculate principles of morality, and that is probably either impossible, laughable, or boring.

Something like this does indeed happen sometimes, but it is not what Lewis had in mind. In order to understand Lewis' viewpoint, it is worth thinking about one such attempt to teach morality which goes by the name of "values-clarification."[48] A student might, for example, be confronted with questions such as these:

(1) Under what circumstances would you try to pass a toll machine without paying the fee?
　　(a) Only if I was certain that I would not be caught.
　　(b) If I felt I had a good chance of not being caught.
　　(c) Never, under any circumstances.
　　(d) Only if I needed the money desperately, like for family food supplies.
(2) Write down 20 things you love to do. . . . Now that you have all made your lists, state the five things you love to do best of all.... Check the things you love to do alone.... X the things you love to do with other people.... Underline the things that cost less than $3 to do.

The purpose of such an approach to moral education is to make the student aware of what he values. It is not to instill any particular values but to help the student discover

---

[47]My treatment of Lewis' resolution of the antinomy between freedom and reason has been influenced by Glenn Graber's explication and discussion of what seems to be a similar problem in Tillich's thought. Cf. his article, "The Meta-ethics of Paul Tillich," *The Journal of Religious Ethics*, 1 (1973), pp. 113–33, esp. p. 122.

[48]I rely for my examples on Amitai Etzioni, "Do as I say, not as I do," *The New York Times Magazine* (September 26, 1976), 44ff.

the ones he already has. So any and all answers are right—
so long as one is ready to give a reason for them. What we
have here are examples of Hare's moral explorers at work.
We can understand why such an approach to moral education might become popular in a pluralistic society. It permits us to believe that we are improving the moral tone of
our society without destroying the freedom and autonomy
of moral agents.

Whatever may be the benefits of such an approach, this
is not what Lewis means by moral education. Indeed, from
his perspective its basic approach is misguided; for it fails
to suggest that some exercises of our freedom to choose,
though logically possible, would be ontologically disastrous. It encourages the picture of the person as moral
explorer, standing outside the realm of values and then
deciding the terms upon which he will enter it. It is not that
the approach is "relativistic," as a concerned parent might
argue before the school board. It is, rather, that it has not yet
risen to the level of moral education at all. The student is
being asked only to express and explore his inclinations and
desires—not to control, discipline, and shape them.

Moral education which interests Lewis does not look
much like teaching. One cannot have classes in it. It involves the inculcation of proper emotional responses and is
as much a "knowing how" as a "knowing that." It cannot be
taught by listening to a lecture or filling out a worksheet.
The picture we get when we think of "knowing how" is the
apprentice working with the master. And inculcation of
right emotional responses will take place only if the youth
has around him examples of men and women for whom
such responses have become natural—persons whose vision of human nature is shaped in accordance with the *Tao*.
The pursuit of the moral life is not an isolated pursuit.
Lewis, like Aristotle, believes that moral principles are
learned indirectly from others around us, who serve as
exemplars. And he, again like Aristotle, suggests that it will
be extremely difficult to develop virtuous individuals apart
from a virtuous society.

This is also the clue to understanding the place of the

Chronicles of Narnia within Lewis' thought. They are not just good stories. Neither are they primarily Christian allegories (in fact, they are not allegories at all). Rather, they serve to enhance moral education, to build character. They teach, albeit indirectly, and provide us with exemplars from whom we learn proper emotional responses. We can think once more of one of the principles of the *Tao*, the law of magnanimity, willingness to expend oneself in a good cause. This is, after all, what that Roman father was appealing to when he tried to teach his son that it was a sweet and seemly think to die for one's country. It is, Lewis thinks, a message best communicated indirectly: through the father's own example, and also through the stories read to his son. The father's message may well be communicated through a story like *The Last Battle*. There, in a passage cited at the outset of this chapter, Roonwit the Centaur, while dying, sends a message to King Tirian telling him "to remember that all worlds draw to an end and that noble death is a treasure which no one is too poor to buy" (p. 86). To overlook the function of the Chronicles of Narnia in communicating images of proper emotional responses is to miss their connection to Lewis' moral thought.

In the second chapter we discussed the reality principle which informs Lewis' vision of community—the principle that human beings are made for fellowship with God and one another and can only achieve the fruition of their nature in such fellowship. We can close our discussion of Lewis' understanding of morality by making a similar move. To see by means of but not to see through the *Tao;* to act within the limitations it imposes, is part of what it means to be human. For Lewis, the *Tao* is "the concrete reality in which to participate is to be truly human" (*AM*, p. 86). Lewis' understanding of morality is more than an argument; it too involves a vision of human nature. It is instructive to remember the last chapter of *The Discarded Image*. There, having described in previous chapters some of the salient features of the Medieval Model of man and the universe, Lewis concludes that all such models ought to be respected and none idolized.

> No Model is a catalogue of ultimate realities, and none is a mere fantasy. Each is a serious attempt to get in all the phenomena known at a given period, and each succeeds in getting a great many. But also, no less surely, each reflects the prevalent psychology of an age almost as much as it reflects the state of that age's knowledge. Hardly any battery of new facts could have persuaded a Greek that the universe had an attribute so repugnant to him as infinity; hardly any such battery could persuade a modern that it is hierarchical. (p. 222)

This cast of Lewis' mind has been implicit in the entire course of our discussion. Of arguments he presents plenty, and he is not in any sense hesitant to defend views he deems correct. But at several key places we have seen him admit the lack of any logically compelling evidence. He grants that one can, for example, divest the world of any values by analyzing human nature from the perspective of an external observer rather than that of the moral agent. There is no compelling argument that this should not be done, just as there is no way to convince the brutal man of the difference between lust and love. Similarly, one can view man simply relative to his freedom; as "an isolated principle of will."[49] But not from within the *Tao*. For Lewis, therefore, the primeval moral platitudes circumscribe and help to define what it means to be human. They characterize the human reality—applying, as they do, to all persons: past, present, and future. And that, in his view, is what morality is about: "men transmitting manhood to men" (*AM*, p. 33).

NORMATIVE ETHICS

At one point Lewis summarizes, simply and briefly, three aspects of morality. It is, he says, concerned with (1) fair play and harmony between individuals (which involves what he elsewhere calls the maxims of the *Tao*); (2) harmonizing and controlling the inner life of the individual; and (3) the general purpose of human life as a whole (*MC*, p. 57). He provides a homely illustration of the point.

[49]The phrase is Murdoch's in *The Sovereignty of Good*, p. 48.

You can get the idea if you think of us as a fleet of ships sailing in formation. The voyage will be a success only, in the first place, if the ships do not collide and get in one another's way, and, secondly, if each ship is seaworthy and has her engines in good order. As a matter of fact, you cannot have either of these two things without the other. . . .

But there is one thing we have not yet taken into account. We have not asked where the fleet is trying to get to. . . . And however well the fleet sailed, its voyage would be a failure if it were meant to reach New York and actually arrived at Calcutta. (*MC*, pp. 56f.)

The third of these aspects will relate most clearly to our discussion of the relation between religion and morality. The first two will be our concern here.

The second aspect—harmonizing the inner life of the individual—might equally well be called the development of virtuous habits. Nowhere does Lewis provide an extended discussion of a morality of virtue; yet, it is a matter of concern to him. This indeed is what moral education involves for Lewis: not simply inculcation of principles but, more centrally, development of appropriate emotional responses (*AM*, p. 31). Furthermore, there seems little doubt that Lewis' work in several genres is intended at least partially to provide such moral education. It is quite true to say that central Christian doctrines are embedded in the Chronicles of Narnia, but it is at least as true to say that the delineation of character (in figures such as Lucy, Edmund, Reepicheep, Puddleglum) may serve to mold and shape virtuous habits of behavior in the sympathetic reader. If we are concerned to become people of a certain kind, it will not be sufficient to concern ourselves with basic principles of morality. Shaping of character will be even more fundamental.

There is a difference between doing some particular just or temperate action and being a just or temperate man. Someone who is not a good tennis player may now and then make a good shot. What you mean by a good player is the man whose eye and muscles and nerves have been so trained by making innumerable good shots that they can now be relied on. They have a certain tone or quality which is there even when he is not playing. . . . In the same way a man who perseveres in doing just actions gets in the end a certain quality of character. Now it is the quality rather than the particular actions which we mean when we talk of "virtue." (*MC*, pp. 62f.)

Lewis also uses the picture of an ugly person wearing a beautiful mask for years, finally removing the mask, and finding that his face has grown to fit the mask—that the disguise has become a reality (*MC*, p. 146). Whether it is wise to talk about the development of virtue in terms of disguise or pretense might be questioned, but Lewis' point becomes clearer in a passage from *Surprised by Joy*. There he recounts how he came to know a young man (whom he calls 'Johnson') in his battalion in the army. Common intellectual interests drew them together, but what most impressed him was the fact that Johnson was a man of conscience. Lewis felt deeply inferior.

> There was no discussion between us on the point and I do not think he ever suspected the truth about me. I was at no pains to display it. If this is hypocrisy, then I must conclude that hypocrisy can do a man good. To be ashamed of what you were about to say, to pretend that something which you had meant seriously was only a joke—this is an ignoble part. But it is better than not to be ashamed at all. And the distinction between pretending you are better than you are and beginning to be better in reality is finer than moral sleuthhounds conceive. (*SJ*, p. 192)

Lewis consistently maintains that the appetites and emotions must be controlled and molded if virtuous habits of action are to be instilled in a person. And this must take place over a period of time.

Despite his belief in the importance of moral education in the formation of goodness of character, Lewis does not present any detailed theory of the virtues. He does, however, express one interesting opinion. Lewis believes that no other virtue will survive (except, perhaps, accidentally) unless the virtue of courage is also present. He comments at one place after a very brief discussion of the cardinal virtues that "you cannot practise any of the other virtues very long without bringing this one into play" (*MC*, p. 62). Screwtape counsels Wormwood that

> courage is not simply *one* of the virtues, but the form of every virtue at the testing point, which means, at the point of highest reality. A chastity or honesty or mercy which yields to danger will be chaste or honest or merciful only on conditions. Pilate was merciful till it became risky. (*SL*, pp. 137–38)

This is interesting when we ask ourselves to what degree Lewis' ethic should be characterized as "intellectualistic." His belief that courage is the form of every virtue at the testing point is an important element in the total picture. Courage involves a willingness to face danger and endure pain, either of which will often involve a suppression of impulses which are purely self-regarding. Even an intellectual virtue such as prudence will require courage if it is to endure. Here again moral discernment is not isolated from the will and emotions, and in our total assessment of Lewis' position we ought not forget the important place he assigns to courage.

If one thinks of the Chronicles of Narnia as an opportunity for schooling in virtue, it becomes clear that at least two figures—Lucy and Reepicheep—demonstrate character in which courageous action has taken on the steady character of a habit.[50] Reepicheep's character makes clear that even if courage is the form of every virtue at the testing point, it is not the whole of virtue. It may be that courage must always be present if another virtue such as prudence or humility is to be consistently displayed in a person's life. That does not mean, however, that nothing more than courage need be present. Evidently each of the virtues has its own objective end. Courage does not enter into the definition of the other virtues; rather, it is necessary to sustain them. Reepicheep is not always prudent, nor is he always humble. The delineation of his character indicates that, even if courage is necessary to sustain the other virtues, there are other ways besides courage in which goodness of character will manifest itself.

To return to Lewis' analogy: The internal workings of

---

[50]Kathryn Lindskoog calls attention to Reepicheep as a personification of knightly valor in *The Lion of Judah in Never-Never Land* (Grand Rapids: Eerdmans, 1973), pp. 104–106.

the ships in the fleet must be in good repair if the voyage is to be successful. That was the second aspect of morality isolated by Lewis, and we have discussed it relative to his treatment of the virtues. The first aspect is equally important. The ships cannot collide and get in one another's way. In other words, certain principles concerning fairness and appropriate conduct will have to be generally accepted. For Lewis these principles are the maxims of the *Tao*, and we have already discussed the way in which he finds these normative principles embedded in the nature of morality itself.

Perhaps the most important feature of this aspect of Lewis' normative ethic is its non-utilitarian character. For Lewis, consideration of consequences—though an element in moral reflection—is by no means the most important factor. Indeed, what the maxims of the *Tao* lay down are ways in which no one's nature ought to be violated for the sake of future benefits alone. What is meant by the non-utilitarian character of Lewis' ethic is the fact that he does not want the primeval moral platitudes violated for the sake of the happiness of the human community or even for the sake of its survival. The rightness of an action is not a function of its consequences alone.

> I care far more how humanity lives than how long. Progress, for me, means increasing goodness and happiness of individual lives. For the species, as for each man, mere longevity seems to me a contemptible ideal.[51]

Thus, the happiness and survival of the community may be pursued, but not at all costs. There are controls placed upon the manner in which that pursuit can be carried out—controls dealing with mercy, justice, human dignity, and veracity.[52]

The scientist Weston in *Out of the Silent Planet* is an example of one who has abandoned such controls in his pursuit of the survival of the human species. He was willing to kidnap Ransom and offer him to be (as he supposed) a human sacrifice for the inhabitants of *Malacandra* if that

[51]*God in the Dock*, p. 311.
[52]*Ibid.*, p. 296.

was the price for the success of his endeavor. His commitment to the survival of mankind overrides the claims of any
particular individual upon him. His hope is that the human
race—however greatly it may have to be changed to make
this possible—will last forever (pp. 123, 138). The Oyarsa of
Malacandra is quite honestly puzzled by Weston's attitude.
He extracts from Weston the admission that he has no idea
what future forms of human life will be like. At one point
Ransom translates Weston's view as follows: "He wants the
creatures born from us to be in as many places as they can.
He says he does not know what kind of creatures they will
be" (p. 137). At another point Ransom can only translate
Weston as saying "that the only good thing is that there
should be very many creatures alive" (p. 136). This puzzles
the Oyarsa. Weston is attached neither to the human body
nor to the human mind; for he grants that these may be very
different in future generations. Nor is he attached to particular individuals, as his attitude toward Ransom
demonstrates.

> "Strange!" said Oyarsa. "You do not love any one of your
> race—you would have let me kill Ransom. You do not love the
> mind of your race, nor the body. Any kind of creature will
> please you if only it is begotten by your kind as they now are. It
> seems to me, Thick One, that what you really love is no com-
> pleted creature but the very seed itself; for that is all that is
> left." (p. 138)

Weston's character makes Lewis' point very clear, but we
may be tempted to think of it as applying to a rather extreme
case. We do well, therefore, to remember some of the
themes from the second chapter; in particular, the place of
animals. Lewis' condemnation of vivisection is a good illustration of his unwillingness to approve certain sorts of action even if their potential benefit to the human race is
great.

In *That Hideous Strength* Lewis turns to a related
theme, what we today might call "genetic engineering."

> The N.I.C.E. was the first-fruits of that constructive fusion
> between the state and the laboratory on which so many
> thoughtful people base their hopes of a better world. It was to

be free from almost all the tiresome restraints . . . which have
hitherto hampered research. . . . (p. 23)

In the course of the story Mark Studdock learns something
about the program the leaders of the N.I.C.E. have in mind.
They are ready to take the last and fatal step in the control
and shaping of nature. They are, that is, ready to view
human beings simply as natural objects. Man is to take
control of his destiny and reshape his nature. Some of the
leaders, at least, are clear about what this means, as one of
them says to Mark, "Man has got to take charge of Man. That
means, remember, that some men have got to take charge of
the rest . . ." (p. 42).

Lewis subtitled *That Hideous Strength* "A Modern
Fairy-Tale for Grown-Ups." In his preface, however, he
writes that the story has behind it a serious point which he
had tried to make in *The Abolition of Man*. And in *That
Hideous Strength* he makes exactly the same point: that
"the power of Man to make himself what he pleases means
. . . the power of some men to make other men what *they*
please" (*THS*, p. 72). Mark learns from Filostrato, the mad
clergyman, that the N.I.C.E. program involves the destruction of all organic life. After all, Filostrato implies, life
would be so much more rational that way. He expects a day
when artificial metal trees will replace the real ones. It
commends itself as a very rational procedure. If we tire of
the tree in one place, we simply get several workmen to
move it elsewhere. "It never dies. No leaves to fall, no
twigs, no birds building nests, no muck and mess" (p. 172).

Applied to man the theory is striking. "What are the
things that most offend the dignity of man? Birth and breeding and death" (*THS*, p. 174). Organic life has done its work
in producing mind; it can now, therefore, be eliminated.
Death will be conquered and reproduction will no longer
involve copulation. Mariann Russell has pointed out the
interesting fact that at Belbury the library is the center of
life while the kitchen is central at St. Anne's.[53] The program
of the N.I.C.E. aims at the extinction of all organic life. But

[53]In her unpublished dissertation, *The Idea of the City of God*, p. 162.

at St. Anne's, where a different vision of what is human prevails, the body is celebrated.

Perhaps, though, it is not quite correct to say simply that a different vision of what is *human* rules at Belbury. Lewis implies that this is not the case but, rather, that on the altar of mankind's future everything specifically *human* is to be sacrificed. And behind this effort lies an impulse which, though seemingly religious, is inhuman.

> The physical sciences, good and innocent in themselves, had already, even in Ransom's own time, begun to be warped, had been subtly manoeuvred in a certain direction. Despair of objective truth had been increasingly insinuated into the scientists; indifference to it, and a concentration upon mere power, had been the result. . . . Dreams of the far future destiny of man were dragging up from its shallow and unquiet grave the old dream of Man as God. The very experiences of the dissecting room and the pathological laboratory were breeding a conviction that the stifling of all deep-set repugnances was the first essential for progress. (*THS*, p. 203)

Lewis took his title *That Hideous Strength* from a line describing the tower of Babel in Sir David Lyndsay's *Ane Dialog:* "The Shadow of that hyddeous strength/sax myle and more it is of length." In refusing to accept the limitations inherent in our creaturely condition we may, Lewis implies, become less than human. We may find that we have achieved only the abolition of man.

Birth, breeding, and death—for Lewis these are abiding elements in our nature. Man is not an isolated principle of will. Though he is free to destroy these fundamental structures of human life, he is not free to remain human while doing so. What is at issue involves different understandings of rationality. Thus, for example, a recent writer on genetic control who states that he will take as his ideal "what is humane and rational" can also write: "Our notion of avarice may have to be broadened to condemn the *selfishness* of keeping our sperm and ova to ourselves exclusively."[54] Lewis takes such views seriously, seriously enough to op-

---

[54]Joseph Fletcher, *The Ethics of Genetic Control: Ending Reproductive Roulette* (Garden City, N.Y.: Doubleday, 1974), pp. xix, xiv.

pose them as fundamentally *in*humane and *ir*rational. Our goal ought not be, he thinks, to do something rational to the abiding elements of our nature. Any ideal of a better, more efficient existence which requires this is not for him an ideal of *human* existence. Instead, he counsels that we should learn to regard these structures as part of the mystery of what it means to be human.

> For the wise men of old the cardinal problem had been how to conform the soul to reality, and the solution had been knowledge, self-discipline, and virtue. For magic and applied science alike the problem is how to subdue reality to the wishes of men: the solution is a technique. . . . (*AM*, p. 88)

There may be a tendency to claim that this older view which Lewis espouses cannot be genuinely rational. Hence, attempts to alter the basic character of birth and breeding are seen as the product of rational investigation; while a claim that there may be knowledge of this sort which we do not want, though such a claim may strike some deep chord within us, will seem to many an attack on reason. But Lewis contends that if man is nothing more than his freedom to reshape himself; if his nature is merely to be an isolated principle of will, then there can be no *reason* to shape himself after one pattern rather than another. The view we think rational turns out, he suggests, to be precisely the opposite.

It should be evident that the basic reason for Lewis' anti-utilitarian position is deeply embedded in his ethic and is non-theological in character: The maxims of the *Tao* are expressions of truths about human nature. They express ways in which the dignity of any human being ought not be violated. Within the total context of Lewis' thought, however, there are several other reasons—more theological in character—which support this unwillingness to make consideration of consequences the determinative factor in our moral assessments. These other reasons seem to grow out of his understanding of Christian teaching about creation and eschatology.

Screwtape provides Wormwood (and us) with some insight into what it means to be a creature. The Enemy's wish for his creatures, Screwtape writes, is that they be con-

cerned either with the Present or with Eternity — with the
Enemy himself (*SL,* pp. 67f.). His desire is that they either
be directing their attention to him "or else obeying the
present voice of conscience, bearing the present cross, receiving the present grace, giving thanks for the present
pleasure" (*SL,* p. 68). To be a creature, therefore, is to be
responsible to the Creator and responsible for one's activity
in the present moment. (Lewis is careful to point out that
some present activity may legitimately concern itself with
planning for the future. We are not, in his opinion, required
to ignore future consequences.) Since it is the business of
Wormwood to bring his patient to act as if he were the
Creator rather than a creature, Screwtape recommends that
Wormwood focus the patient's attention elsewhere than on
the Eternal One or the present duty. To achieve this, Screwtape recommends that Wormwood inspire his patient to
concentrate on the Future. Nearly all vices, he writes, are
rooted in that attitude. "Gratitude looks to the Past and love
to the Present; fear, avarice, lust, and ambition look ahead"
(*SL,* p. 69). Thus, writes Screwtape,

> we want a man hagridden by the Future—haunted by visions
> of an imminent heaven or hell upon earth—ready to break the
> Enemy's commands in the Present if by so doing we make him
> think he can attain the one or avert the other—dependent for
> his faith on the success or failure of schemes whose end he will
> not live to see. We want a whole race perpetually in pursuit of
> the rainbow's end, never honest, nor kind, nor happy *now,* but
> always using as mere fuel wherewith to heap the altar of the
> Future every real gift which is offered them in the Present.
> (*SL,* pp. 69f.)

A creature, Lewis is implying, does not plan the drama of
human history. He acts the part given him, his present duty.

Human existence is limited not only in its beginning but
also in its ending. Lewis believes that the doctrine of a
second coming of Christ and a final judgment—of an end to
the world and human society as we know it—must have an
effect on what we think it right to do. As Weston explains to
the Oyarsa his plan for human life to hop from a dying world
to a younger one and thence to another, he meets just this
objection.

"But do you not know that all worlds will die?"
"Men go jump off each before it deads—on and on, see?"
"And when all are dead?" (p. 139)

Human life is, for Lewis, like a drama in which we are
characters who do not know the plot. We do not even know
who are the major and minor characters, nor do we know
whether we are in Act I or Act V. "The playing it well is
what matters infinitely."[55] Lewis provides an example
taken from a drama.

> In *King Lear* (III:vii) there is a man who is such a minor
> character that Shakespeare has not given him even a name: he
> is merely 'First Servant.' All the characters around him—
> Regan, Cornwall, and Edmund—have fine long-term plans.
> They think they know how the story is going to end, and they
> are quite wrong. The servant has no such delusions. He has no
> notion how the play is going to go. But he understands the
> present scene. He sees an abomination (the blinding of Old
> Gloucester) taking place. He will not stand it. His sword is out
> and pointed at his master's breast in a moment: Then Regan
> stabs him dead from behind. This is his whole part: eight lines
> all told. But if it were real life and not a play, that is the part it
> would be best to have acted.[56]

The limits at both ends of man's existence are there to

---

[55]"The World's Last Night," *The World's Last Night . . .* , p. 106. There
are Augustinian overtones to this view, but they should not be pressed,
since Lewis does not commit himself to Augustine's understanding of
predestination. Nevertheless, it is interesting to note a statement like the
following from Charles Moorman's *The Precincts of Felicity* (p. 9): "St.
Augustine's theory of predestination thus makes of history a cosmic *drama*
conceived and executed by God about a central theme—the Fall and
Redemption of Man. This great *drama,* moreover, was composed before
the creation of man, and man's function in the scheme of things is simply to
play his part as it is assigned to him" (italics added). Gunnar Urang, who
prefers a process theology stressing openness to the future, has criticized
Lewis on these grounds in *Shadows of Heaven* (p. 161): "We are not
willing to say that we are simply *in* a tale, even one told by a loving
all-powerful God. We do not simply choose whether or not to play our
appointed parts in a story already composed; we are helping to *invent* the
incidents and the plot." Both writers perhaps miss the point that Lewis'
concept of human beings as participants in a cosmic drama is not actually
grounded in a doctrine of predestination (though, of course, one could be
implied). He normally uses the analogy when discussing creation and
eschatology.
[56]*Ibid.,* pp. 104f.

remind him of what it means to live as a creature and to guard against a deification of the human agent in matters of morality.

Lest he seem to be counseling a disregard for posterity, Lewis points to another aspect of this same theological dogma. According to Christian teaching, "the world's last night" will not only be an end but also a judgment. Happy are those who are found laboring in their vocations—and, as Lewis recognizes, some vocations may entail a good bit of planning for the future. However, the rightness of one's action cannot simply be entrusted to the future. To face not only one's end but also one's judgment in such a moment might be precarious. What is permitted, though, is "sober work for the future, within the limits of ordinary morality and prudence."[57]

It must be remembered that a utilitarian ethic does at least provide a principle—however difficult its application may be—which is intended to offer some way of resolving conflicts among duties. Lewis' ethic, consisting as it does of a number of principles which can conflict with one another, seems to offer little hope in this regard. A common way of trying to solve this difficulty would be to establish priority rules so that in cases of conflict one could decide which maxims of the *Tao* were more fundamental. However, Lewis makes no serious attempt to do this. He does believe that some duties are more fundamental (for example, that the demands of justice are more fundamental than the claims of kinship), and he recognizes that one way of resolving such conflicts is to show that one "precept in question conflicts with some precept which its defenders allow to be more fundamental" (*AM*, p. 60). But he makes no rigorous attempt to establish such priority rules; that is, Lewis shows little concern to demonstrate that there are any exceptionless moral rules (which is not, of course, to say that he thinks there are none).

Here also we could say that Lewis remains faithful to Aristotle, who seems to have been the chief influence on

[57]*Ibid.*, p. 111.

Lewis' understanding of morality and his normative ethic.[58] He is at pains to make clear that he does not think his defense of "traditional morality" will provide an answer to every particular moral problem we face. Indeed, moral codes create rather than solve many moral problems.

> Obviously it is moral codes that create questions of casuistry, just as the rules of chess create problems. The man without a moral code, like the animal, is free from moral problems. The man who has not learned to count is free from mathematical problems. A man asleep is free from all problems. Within the framework of general human ethics problems will, of course, arise and will sometimes be solved wrongly. This possibility of error is simply the symptom that we are awake, not asleep, that we are men, not beasts or gods.[59]

Thus, like Aristotle, he seeks no more certainty than ethics allows and seems quite content to recognize the limits of his *own* normative ethic.

It remains true that none of the principles of the *Tao* can simply be discarded, and if they cannot, we might ask whether any real development could ever take place in our moral understanding. Lewis thinks that no radically new judgment of value is possible, but he also thinks that one

[58]Corbin Carnell reports Lewis' answer to him when Carnell had written Lewis to inquire about the influence of Aquinas on his thought: "In answer to those who have read his books as modern restatements of Aquinas, Lewis says that the appearance of a strong Thomist influence is really due to the fact that he has often (especially on ethics) followed Aristotle where Aquinas also followed Aristotle. 'Aquinas,' he says, 'and I were, in fact, at the same school—I don't say in the same class! And I had read the *Ethics* long before I ever worked at the *Summa*' " (*Bright Shadow of Reality*, pp. 70–71).

[59]"On Ethics," *Christian Reflections*, p. 56. If we try to characterize Lewis' normative ethic relative to the options considered today by moral philosophers, we might call him an act deontologist. That he is—if the choice is made this simple—a deontologist rather than a utilitarian is clear: he does not think that the rightness of an action is a function of its consequences alone. Whether he is an *act* deontologist—one who believes that the right act in any situation cannot be determined by reference to any rule or set of rules—is less clear. Rarely does he concern himself with this problem. However, since Lewis does not altogether rule out considerations of consequences, one might label his view as (in Frankena's terms) a "mixed deontological theory" (cf. Frankena, *Ethics*, p. 35). Nevertheless, there can be little question that the major emphasis in Lewis' ethic does not lie in considerations of utility.

who is sincerely practicing the *Tao* will find that it admits of "development from within" (*AM*, p. 58). He recognizes that there will be great differences among the many traditional moralities from which he draws his conception of the primeval moral platitudes. To illustrate his conception of development from within he turns to another subject about which he knows a great deal.

> A theorist about language may approach his native tongue, as it were from outside, regarding its genius as a thing that has no claim on him and advocating wholesale alterations of its idiom and spelling in the interests of commercial convenience or scientific accuracy. That is one thing. A great poet, who has 'loved, and been well nurtured in, his mother tongue,' may also make great alterations in it, but his changes of the language are made in the spirit of the language itself: he works from within. The language which suffers, has also inspired, the changes. That is a different thing—as different as the works of Shakespeare are from Basic English. It is the difference between alteration from within and alteration from without: between the organic and the surgical. (*AM*, pp. 57–58)

Lewis recognizes that it will be "a matter of some delicacy" to decide which of these is taking place on some occasions. Nor is there any test to determine this except the test of seeing how the moral innovator approaches the precepts of the *Tao*. However, to challenge these precepts simply to produce their credentials will always be an unacceptable approach.

As an example of such moral advance, Lewis cites the difference between the Confucian "Do not do to others what you would not like them to do to you" and the Christian "Do as you would be done by" (*AM*, p. 58). He suggests that only a person who accepted the first maxim would see any reason to accept the second. However, in addition, if one who accepted the first wanted to reject the second, how would he do so? Not, says Lewis, by simply rejecting it but by claiming that it was superfluous (*AM*, p. 58).

In a sense, therefore, we return to the central importance of moral education in Lewis' normative ethic.

> From within the *Tao* itself comes the only authority to modify the *Tao*. This is what Confucius meant when he said, 'With

> those who follow a different Way it is useless to take counsel.'
> This is why Aristotle said that only those who have been well
> brought up can usefully study ethics. . . . (AM, p. 59)

To educate the youth in the primeval moral platitudes is to
lead him into his human inheritance. This heritage frees
him even as it binds him, for in binding him to a vision of
what it means to be human it frees him for the only kind of
moral development possible.

RELIGION AND MORALITY

In *The Problem of Pain* Lewis interprets religion as man's
experience of the numinous, an experience of dread and
awe before the uncanny. In such an instance one would feel

> wonder and a certain shrinking—a sense of inadequacy to cope
> with such a visitant and of prostration before it—an emotion
> which might be expressed in Shakespeare's words "Under it
> my genius is rebuked." (p. 17)

This, Lewis says, is different from the moral experience of a
claim upon one which is at once acknowledged but at the
same time disobeyed. It is possible to look upon the
Numinous Power as the guardian of morality, but it is not
necessary. "In many forms of Paganism the worship of the
gods and the ethical discussions of the philosophers have
very little to do with each other."[60] Hence, on these definitions morality can remain quite independent of religion. On
another occasion, however, Lewis incorporates moral
evaluations into his definition of religion. In the context he
is denying that religion is adequately described as belief in
God and immortality; however, he suggests that

> the essence of religion . . . is the thirst for an end higher than
> natural ends; the finite self's desire for, and acquiescence in,
> and self-rejection in favour of, an object wholly good and
> wholly good for it.[61]

[60]*PP*, p. 22. This is, in fact, the case in the kingdom of Glome, which
Lewis creates in *Till We Have Faces*. Part of Orual's struggle is to reconcile
the truth in the Fox's teaching with the truth in the teaching of the priest of
Ungit.

[61]*God in the Dock*, p. 131.

Our concern here is not to arrive at a suitable definition of religion against which no counterexamples can be produced, nor is it simply to pin an inconsistency on Lewis. Instead we should ask what these two definitions tell us about Lewis' view of the relation between religion and morality.

What they seem to indicate is this: that God understood as a Commander of moral rules is irrelevant for morality.[62] Lewis nowhere formulates a thesis in precisely those terms, but it accurately characterizes his view. There is a passage in *The Pilgrim's Regress* which nicely illustrates one of the reasons behind the irrelevance for morality of God as Commander. In the context John is conversing with Wisdom (a representative of philosophical idealism) about the rules the Landlord has made for the land. The question is, why should we keep them? And Wisdom says this:

> There can be only two reasons. Either because we respect the power of the Landlord, and are moved by fear of the penalties and hopes of the rewards with which he sanctions the rules: or else, because we freely agree with the Landlord, because we also think good the things that he thinks good. But neither explanation will serve. If we obey through hope and fear, in that very act we disobey: for the rule which we reverence most ... is that rule which says that a man must act disinterestedly. To obey the Landlord thus, would be to disobey. But what if we obey freely, because we agree with him? Alas, this is even worse. To say that we agree, and obey because we agree, is only to say again that we find the same rule written in our hearts and obey *that*. If the Landlord enjoins that, he enjoins only what we already purposed to do, and his voice is idle: if he enjoins anything else, his voice is again idle,

---

[62]It is, of course, true that within a system of religious belief this may not be the case. If one is already committed to fidelity to the Christian God, one will want to know what that fidelity involves. To serve one's neighbor, for example, would require knowledge about the nature of a human being in God's sight. And it is conceivable that some of God's commands might be a source of such knowledge. In that context, however, they would be providing information rather than simply issuing requirements. The command prohibiting adultery, for example, would be construed as providing information about what a fully human relation between a husband and his wife would be like. Insofar as it was still felt and interpreted as requirement rather than information, this would be a result of a commitment to God which was not yet whole and entire.

230   THE TASTE FOR THE OTHER

> for we shall disobey him. In either case the mystery of the
> rules remains unsolved, and the Landlord is a meaningless
> addition to the problem. (pp. 127–28)

In other words, God understood as Commander of the rules
can provide no acceptable reason for obeying them. As
Commander he can enjoin actions which we either (morally) approve or disapprove. If we obey it will be because
we freely consent, not because we bow before an external
command. To think that we should obey even if we disagree
would be to put ourselves into the position of Weston in
Perelandra. His philosophy was changed somewhat when
he was committed to the Life-Force, a "blind, inarticulate
purposiveness thrusting its way upward" (p. 91). This
Life-Force incorporated within itself both what Ransom
called God and what he called Devil (p. 93). Ransom in-
quired as to what Weston would be willing to do if prompt-
ed by the Life-Force. Would he murder Ransom? Yes.
Would he sell England to the Germans? Yes. Would he print
lies as serious research? Yes. " 'God help you!' said Ransom" (p. 95).

    It is, of course, true that in any particular instance when
faced with a command of God contrary to our moral beliefs
we might decide that our beliefs were in need of revision.
Indeed, that would be a serious possibility for anyone who
believed that the human race was a kind of local pocket of
evil in the universe, "an isolated bad school or regiment
inside which minimum decency passes for heroic virtue
and utter corruption for pardonable imperfection" (*PP*,
p. 62). But, Lewis thinks, some correct sense of minimal
decency would have to exist. For if God's moral judgment
differs entirely from ours so that what we call 'good' he calls
'bad' and vice versa, it could mean nothing for us to say
that he is good. Hence, those particular instances when—
faced with his command—we revise our moral judgments
should be interpreted in light of the analogy of what happens
when a man of inferior moral standards enters the society
of those better than he and gradually accepts their standards.
This is not like being asked to do an about-face. One sees

that the direction in which one is moving is indeed the direction one calls 'better,' and this explains why a sense of guilt accompanies recognition of the new standards (*PP*, pp. 38–39). Or, to take another analogy Lewis uses, God's goodness differs from ours:

> not as white from black but as a perfect circle from a child's first attempt to draw a wheel. But when the child has learned to draw, it will know that the circle it then makes is what it was trying to make from the very beginning. (*PP*, p. 39)

Thus, the fact that in any particular instance we might revise our judgment so as to bring it into agreement with God's command does not demonstrate that the divine command alone will do as a basis for morality. We might, however, take Wisdom's other option and suggest that we ought to obey God either out of fear of his penalties or hope of his rewards. The difficulty with this, as Wisdom notes, is that it is one of our basic moral convictions (and one of God's commands) that we should obey disinterestedly rather than from such self-regarding motives. We can relate this to Lewis' belief that morality itself requires that morality be transcended. What he means by this can perhaps become clearer if we consider a passage in which he explicates Tyndale's teaching that *(coram deo)* the deed is good because of the man, not the man because of the deed.

> In reality Tyndale is trying to express an obstinate fact which meets us long before we venture into the realm of theology; the fact that morality or duty (what he calls 'the Law') never yet made a man happy in himself or dear to others. It is shocking, but it is undeniable. We do not wish either to be, or to live among, people who are clean or honest or kind as a matter of duty: we want to be, and to associate with, people who like being clean and honest and kind. The mere suspicion that what seemed an act of spontaneous friendliness or generosity was really done as a duty subtly poisons it. In philosophical language, the ethical category is self-destructive; morality is healthy only when it is trying to abolish itself. In theological language, no man can be saved by works. The whole purpose of the 'gospel', for Tyndale, is to deliver us from morality. Thus, paradoxically, the 'puritan' of modern imagination—the cold, gloomy heart, doing as duty what happier and richer

souls do without thinking of it—is precisely the enemy which historical Protestantism arose and smote. What really matters is not to obey moral rules but to be a creature of a certain kind.[63]

Here we get an inkling of what Lewis means by saying that morality must be transcended in religion. What he means is that a person must learn to think of God as something other than Commander—as, let us say, Lover—and learn to see his activity as growing out of this perception of God.

Perhaps now we can explain the inconsistency in Lewis' definitions which we noted at the beginning of this section. When he defines religion as the numinous, there is little problem in keeping religion and morality (logically) separate. When he brings moral evaluations into his definition of religion, God is being understood as both Lover and Beloved. What Lewis does not try to do is make a connection—at the level of our most basic moral evaluations—between morality and an understanding of God as Commander. That he believes to be impossible, for such a connection will either destroy morality (by keeping us from acting disinterestedly) or destroy religion (by making God an unnecessary hypothesis). Thus, God's commands are not necessary as a source of (at least some of) our moral knowledge. Indeed, to some extent religion may be said to be dependent on morality, since our evaluation of God as good rests on fundamental moral beliefs.

Nevertheless, there are ways in which Lewis thinks morality is dependent on religion. *Some* of our moral views will be affected by our religious beliefs. Lewis does not regard this as any more surprising than a lawgiver ceasing to make statutes against witchcraft when he ceases believing that witches exist, or making vaccinations compulsory when he begins believing that it will prevent smallpox (*SW*, p. 201). If, as Lewis understands Christianity, every person is destined to live forever, one may come to think that the individual is incomparably more important than nations, societies, or civilizations (*MC*, p. 59). Or again, it is not self-contradictory or silly to think that an act can be wrong

---

[63]*English Literature in the Sixteenth Century Excluding Drama*, p. 187.

only if it hurts someone else. But if a person believes that he is not the owner of his mind and body but that he belongs to someone else, his judgment of such actions might be altered (*MC*, pp. 58f.). There are ways, then, in which one's total religious viewpoint might have a bearing on his total moral stance.

In addition, and more important to Lewis, we have already seen a sense in which the very fulfillment of morality depends on its being transcended. The moral law demands that we cease to rely on our ability to keep it. But this is not within our power, and, therefore, at its deepest level the moral law requires that we be reborn. This, Lewis thinks, corresponds well to the experience of the early Christians. Screwtape counsels Wormwood to inspire his patient to think of Jesus as essentially a moral teacher. If Wormwood can manage that, he will have succeeded in placing the emphasis at just the place where (from the Enemy's point of view) it does not belong.

> The earliest converts were converted by a single historical fact (the Resurrection) and a single theological doctrine (the Redemption) operating on a sense of sin which they already had—and sin, not against some new fancy-dress law produced as a novelty by a "great man," but against the old, platitudinous, universal moral law which they had been taught by their nurses and mothers. (*SL*, p. 108)

The demand of repentance and the offer of forgiveness assume a moral law already known and broken. What the Christian faith offers, therefore, is a chance to be reborn and forgiven.

The analogy with the fleet of ships will, finally, not do. For, even if morality is necessary to provide some possibility of success for the fleet as a whole, it cannot make any guarantees for the individual ships. This is the lesson Mark learns in *That Hideous Strength* when Frost brings him to the last stage of his training in "objectivity." He is asked now to trample on a crucifix. Although not a Christian, Mark is reluctant to obey. The cross is not itself an image of the Straight. Yet, it seems opposed to crooked Belbury. And suddenly Mark understands why.

> It was a picture of what happened when the Straight met the Crooked, a picture of what the Crooked did to the Straight—what it would do to him if he remained straight. It was, in a more emphatic sense than he had yet understood, a *cross*. (p. 336)

If this is the fate that awaits "the Straight," how is it possible to retain a commitment to it? That is the question Mark faces.

> But this raised a question that Mark had never thought of before. Was *that* the moment at which to turn against the Man? If the universe was a cheat, was that a good reason for joining its side? Supposing the Straight was utterly powerless, always and everywhere certain to be mocked, tortured, and finally killed by the Crooked, what then? Why not go down with the ship? (p. 337)

To make that decision requires an abandonment of the claims and desires of self. Or, to put it more positively, it requires that one be moved by a self-giving love. Only that makes complete commitment to the Good possible. Thus, to be reborn is not simply to come to perceive God as Lover rather than Commander. It is to be changed; changed from one who desires to be moral into one who is above all a lover of the Good.

Conclusion

The social and ethical themes discussed in preceding chapters form the center of Lewis' theological vision. His essential concern is to perceive the whole of human life in relation to God, the Creator and Redeemer, and his views are best described as, quite simply, Augustinian. On the great issues which divided Christendom in the 16th century Lewis demonstrates sensitivity to both Catholic and Protestant emphases—precisely what one might expect, since Augustine, whose thought shaped so much in medieval Christendom, was almost equally influential in shaping Luther and Calvin. Lewis' views are best characterized not by reference to contemporary thinkers but—which perhaps explains the breadth of his vision—by reference to Augustine, Plato, and Aristotle. Any reader who has entered Narnia will have learned a great deal about this enduring vision of human nature and community. He will have inhabited a world in which that vision makes sense and will have learned how to envision his own world in a new way.

One thing the reader should achieve is some sense of what it means to be a creature: to exist at Aslan's pleasure and to achieve self-fulfillment only in right relation to him. This belief is central in Lewis' vision. No creature, no relation among creatures, no created thing can be properly itself when isolated from the Creator who is both source and destination of his creation. When in *The Silver Chair* Jill Pole is taken by magic into Narnia for the first time, she experiences for herself the great reality principle of the universe. She is thirsty and goes in search of running water to drink. At last she finds a stream.

> But although the sight of water made her feel ten times thirstier than before, she didn't rush forward and drink. She stood as still as if she had been turned into stone, with her mouth wide open. And she had a very good reason: just on this side of the stream lay the Lion. (p. 15)

She stands transfixed, unable to move toward the water and unable to run away. At last the Lion speaks. "If you're thirsty, you may drink" (p. 16). She remembers that Eustace had told her how animals speak in this country; yet she is scarcely able to move.

> "Are you not thirsty?" said the Lion.
> "I'm *dying* of thirst," said Jill.
> "Then drink," said the Lion.
> "May I—could I—would you mind going away while I do?" said Jill. (p. 16)

The sound of the running water is driving Jill nearly frantic. She tries to extract from the Lion a promise that he will not do anything to her if she comes near the water, but he will make no promise.

> "I daren't come and drink," said Jill.
> "Then you will die of thirst," said the Lion.
> "Oh dear!" said Jill, coming another step nearer. "I suppose I must go and look for another stream then."
> "There is no other stream," said the Lion. (p. 17)

That is Lewis' message: that in the whole universe no other stream is to be found, but also that anyone who (like Emeth in *The Last Battle*) truly seeks will find it. When Jill finally does kneel down to drink the water she finds it is "the coldest, most refreshing water she had ever tasted" (p. 17).

All are created to drink of that water, to share in the divine fellowship. But the journey to that destination is a long one and requires self-renunciation. No one finds his life unless he loses it. All are pilgrims along this path. In *The Horse and His Boy* Shasta and the talking horse Bree are trying to make their way back to Narnia, from which they had been taken captive. Their journey is a long and perilous one, during which Bree realizes that the greatest danger to him lies not in their enemies but in his own vanity. Part of the plan of escape is to disguise Bree (and the other horse, Hwin) so that they will not be recognized as warhorses. This involves cutting their tails to make them shorter and ragged. Bree heartily objects to this suggestion by Hwin.

> "My dear Madam," said Bree. "Have you pictured to your-self how very disagreeable it would be to arrive in Narnia in *that* condition?"
> "Well," said Hwin humbly (she was a very sensible mare), "the main thing is to get there."[1]

When they are making their escape, Bree decides at one point that he simply cannot go on any longer without stop-ping for a rest and a snack. Hwin, though equally tired, suggests that (since they do not know how near their enemies may be) they ought to push toward Narnia as quickly as possible. But Bree objects, and the result is that his rest is almost the cause of their capture by the enemy. Only because of Shasta's bravery are they safely rescued. Still, when all is safe, Bree suggests that there is no need to hurry on immediately into Narnia. The others do not at first understand his reticence, and Hwin asks why he would want to delay.

> "M-m-m, broo-hoo," muttered Bree. "Well, don't you see, Ma'am—it's an important occasion—returning to one's own country—entering society—the best society—it is so essential to make a good impression—not perhaps looking quite our-selves, yet, eh?" (p. 168)

Suddenly the others realize the reason for Bree's reluc-tance: he is embarrassed to be seen while his tail remains short. It is only when he meets Aslan that Bree learns to say, "I'm afraid I must be rather a fool" (p. 170). But then, that confession *is* a part of the journey back to Aslan.

Lewis never loses sight of what it means to be human. "We were made to be neither cerebral men nor visceral men, but Men. Not beasts nor angels but Men—things at

[1] *The Horse and His Boy* (New York: Macmillan, 1954), p. 39.

once rational and animal."[2] If, letting Lewis mold our vision, we were to understand ourselves and our world from the viewpoint of the Christian story, we would see ourselves as creatures: beings who cannot be fulfilled apart from fellowship with God and one another; beings who, nevertheless, fight against what we need, who try to live out of our own resources; beings, therefore, for whom the journey home is likely to be painful. We lose our humanity, finally and completely, only when we lose that "taste for the *other*" which draws us out of ourselves (*PP,* p. 123). For Lewis, self-giving love is the bond which makes fellowship possible. Indeed, the law of self-giving is, he thinks, written into the very nature of the universe. Without it joy is impossible; for one can only enjoy what is other than the self. Lewis even applies this belief to literature and permits it to illuminate what was for him more than "subject matter." In a passage which comes very near the heart of his thought he writes:

> Good reading, therefore, though it is not essentially an affectional or moral or intellectual activity, has something in common with all three. In love we escape from our self into one other. In the moral sphere, every act of justice or charity involves putting ourselves in the other person's place and thus transcending our own competitive particularity. In coming to understand anything we are rejecting the facts as they are for us in favour of the facts as they are. The primary impulse of each is to maintain and aggrandise himself. The secondary impulse is to go out of the self, to correct its provincialism and heal its loneliness. In love, in virtue, in the pursuit of knowledge, and in the reception of the arts, we are doing this. Obviously this process can be described either as an enlargement or as a temporary annihilation of the self. But that is an old paradox; 'he that loseth his life shall save it'.[3]

For a fallen creature—one whose primary impulse is self-aggrandizement, one who is separated from *the* Other—it is no easy matter to escape from self. It is a process which must, according to Lewis, take place over time, and he thinks of the believer as a pilgrim who must

---

[2]"Preface" to *The Pilgrim's Regress,* p. 13.
[3]*An Experiment in Criticism* (Cambridge, 1961), p. 138.

learn self-giving during his sojourn. The sojourn *is* the way
to self-fulfillment, but in our present pilgrim condition we
cannot necessarily experience it as such. Hence, a sense of
the Christian as one whose life is limited by the contours of
his journey accounts for many of the tensions within Lewis'
thought. His several definitions of love—one of which may
permit great harm to be done for the sake of the other's
good—reflect the distinction between what we can (in the
midst of our sojourn) experience and what, as those who
journey toward fulfillment in fellowship with God, we can
believe to be the case. His ambiguities about self-love reflect the same distinction: what must be experienced as
self-renunciation can be believed to be self-fulfillment. The
dialectical attitude of enjoyment and renunciation toward
created things is the attitude of one who knows that these
things image the Creator and are rightly received only as
his trust. The creature must give himself to others in the
earthly loves and yet be willing, if necessary, to give up
these loves for God's sake. The loves cannot exist apart from
divine love; yet it sometimes seems that they cannot coexist
with it either. We may *believe* in the harmony of human and
divine love. We are likely to *experience* the "tether and
pang of the particular." And if Lewis' normative ethic is less
obviously theological, it is nevertheless an ethic for those
who know themselves as creatures and recognize in themselves and others that impulse toward self-aggrandizement
which must be disciplined, controlled, and destroyed.

Lewis offers a vision of harmonious fulfillment and a
(Christian) story which tells us that we have not yet reached
that destination. We could put it in very Augustinian terms:
The vision is of the restless heart finding its longing fulfilled as it rests in God. The story is that of God at work
building the city of his love. There is no way to save one's
humanity except by giving it in love to God and one's
fellows. To claim independence is to make war on the great
reality principle of the universe. Yet, to accept that reality
may mean the death of the worlds we have constructed to
keep ourselves secure. The lessons of humility and the
pattern of love are not easily or painlessly learned. Orual

asks the Fox the pilgrim's question and hears (from the Fox!) faith's answer:

> "And will the gods one day grow thus beautiful, Grandfather?"
>
> "They say . . . but even I, who am dead, do not yet understand more than a few broken words of their language. Only this I know. This age of ours will one day be the distant past. And the Divine Nature can change the past. Nothing is yet in its true form."[4]

But while waiting for that day and the community it brings, it is never wrong, Lewis thinks, for a creature to mourn the passing of what is local and unique. As Tirian says when Narnia and all worlds come to an end and he and the children enter Aslan's world, "I have seen my mother's death. What world but Narnia have I ever known? It were no virtue, but great discourtesy, if we did not mourn."[5] That, Lewis means to say, is quite appropriate for one who has not turned from the fellowships offered a creature but has throughout his sojourn nourished within himself "the taste for the other."

A good many pages have come and gone since we noted that Lewis does not strive for theological originality. In the chapters that followed we unfolded and, on certain occasions, evaluated the social and ethical thought which make up so important a part of Lewis' work. It is now possible to say that Lewis both has and has not been original. He has seldom tried to do more than articulate a view which he believes to be integral to the Christian tradition. Yet, in that very attempt he has so given himself to the tradition that he seems undeniably successful in the task of handing on what he has received. Of course, his views are not always clear, and they are sometimes inadequate. There is, in addition, much that he leaves undone. Yet he is, by and large, a capable and insightful explicator of the tradition. He also seeks to defend what he passes on. However, he does this less often than many have imagined. More often he helps us step inside the tradition, and in doing so, he enlarges our

[4]*Till We Have Faces*, p. 305.
[5]*The Last Battle*, p. 150.

vision. He does this uncommonly well—so well, in fact, that one is tempted to speak of his originality and to suggest that he has enriched what he passed on. However, it is better to interpret him in the light of his own statement about the medieval authors whom he studied. They were, he writes, more apt to conceal than to feign originality. For their aim is not self-expression but to hand on worthily the matter they have received; "not worthily of your own genius or of the poetic art but of the matter itself."[6] And, writes Lewis, "the paradox is that it is just this abdication of originality which brings out the originality they really possess."[7] That is what we should finally say about Lewis. And we ought not miss in this note of continual abdication that mystical death which is, for Lewis, the secret of life. The taste for the other is present also in his theological reflection about human nature and community. He gives himself to his experience and to the Christian tradition, using the latter to sharpen his vision of the former. That is to say, his manner of thinking theologically seems itself to be consistent with the matter of his theology. And that, perhaps, is as it should be—at least when we are discussing a matter as important as how a man should live.

[6]*The Discarded Image*, p. 211.
[7]*Ibid.*, pp. 211–12.

Index

244 THE TASTE FOR THE OTHER